THE **ULTIMATE** GUIDE TO USING THE
REVOLUTIONARY CAMERA

Noah Kadner

Peachpit
Press

RED
The Ultimate Guide to Using the Revolutionary Camera
Noah Kadner

Peachpit Press
1249 Eighth Street
Berkeley, CA 94710
510/524-2178
Fax: 510/524-2221

Find us on the Web at www.peachpit.com
To report errors, please send a note to errata@peachpit.com

Peachpit Press is a division of Pearson Education
Copyright © 2010 by Noah Kadner

Senior Editor: Karyn Johnson
Development Editor: Corbin Collins
Production Editor: Lisa Brazieal
Copy Editor: Kim Wimpsett
Technical Editors: Leo Ticheli, Joe Walker, Gunleik Groven
Compositor: Danielle Foster
Proofreader: Kelly Kordes Anton
Indexer: Valerie Perry
Interior Design: Danielle Foster
Cover Design: Aren Howell and Aaron Lea
Cover Production: Andreas deDanaan
Cover Image: Zacuto RED ONE Filmmaker package featuring ZRED EVF monitor mount,
courtesy of Zacuto

NOTICE OF RIGHTS   All rights reserved. No part of this book may be reproduced or transmitted in any form by any means, electronic, mechanical, photocopying, recording, or otherwise, without the prior written permission of the publisher. For information on getting permission for reprints and excerpts, contact permissions@peachpit.com.

NOTICE OF LIABILITY   The information in this book is distributed on an "As Is" basis without warranty. While every precaution has been taken in the preparation of the book, neither the author nor Peachpit shall have any liability to any person or entity with respect to any loss or damage caused or alleged to be caused directly or indirectly by the instructions contained in this book or by the computer software and hardware products described in it.

TRADEMARKS   RED™ and its associated products are trademarks of Red.com, Inc. Many of the designations used by manufacturers and sellers to distinguish their products are claimed as trademarks. Where those designations appear in this book, and Peachpit was aware of a trademark claim, the designations appear as requested by the owner of the trademark. All other product names and services identified throughout this book are used in editorial fashion only and for the benefit of such companies with no intention of infringement of the trademark. No such use, or the use of any trade name, is intended to convey endorsement or other affiliation with this book.

ISBN-13:   978-0-321-61768-2
ISBN-10:   0-321-61768-1

9 8 7 6 5 4 3 2 1

Printed and bound in the United States of America

"If you want to dive in and starting using the RED, look no further. This book is the next best thing to having a top-notch production crew with RED experts working by your side."

—Arthur Albert, Director of Photography, *ER*

"An essential guide loaded with knowledge, I recommend it as the first purchase for any filmmaker who is thinking about owning or currently owns the RED."

—Rodney Charters, ASC, Director of Photography, *24*

"If you're planning to shoot with the RED camera, this is the book to get!"

—Rob Cohen, Director, *The Fast and the Furious*

"Noah Kadner takes the best practices of using the RED camera and shares them with the rest of us in this indispensable guide."

—Simon Duggan, ACS, Director of Photography, *Live Free or Die Hard, Knowing*

"Written in an easy-to-follow style, yet thorough in covering everything from production to postproduction to making money from your investment, this is a book that should be on every filmmaker's desk and in their kit bag."

—Norman Hollyn, film editor, instructor, and author of
The Lean Forward Moment

"If you want to see how the pros are using the RED camera, you need this book."

—Nancy Schreiber, ASC, Cinematographer, *Every Day*

To Mónica y Max

Acknowledgments

I want to thank, above all, my family: my wife, Mónica, and son, Max. They gave their infinite love, support, and encouragement during all those late nights and missed vacations to the beach while I was writing this book. I thank my mom and dad (Steve and Kathy) for supporting me for so many years before passing the baton over to Mónica. I thank my father-in-law, Dr. Bernardo Reina, who is the very essence of a gentleman and an intellectual. I wrote this to try to make you guys proud.

I'd also like to thank the good folks over at Peachpit Press: my editor Karyn Johnson for believing in this idea from the start and giving expert advice and support along the way, development editor Corbin Collins for his unwavering commitment to excellence in writing, production editor Lisa Brazieal for the great graphic look, and Danielle Foster for a beautiful layout.

The good folks at RED were also a big help, especially Jarred, Graeme, Deanan, Stuart, Kelly, and Ted. The "chicos" at Simplemente were gracious enough to offer a ton of hands-on camera support, including Rune Hansen, Iris Mendieta, and Carlos Martínez Torres. And last but not least, I want to thank Jim Jannard for having the vision of a no-compromises movie camera for the masses and for following through on that vision.

About the Author

Noah Kadner was born in New Jersey and raised in the American Southwest. He graduated from the MFA program in film production at the USC School of Cinema-Television. Noah runs Ternura Corporation, a film, television, production, and postproduction company. He made his feature-film directing debut with *Formosa*, a 1950s-style romantic comedy shot on location in Albuquerque and Los Angeles.

In 2006, Noah cofounded Call Box (www.callboxlive.com), an interactive training company. Call Box produces and distributes a successful line of courses on DVD for independent filmmakers and broadcast producers. He also administers several online moviemaking and postproduction forums, including 2-pop, Creative Cow, and DVXuser. Noah writes for industry magazines such as *Videography*, *HD Video Pro*, and *American Cinematographer*, as well as for various industry Web sites, including Apple.com. Noah wrote the *American Cinematographer* cover stories for *Pirates of the Caribbean: At World's End* and *Indiana Jones and the Kingdom of the Crystal Skull*.

In 2007, Noah's wife and her partner, Rune Hansen, acquired two RED cameras for their company Simplemente in Mexico City. Since then, Noah has worked with the cameras on many different projects, mastering hands-on production techniques and postproduction workflows.

Contents

INTRODUCTION

You probably remember the first movie you saw in a theater. Maybe you recall only a few moments that made an impression, or perhaps you can recite every line of dialogue. I was 5 years old, and the movie was *Star Wars*. Many people were blown away by the opening scene, where the giant spaceship rumbles overhead, but I remember seeing Luke Skywalker on his desert home planet for the first time. I was living in El Paso, deep in the hot desert badlands of West Texas and really the middle of nowhere. My reaction was, "Hey, this planet looks just like home. I could be Luke's next-door neighbor. I could be up there on that screen." Chances are, if you're interested in the RED camera, you've probably dreamed of being up there on the big screen, too, somehow.

Until a couple of years ago, if you wanted to make a movie for theaters, you had two choices, both fraught with compromise. Either you could try to get a big-budget studio interested in financing your project or you could shoot it on your own. If you went the studio route, you were likely to be compromised creatively, because even the most benevolent film studio in the world cares more about demographics and marketing than about your story. Let's face it, it's called show *business*, and movie studios must produce hit movies to remain in business.

If you tried to make a movie on your own, your compromise was more on a technical level. Sure, you could make any story you wanted to, but unless you were fabulously wealthy, you'd likely be shooting with something less than a 35mm film camera and would wind up with a final product that wasn't going to look so great up on that big movie theater screen.

With the advent of the RED ONE digital motion-picture camera, you're finally able to avoid those two compromises. It gives you the same visual quality as a professional film camera, but is much more affordable and requires none of the attendant expenses of buying film stock, processing, transferring, negative cutting, answer printing, and so on. In other words, you can now shoot a project without many technical or creative compromises and fulfill that dream of finally putting your story up on the big screen.

Who This Book Is For

This book is intended for anyone with a direct or even peripheral interest in the RED camera. "Yeah, but I'm not just anyone," you may say. Let's get into the specifics of who this book is really designed for.

NEW OWNERS

You've just gotten your delivery from the good folks in Orange County (that would be the RED folks), and you're feeling a little overwhelmed by all that gear. Take a deep breath, leave the camera in its box for a little while longer, and grab a cup of coffee. Spend a few hours flipping through this book, and I can absolutely promise you'll save yourself untold time and money. If you read this book from cover to cover, you'll leapfrog over weeks and months of the learning time you would have spent figuring out all this stuff on your own.

LONGTIME OWNERS

Let's say you've had the camera for a few months or a year and are getting pretty good results with it already, but now you'd like to take things to the next level. Maybe you have a modest camera package and are trying to decide what's the wisest equipment to purchase next. Perhaps there's always been one aspect of using the camera you just can't seem to get right, or maybe you want to improve your postproduction efficiency. This book can help you with all of those concerns, and then some.

EDITORS AND POSTPRODUCTION TEAMS

A hard drive has just landed on your desk with raw footage from a RED shoot, and you're wondering where to start. You're an Avid, Apple Final Cut Pro, or Adobe Premiere Pro editor, and you're expected to have the project edited and output to DVD or Blu-ray by Friday. This book can help you. Or maybe you're a visual effects artist, and you're a little confused about the file requirements of integrating your animation into a 4K RED background plate. Bingo— you should delve right into the later chapters of this book, which cover postproduction techniques for a wide variety of editing and finishing applications. If you have a little extra time, the production chapters can also shed some light onto that age-old postproduction question, "Why did they shoot it like that?!"

RENTERS

If you're planning to rent the RED for an upcoming shoot or if you already rented one and have started scratching your head, this book is also for you. The RED comes with a detailed instruction manual, but the manual functions as a reference guide, dealing more with the camera's operations than with overall workflow. This book is not a substitute for reading the manual, but it can be used to get you up to speed on what you need to know to use the camera quickly.

SCARLET AND EPIC OWNERS

So, you've gotten your hands on one of the *newer* cameras from RED that were still being developed when I was writing this book. Lucky you! Even though I could only make edu-cated guesses about some details, the RED ONE shares a lot of DNA with Scarlet and EPIC (especially EPIC). The RED ONE offers similar frame resolutions, postproduction methodology, and general production approaches with the newer models. So, wherever you read "RED ONE," just substitute "Scarlet" or "EPIC" in your head, and you'll still get a lot out of this book.

ENTHUSIASTS

Maybe you can't really afford to buy or even rent a RED ONE (or a soon-to-release Scarlet or EPIC) camera right now. Or perhaps you're in a totally unrelated line of work, but you're still passionately interested in the camera on a technical or creative level. In this book, you'll learn how the RED operates and get a firsthand tour through every step of production and postproduction. And just maybe you'll get inspired enough to realize that your dream isn't as far out of reach as you thought, and you'll move from being merely enthusiastic to being in production.

How to Use This Book

RED: The Ultimate Guide to Using the Revolutionary Camera is organized into two basic sections: production and postproduction (after a quick chapter on some history of the camera). I recommend reading as much of this book from start to finish as you can. Some of the later postproduction chapters may not directly apply to you. For example, if you're an Avid editor, you can probably skip the Final Cut Pro and Premiere Pro chapters (unless you want to see how the other half lives).

The book covers the whole process from start to finish in order, beginning with what the camera is and how to put together a package and then following through with production techniques and on-set data management strategies. In the postproduction section, you'll learn how to bring RED footage into your editing software, how to edit, and how to color-correct footage. Then we'll look at exporting completed projects for film, HD, the Web, and more. The book concludes with a look into how you can use the RED in your business and in future projects.

You can also use this book like a film school in a box. I went to film school at the University of Southern California (USC, alma mater of folks such as George Lucas, Robert Zemeckis, and Ron Howard), and I've attempted to bring into this book some of what I learned at USC whenever it's appropriate to the RED discussion. I'm a firm believer in learning from the experience of others, and that's why you'll find POV (Point-of-view) interviews with some of the top professionals in the industry at the ends of most chapters. Some of those POVs directly relate to the chapters they follow, others are there for general insight.

I recommend keeping the book with your camera or next to your system if you're working in postproduction. You can easily flip through the index and use this book as a handy quick-reference guide. The complete camera menu map in the appendix at the back of the book is reason alone to pack it with your camera. (The book is also very lightweight compared to most of the other gear you'll need, so no excuses for not sticking it into your camera case!)

DEFINING WORKFLOW

You're going to read the term *workflow* over and over again in this book. So, what exactly is a workflow, and why is it so important? In broad terms, a workflow is a sequence of processes through which a piece of work passes from initiation to completion.

In this case, the initiation occurs as you hit the record trigger on your RED ONE, and the completion happens when a theater audience applauds at the end of your movie (or appreciates it via DVD or downloaded webisode—you get the idea). Between initiation and completion lie a lot of technical skills, equipment requirements, and production and postproduction concepts. The RED workflow is an A to Z process that you'll explore and master over the course of this book. It's a lot to take in, but I've done my very best to make everything easy to understand and enjoyable.

COMPANION WEB SITE

The great thing about RED is that the company is always working on new developments. It would be impossible to keep this book up-to-date on all fronts; therefore, you'll also find it useful to visit the companion Web site (www.peachpit.com/red), which contains helpful links, updated information, and documents you can use as part of your productions. Throughout the book you'll find pointers to the Web site for further updates.

1 THE HISTORY OF THE FUTURE

The idea for the RED camera began, as many innovations do, with one person's intense frustration with the status quo. In this case, that person was Jim Jannard, CEO of Oakley, Inc., a sunglasses and apparel company. The status quo in 2004 was the unavailability of a digital video camera that could produce the same quality as 35mm film. Jannard recognized a disparity between what was possible photographically with a 35mm motion picture camera and what could be done with a semi-professional, high-definition (HD) camera that an average person could actually afford.

He also noted that digital still cameras already existed with resolutions much higher than high-definition, plus had the ability to shoot in RAW (or digital negative) format. He reasoned that with enough know-how and capital investment, a digital motion-picture camera could be built that is not only as good as 35mm film cameras but at a much lower cost, enabling anyone to shoot high-quality movies. Before we dive into using the camera and working with footage, let's take a look at how this phenomenal camera came about and how it's currently being used.

Assembling the Team

In order to get his idea off the ground, Jannard contacted a couple of industry experts. The first was Frederic Haubrich, creator of the Lumiere HD plug-in, which Jannard was using to transfer footage from HD cameras into his computer. The second was Ted Schilowitz, a marketing expert and designer who had launched hardware used for content creation, such as AJA's video editing converter cards and G-Tech's hard drive storage.

The RED group expanded to include more industry experts whose specialties would be needed to deliver a camera others had said could not be built. One of these experts was Stuart English, who had been a workflow expert at Panasonic supporting the company's VariCam HD camera and the enabling of HD footage transfer over FireWire.

Another early team member was Graeme Nattress, a programmer who had spent years developing plug-ins for editing software and researching video compression and image-processing technologies. Nattress would be instrumental in the development of RED's onboard compression software called REDCODE. Jarred Land, an Internet developer and part-time product designer who had launched the popular filmmaking portal DVXuser (www.dvxuser.com), also joined the team. Land would create REDuser (www.reduser.net), a Web site that became an important part of RED's marketing success. (You'll learn more about REDuser later in this chapter.)

Technical Specs

The RED team worked from a design edict that called for several key elements in the finished camera, all of which would be necessary to enable image quality that could rival that of film. These requirements included a very high-resolution image sensor that could shoot at 4K (4,000 pixels of horizontal resolution). For comparison, most other digital cameras shoot at well under 2K.

The second mandate was that the camera use the same lens mount as a 35mm film camera so that it would have access to the same high-quality optics and be able to achieve comparable cinematography. The internal electronics would need to control the camera's operation while capturing and compressing 4K footage with efficiency and high quality. Jannard also wanted the camera to be able to store footage as RAW data, which he was accustomed to working with on digital still cameras.

The result? Table 1.1 lists the eventual specifications that came out of the team's work. (For more technical details on the camera, see Chapter 2.)

TABLE 1.1   RED ONE SPECIFICATIONS

Item	Description
Sensor	12 Megapixel Mysterium (24.4mm x 13.7mm)
Resolution	4K (4520 x 2540 pixels)
Depth of field	35mm cinema equivalent
Frame rate	23.98, 24, 25, 29.97, 30, 50, 59.94, 60, and variable (1 up to 120 in 2K for slow motion)
Format	REDCODE 12-bit RAW at 4K, 3K, and 2K
Data rate	36 MB/second (REDCODE 36) and 28 MB/second (REDCODE 28)
Audio	4-channel uncompressed, 24-bit, 48kHz
Weight	10 lbs (body only)
Base price	$17,500 (body only)

The RED Phenomenon

At a certain point during development, Jannard realized his team had succeeded in design-ing the camera and that it would work, but the next big question was, would anyone want it? Another challenge RED encountered from the outset was mounting industry skepticism. From the moment RED was announced until cameras started to ship (and even at the time of this writing), some industry pundits have decried the company's efforts.

The criticisms split into two primary concerns. First, the camera was *vaporware* and could never be delivered with those specifications at that price point. Second, the camera might be possible, but despite the specifications on paper, its image quality would never rival that of 35mm film. With motion-picture film's nearly 110-year head start (dating from Louis Lumi-ere's motion-picture film camera invention of 1895), Jannard and his team had their work cut out for them.

NOTE *Vaporware* is a computer-industry term used to describe products that are announced but never actually released.

PUBLIC DEBUT: NAB 2006

Much of what you've read up to this point about the development was not public knowledge. That changed on April 24, 2006, in Las Vegas, Nevada. At the annual National Association of Broadcasters (NAB) convention, RED made its public debut, announcing camera specifications and pricing. Initially, the team had little to show in their modest booth on the show floor, in the shadow of the film and video industry's heavyweights (**Figure 1.1**).

Figure 1.1 RED's first booth at NAB 2006, just before the doors opened to the public.

Figure 1.2 RED's titanium "R" sculptures were given to the first 1,080 reservation holders.

All the company could offer during its first NAB show were brochures and a reservation policy. For $1,000, any interested party could put down a reservation for the right to purchase the eventual camera RED was proposing. In return, they received a serial number and a small titanium sculpture (**Figure 1.2**). Though the criticism from skeptics only intensified, Jannard's vision was vindicated: By noon on the first day, RED already had more than 100 reservations.

Figure 1.3 The RED "milk girls" footage was part of the first presentations shown to the public.

Figure 1.4 "Frankie" was the first working prototype of the RED ONE, switched on in August 2007. (Photo by Robert Rex Jackson.)

RED left NAB in 2006 with lots of hype and expectation, but the year ahead proved especially challenging. Internally, development was moving as quickly as possible both on a technical level and an organizational level as the company rapidly grew to include more engineers and support personnel. On the outside, speculation was rampant among critics and enthusiasts. This was somewhat alleviated by marketing professional Schilowitz offering seminars and demonstrations of footage and prototypes (**Figure 1.3** and **Figure 1.4**).

REDUSER FORUM

Meanwhile, to stimulate dialogue with the public, Land launched REDuser in December 2006 (**Figure 1.5**). The site became the clearinghouse for all information from RED and a portal into the company's inner workings. Reservation holders, RED employees, enthusiasts, and critics alike were all invited to discuss anything related (or even completely unrelated) to RED on the site's forums.

NOTE REDuser was later joined by Scarletuser (www.scarletuser.com) to cover RED's new prosumer camera, Scarlet.

Figure 1.5 The home page of REDuser.

Remarkably, as of this writing, RED has yet to purchase any advertising—despite having one of the highest levels of brand awareness and interest in the industry. That's due in large part to the popularity of RED's outreach on the Internet via REDuser and the stories, analyses, forum discussions, and blog posts it generates. The site also offers a direct conduit between Jannard and the public, who are welcome to comment, question, and argue with him.

NAB 2007

RED returned to NAB in April 2007 with more than 1,000 reservations received. The company still lacked a shipping camera, but this time it had an expanded booth and a secret weapon provided by director Peter Jackson (*King Kong, The Lord of the Rings* trilogy). Jackson evinced an interest in RED since it had first been announced and had contacted Jannard to stay apprised of the project's progress. By March 2007, RED had developed working prototypes of the camera and arranged to fly two of the cameras (nicknamed Boris and Natasha) to Jackson in New Zealand for testing (**Figure 1.6**).

Figure 1.6 The Boris and Natasha camera prototypes used by Peter Jackson. (Photo by Robert Rex Jackson.)

Rather than just do a regular camera test, Jackson chose to shoot an actual short movie. The film was an action-adventure set along a front line in World War I, featuring explosions, tanks, and biplanes. Jackson shot over two days and then put the results through post-production, adding more explosions, animated machine-gun fire, sound effects, and music (borrowed from James Newton Howard's score for Jackson's *King Kong*). *Crossing the Line* was delivered the night before NAB opened and became the demo footage for RED's booth (**Figure 1.7**).

Figure 1.7 A 4K still frame from *Crossing the Line*.

Viewers of *Crossing the Line* were impressed by both the proof that the camera delivered exceptional imagery and the quality of the production Jackson had achieved on a fast turnaround. RED's 2007 booth also included working models of the camera in its near-final body design, along with viewfinders and monitors (**Figure 1.8**). This went a long way toward quelling controversy. Reservations for the camera were again opened, though the big question remained: When would the camera actually ship? That was finally answered on August 31, 2007, when the first 25 reservations were filled with shipping cameras.

Figure 1.8 RED's Booth at NAB 2007 became a popular destination for enthusiasts and skeptics alike. (Photo by Robert Rex Jackson.)

RED DAY

For its early reservation orders, RED offered "RED Day" seminars, conducted at its headquarters in Lake Forest, California. These sessions included an introduction to the camera and its workflow, along with hardware delivery and accessory consultations. For many owners, this was the first time they got their hands on the camera they'd been waiting more than a year to receive. RED Days continued throughout 2007 and 2008. By early 2009, the company had caught up with its reservations and was able to ship a camera upon order.

TAKING A PERSONAL RED DAY

I went to the third RED Day in October 2007. My wife, Mónica, and her business partner, Rune Hansen, held reservation numbers 84 and 85. The two cameras were destined for the rentals department at Simplemente, their production house in Mexico City. RED Day involved meeting Jim Jannard and members of the engineering team to chat about the camera (Figure 1.9). We were also given some workflow demonstrations and received our cameras along with lenses and accessories.

Figure 1.9 The author (right) with his wife, Mónica, and Jim Jannard at a RED Day in October 2007.

INDUSTRY ACCEPTANCE

The RED ONE is now in use on a variety of music videos, TV series, commercials, and features. You'll meet some of the professionals shooting these projects in the point-of-view (POV) sections throughout this book. Table 1.2 lists some of the projects that have been shot on the RED.

TABLE 1.2   PRODUCTIONS SHOT ON THE RED

Project	Description
Knowing	Feature, directed by Alex Proyas
The Book of Eli	Feature, directed by the Hughes Brothers
Che	Feature, directed by Steven Soderbergh
My Bloody Valentine 3D	Feature, directed by Patrick Lussier
The Informant	Feature, directed by Steven Soderbergh
ER	TV Series, NBC
Southland	TV Series, NBC
Sanctuary	TV Series, SciFi Channel
Leverage	TV Series, TNT
The Cleaner	TV Series, A&E

In addition to the Scarlet and EPIC cameras mentioned in the introduction, RED has plans for more motion-picture equipment. These include a disc-based 4K-playback device called RED-RAY, 4K projectors, and lenses at lower than the industry-standard prices. (To read more about RED's future, visit this book's companion Web site at www.peachpit.com/red for updates.)

For the remainder of the book, you'll learn how to use the RED ONE, but keep that new gear in the back of your mind. Now that you know a little more about where the camera came from, who made it, how they did it, and why—let's get to work learning how to actually use it. For those of you with a Scarlet or EPIC, you'll find that a lot of the material in the upcoming chapters applies to you as well.

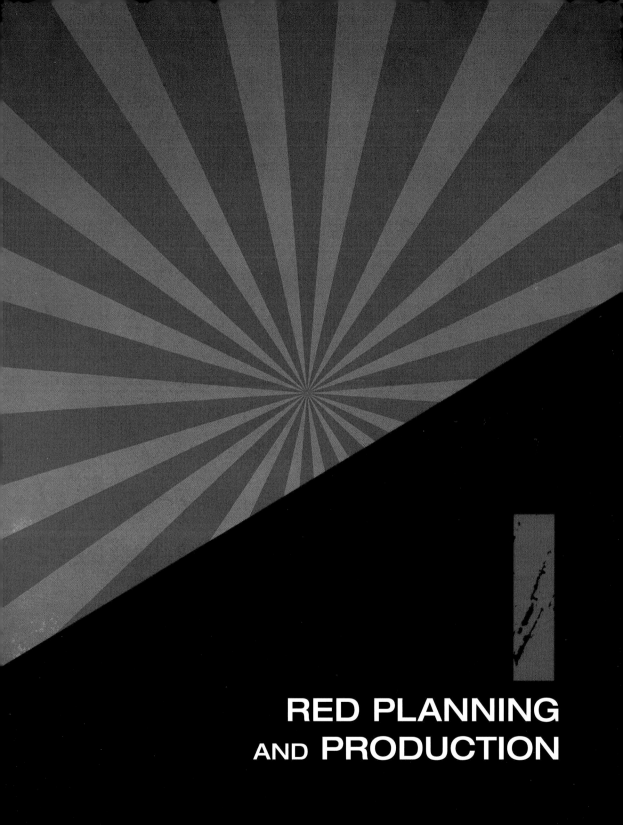

RED PLANNING
AND PRODUCTION

2 OVERVIEW OF THE RED WORKFLOW

One of the first questions many new RED users have is, "How does the camera compare with what I've used already?" That's a complex issue because the RED is similar to many different cameras and yet unlike any single one. Simply stated, the RED combines the working methods of a 35mm film camera with the convenience and advantages of a digital single-lens reflex (DSLR) camera. It also has more in common with a traditional film camera than standard video or high-definition cameras, except you don't pay for processing and printing film.

With that in mind, let's drill a little deeper and compare the RED ONE with other cameras. After that, you'll see an overview of two workflows you'll need to master to get the best images out of the RED: the tapeless workflow and the RAW workflow. The bulk of this book is spent fleshing out those two concepts, so pay rapt attention. At the end of this chapter, you'll learn about metadata and ways you can upgrade your own camera.

Comparing the RED with Other Cameras

To understand what's special about the RED camera, it's best to look at how it is different from and similar to other cameras. Film cameras came first historically, followed by video and later by high-definition (HD) and digital cameras. You could say the RED is in a class of its own by being the first digital camera to compare directly with film cameras in terms of resolution and quality.

VIDEO

Up until a few years ago, the word *video* conjured mental associations of footage from news channels, reality television, or perhaps home video. That association is based on the inter-laced technology used by most video cameras. In National Television System Committee (NTSC) countries, *interlaced* refers to a camera that shoots 60 half frames per second and combines (or interlaces) them to create a moving image. Sixty interlaced halves (or 60i) are played back to create 29.97 frames per second in NTSC. The resulting effect has different motion characteristics than film, which is captured as 24 discrete still frames per second to achieve what some folks would call a *film look* or a *cinematic* appearance. Because a video camera captures motion differently than film, 60i doesn't look like film and is consequently not very cinematic, at least on a purely psychological or aesthetic level (**Figure 2.1**).

Figure 2.1 A progressive video frame (left) compared to an interlaced frame.

To counter this perceived deficiency, creative people shooting on video resorted to all kinds of tricks to attempt to make 60i video look more like 24 frames per second film. This involved the merging of fields into frames with software plug-ins and even special services that charged a hefty hourly sum to attempt the same alchemy via hardware. In the end, the results were never quite right. As a consequence, if you truly wanted something to look cinematic, you needed to shoot on film, which meant much more expense.

That issue was changed forever with the advent of a format for cameras called 24p, which simply means that instead of making *60 half images per second* and recording them to tape, a 24p camera photographs *24 complete still images per second* and records them to tape. The resulting image is far more similar to film because the motion-capture characteristics are emulated. The primary difference is that instead of the photography being captured as brightness values onto a piece of celluloid film, it's captured by an electronic image sensor. Initially 24p was only available on very expensive high-definition cameras that, for most filmmakers, were as far, or farther, out of reach than film cameras.

The first truly affordable video camera equipped with 24p was Panasonic's DVX100, introduced in 2002. For the first time, anyone could shoot with a video camera with results that looked like film without any additional processing. Consequently, this camera became highly popular among indie filmmakers and went on to be used on features, music videos, commercials, and pretty much any video project that wanted to look a little more high-end.

So when we say "video camera," often we're talking about a standard-definition 60i camera, which the RED has almost nothing in common with. But if we're talking about a video camera that shoots 24p, at least in frame rate there's some shared DNA with the RED. The RED shoots 24p—in addition to several other frame rates for different TV standards and for fast- and slow-motion effects—capturing images digitally with a sensor to CompactFlash (CF) cards and hard drives instead of tape. This requires a special workflow to make sure footage is being managed and saved properly.

HIGH DEFINITION

The RED has more in common with HD cameras than standard-definition cameras, at least in terms of resolution. Cameras such as Sony's F-950 and Panavision's Genesis shoot high-definition at 1920 x 1080 pixels (also called 1080p), usually at 24p, and record to Sony's HDCAM tape format. Typically these cameras use 2/3-inch CCD chips (more on sensor chips in the sidebar "What's a CMOS?" in Chapter 4) and produce a reasonably cinematic look, especially when fit with high-end HD lenses. For many filmmakers, the 1080p look of these HD cameras is more than enough to get the job done. In fact, many high-profile TV series and Hollywood features have been shot with HD cameras, such as *Get Smart, Superman Returns, 21,* and *Star Wars Episode III: Revenge of the Sith.*

Prosumer HD cameras such as the Panasonic HVX200 and Sony EX1 have given independent moviemakers a little more opportunity to affordably shoot HD. (*Prosumer* cameras offer certain professional features at a more consumer-friendly price.) These cameras are limited by their image quality compared to the higher-end HD cameras, both with smaller chips and with more compressed video signals. Also, most prosumer HD cameras have permanently affixed lenses of good but not exceptional image quality. It's difficult to achieve extensive creative effects with a standard fixed zoom lens alone.

The RED differs from most HD cameras in resolution and recording format. At its maximum 4K (4096 x 2304 pixels) resolution, the RED has more than twice the resolution of a 1080p HD camera. This means a sharper picture, and it also means much greater potential to enlarge and reframe shots in postproduction without losing apparent image quality. In fact, 4K generally has to be down-converted to 2K in order to be printed back to 35mm film because most film-recording services are based around a 2K workflow. In short, there are a lot of pixels to play with in a 4K image. Because the initial image is twice as large as the 2K frame, footage down-converted from 4K to 2K looks much sharper than footage that originated at 2K.

Because the RED's sensor is so much bigger than an HD camera's, it can approximate the image area of a 35mm frame. That means you can take a lens designed for a 35mm film camera and mount it onto the RED to achieve a very similar shot. You have a similar field of view and also a shallower depth of field—more so than most HD cameras could ever achieve.

Another difference from most other HD cameras is that the RED records to CF cards and hard drives instead of a tape deck. This makes the camera a lot lighter and less mechanically complex; in fact, there are no major moving parts inside the RED ONE. Recording to flash drives also makes the camera body much cheaper, and this is probably the single most important advantage the RED has over most high-end HD cameras: It's affordable. Moreover, because the recording method is digital, the camera can be updated and improved via software updates rather than costly hardware upgrades (see "Uprading Your Firmware," later in this chapter).

FILM

Moving on to 35mm film cameras (**Figure 2.2**), there's a really important difference to get out of the way first: price. Although renting an ARRI or Panavision 35mm body is not really that much more expensive than renting a RED ONE body, the additional purchase of 35mm stock makes it much more costly. Add the costs of developing, transferring to video for editing, negative cutting, answer and release printing, and so on, and you can see that making 35mm features is primarily the domain of deep-pocketed movie studios. If you actually wanted to own a 35mm camera body, you'd discover that most good ones are several times more expensive than the RED (Panavision doesn't even offer its cameras for sale—they are rental-only).

Figure 2.2 An ARRI 435 Xtreme 35mm motion-picture film camera.

So, with the big price difference aside, the RED is actually designed to be as similar to a film camera as possible while leveraging the strengths and cost savings of digital. In addition to being compatible with standard 35mm lenses, the RED is also usable with a huge variety of film accessories, including matte boxes, filters, audio gear, monitors, and more. This is an important advantage, because it means people who have worked over the years on 35mm film productions can segue to RED shoots without unlearning everything they already know. (We'll look at recommended equipment in more detail in Chapters 4 and 5.)

A key question on many filmmakers' minds is, "Can the RED be used to create a motion picture that could be printed back to 35mm film and exhibited theatrically without compromise?" From a resolution and technical standpoint, that answer is a resounding yes. By the time you read this, it will have become increasingly likely that you've already seen a movie in a theater that was shot on the RED.

NOTE   You can see a current list of projects shot on the RED at www.red.com/ shot_on_red

OTHER HIGH-END DIGITAL CAMERAS

A few other high-end cameras are similar to the RED. One is the Silicon Imaging SI-2K camera (www.siliconimaging.com), which was used to shoot sections of 2009's Academy Award Best Picture winner, *Slumdog Millionaire*. The SI-2K (**Figure 2.3**) maxes out at 2K resolution—half that of the RED's but still higher than HD. It also uses PL-mount lenses and a CMOS chip like the RED. It even has the same base body price as the RED at $17,500 (though you also need to purchase a $17,000 recording device to go with the body). In my opinion, the SI-2K compares most favorably with the RED all around.

Figure 2.3 The Silicon Imaging SI-2K camera.

Another camera that's comparable with the RED is the Vision Research Phantom HD (www.visionresearch.com). The Phantom is a specialty high-speed camera that can shoot uncompressed 2K at up to 1,000 frames per second using a massive array of onboard flash memory. Now, this is very cool, but it's also very expensive: The body of the Phantom HD alone costs more than $100,000. But that said, as a rental it's a formidable option. I often set up productions with both the RED and the Phantom. The RED does the bulk of the regular shooting, and the Phantom rolls in as a high-speed B camera to capture stunts, explosions, liquids, and pretty much anything that would look cool in super slow motion.

Finally, I should mention a few other cameras in a similar league to the RED. These are the Dalsa Origin camera (www.dalsa.com), which shoots uncompressed 4K, and the Thomson Viper (www.thomsongrassvalley.com), which shoots up to 1080p. Both of these cameras shoot a great-looking image using cinema lenses. But they are also fairly expensive and use workflows that are not as well-known as the RED's has become.

Exploring the Tapeless Workflow

Some people coming to the RED may find the *tapeless workflow* new and challenging. With film- and tape-based cameras, you are shooting to a medium once, which becomes your de facto backup. You can't shoot film negative twice (unless you're doing multilayered effects in camera, but that's another book), and you don't usually shoot videotape more than once (unless you're really strapped for cash). With the RED, you work with CF cards and hard drives, which are reusable—you use them again and again while storing your footage on other media, typically other hard drives. (For the full lowdown on managing footage on hard drives and preparing archives, check out Chapter 14.)

The most important takeaway as we consider the tapeless workflow is that with the RED the data itself is your "digital negative"—not the medium on which it's stored. You need to put in place procedures to assure that you always know where the hard drive or CF card you're currently shooting on came from. When you're about to format a new drive for shooting, make extra certain that any footage it contains has been safely transferred to another drive and verified for accuracy. Take notes on the set or work carefully with a digital imaging technician (DIT) to establish a workflow.

The tapeless workflow can be as complex as running a spreadsheet on a laptop for every take (**Figure 2.4**) or as simple as putting pieces of red gaffer's tape on hard drives that hold untransferred footage. Whatever you do, devise a clear system that everyone understands. Make sure there's never that sinking feeling on set that you may have just erased something you don't have backed up. Take a look at the point-of-view (POV) experiences in this book as well—the interviews with DITs offer lots of tips for assuring everything is running smoothly with the tapeless workflow.

Figure 2.4 Fotokem camera report, customized for RED. Courtesy of Mike Brodersen, Fotokem, www.fotokem.com/nextlab

NOTE You can download a version of this report at the Web site, www.peachpit.com/red.

MANAGING THE TAPELESS WORKFLOW

Figure 2.5 The HD Monitor Pro wireless Bluetooth logging and proxy creation device.

Red Lightning Software (www.hdmonitorpro. com) offers an interesting wireless device that can help keep track of footage. The HD Monitor Pro Bluetooth remote unit (**Figure 2.5**) connects directly to the RED's GPIO port and automatically transmits a small proxy clip version of every take you shoot. In effect, you'll have a complete database of every shot you make before you even start transferring footage. This doesn't replace the need to carefully manage every hard drive and CF card, but it's a nice supplement.

Exploring the RAW Workflow

Along with the tapeless workflow, the other aspect of working with the RED you need to master is the *RAW workflow*. What does it mean to be RAW exactly? It means that you are getting "raw" sensor data instead of actual video footage. This differs from most DV and HD cameras, where the image you produce is mostly dependent on how you have the camera set up at the time of image capture. For example, you must select your gamma settings, your color values, and your exposure very carefully, because those are recorded as RGB data when you roll to tape. You can do a lot in color correction during postproduction, but once you go too far in any one direction, you'll get noise and greatly reduced image quality.

NOTE RGB stands for red, green, and blue. In an RGB image, each individual pixel is assigned a specific value as an expression of red, green, and blue values. Put those together, and you have created a color. Put a screen full of RGB pixels together, and you have a picture. Shoot 24 pictures a second, and you have motion...you get the idea.

Shooting RAW in the RED is a completely different way of working, because instead of capturing footage that has a certain look locked in, the camera actually records the "raw" data captured by the sensor. Then, using the RED's helper applications (details in Chapter 9), you can manipulate exposure, color, and a host of other attributes to a far greater degree than you ever could with non-RAW video. Shooting RAW is much closer to the concept of shooting 35mm film negative, where you have a massive degree of latitude to alter footage in postproduction.

COMPARISONS WITH DSLR RAW

Figure 2.6 Nikon D200 Digital SLR still camera.

If you've ever worked with a DSLR camera that supports the RAW still image format, you've gotten a sense of its advantages. High-end still cameras from companies such as Nikon (**Figure 2.6**) and Canon offer a choice of different formats, typically including JPEG, TIFF (sometimes), and RAW. JPEG and TIFF take up less space than RAW on a memory card, and both look great— but both are relatively limited in how much manipulation can take place after shooting. In essence, the color temperature, gamma, and exposure settings are "baked in" when you press the shutter release. With the RAW format, the file sizes are much larger, but you retain nearly complete control over those attributes as you grade your images in postproduction.

The engineers of the RED camera set out with a mandate to create a motion-picture camera with this very same RAW approach. In fact, the RED shoots *only* RAW, so whether you realize it or not, you're always working in RAW when you shoot with this camera. What you see on the monitor as you shoot is only one possible interpretation of the raw data. It's a look that you can attach to your footage, which will appear on the QuickTime proxy clips that the camera makes (more on proxies later in this chapter), but the raw sensor data remains intact.

You'll learn more about viewing images on set versus in postproduction in Chapter 6. With RAW, you still need to get a proper focus and exposure and pay attention to color temperature, gamma, and other image qualities. But you'll always know you have significant creative options preserved for you in postproduction.

THE REDCODE RAW NATIVE CAMERA CODEC

In order to deliver on the concept of the RAW workflow, RED devised its own camera codec, called REDCODE RAW, and integrated it into the camera. REDCODE is a wavelet-based codec, which basically means that an image is divided up into very small wave patterns, as opposed to the block patterns of other camera codecs, including digital video (DV). In REDCODE, as the image approaches the limits of its data rate, it becomes softer rather than getting blocky as DV does, so it's a lot more pleasing to the eye. That said, the data rate of REDCODE—at approximately 28 MB per second for REDCODE 28, and 36 MB per second for REDCODE 36—is sufficiently high and I've never seen any compression artifacting (such as pixelation or noise) even in scenes with highly complex motion.

> TIP REDCODE 28 offers a lower data rate for longer recording time, but the difference is small enough you might as well shoot REDCODE 36 for maximum image quality.

Compare REDCODE to some other video formats in **Table 2.1**, and you'll see it actually has a relatively high bit rate. That said, REDCODE also has to account for more than twice the resolution of HD codecs while preserving RAW sensor data. So, you can appreciate the engineering feat that RED's programmers pulled off cramming those huge 4K frames into manageable data sizes.

WHAT'S A CODEC?

Codec is short for compression/decompression and is a specific method for compressing and uncompressing a digital signal. HD and SD video are rarely transmitted or viewed uncompressed, because the data storage and throughput rates would require very fast and expensive hard drives and processors. Visually speaking, it's often hard to tell the difference between well-compressed and uncompressed video. It's like in music: AAC and MP3 audio files are a lot more common than uncompressed AIF or WAV, but to most ears they sound great. In the RED's case, REDCODE RAW is the image codec, and it looks virtually indistinguishable from an uncompressed signal because of its high efficiency.

TABLE 2.1   DATA TRANSFER RATE BY VIDEO FORMAT

Format	Store 1 hour	Transfer rate
REDCODE RAW	Up to 130 GB	28 or 36 MB/second
HD		
HDV	12 GB	3.2 MB/second
AVC-Intra	Up to 54 GB	7.25 or 12.5 MB/second
XDCAM EX	16 GB	4.37 MB/second
DVCPROHD	45 GB	12.5 MB/second
ProRes 422 HQ	99 GB	27.5 MB/second
HDCAM SR	396 GB	110 MB/second
SD		
DV	12 GB	3.2 MB/second
DVCPRO50	27 GB	7.25 MB/second
Uncompressed 8-bit	72 GB	20.2 MB/second
Uncompressed 10-bit	96 GB	26.7 MB/second
ProRes 422 HQ	29 GB	8 MB/second

Table courtesy of www.larryjordan.biz.

Certain codecs are locked to specific data rates, because these are tied to a tape-based camera system. To get more data on a tape, the tape needs to either run faster or be physically larger. With the RED's software-only encoding, there's no physical limitation. The data rate is limited only by the processing capability of the camera's computer and the speed of the memory format to which it's recording. That means that as memory card and hard drive speeds increase, RED could potentially increase the data rate of REDCODE even more, assuming the onboard computer could handle it.

RED FILES, FOLDERS, AND PROXIES

When you work with the RED, you'll notice the camera creates a number of files for each shot. Each shot goes in its own separate folder (**Figure 2.7**) with an RDC file extension. (RDC stands for RED Digital Clip.) In turn, all of those folders filled with RDC files go into a top-level directory with an RDM file extension. (RDM stands for RED digital magazine.) In order to avoid any file-handling errors or trouble importing into your editing software, you should always copy all of these files intact when you are duplicating files.

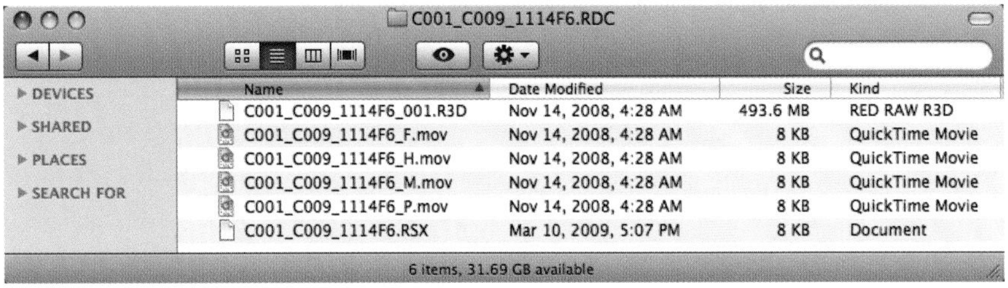
C001_C009_1114F6.RDC
DEVICES
SHARED
PLACES
SEARCH FOR
Name
Date Modified
Size
Kind
C001_C009_1114F6_001.R3D
Nov 14, 2008, 4:28 AM
493.6 MB
RED RAW R3D
C001_C009_1114F6_F.mov
Nov 14, 2008, 4:28 AM
8 KB
QuickTime Movie
C001_C009_1114F6_H.mov
Nov 14, 2008, 4:28 AM
8 KB
QuickTime Movie
C001_C009_1114F6_M.mov
Nov 14, 2008, 4:28 AM
8 KB
QuickTime Movie
C001_C009_1114F6_P.mov
Nov 14, 2008, 4:28 AM
8 KB
QuickTime Movie
C001_C009_1114F6.RSX
Mar 10, 2009, 5:07 PM
8 KB
Document
6 items, 31.69 GB available

Figure 2.7 The folder contents of a single shot from a RED ONE camera.

What's actually in an RDC folder? First, there's the R3D file, which holds all the raw sensor and image data. The R3D is by far the largest file because it contains the full 4K image running at 24 frames per second (or more, depending on your settings).

Next, you'll notice four QuickTime movie files. Those are your proxies. A *proxy* is simply a lower-quality, smaller version of your R3D file that acts as a translator for QuickTime to access the footage. Proxies make viewing and editing each clip much easier. Now, keep in mind that the QuickTime proxies are not RAW—they have the current gamma and color settings "baked in" that you selected when recording the shot.

You can easily open an R3D file in RED's included software such as RED Alert! or REDCINE and create a whole new set of proxies with updated color and gamma settings; this leverages the power of the RAW workflow while producing files you can play back in any QuickTime-aware application. (You'll learn more about that in Chapter 9.) Each QuickTime proxy has a different frame size and corresponding addition to its file name (such as _F for full). They are, in order, as follows:

- _F full
- _H high
- _M medium
- _P proxy

The actual resolution for each set of proxies (**Figure 2.8**) varies with the original shooting format, but in general each format is half the size of the one before it. So, if you shoot 4K, then F is 4K, H is 2K, M is 1K, and P is 1/2K.

TIP   Notice that the proxy files are only a few kilobytes in size. That's because they are really just QuickTime pointer files back to the R3D files. And *that's* why you must copy the entire RDC folder intact. If you just copy the proxy files, they will be blank when you try to open them on another computer without the R3D files.

Figure 2.8 Proxies of the same shot opened in QuickTime Player with P (proxy) on the far left and F (full) at the far right. Note the full-size proxy dwarfs a 30-inch display's desktop.

You might also find an RSX file within the RDC folder. This file contains color-correction data from RED Alert! that appears the moment you open a shot in that application. When this file is in the same folder as the R3D and it's loaded into RED Alert!, you'll see all the most recent color- and gamma-correction data you applied to the shot. (See the "RED Alert!" section of Chapter 9 for more details.) Keep in mind this is nondestructive; in other words, you can easily alter this data or remove it entirely, and the R3D file will return to its original camera settings. That's one of the main benefits of working in RAW: You can change the look of the R3D files to your heart's content, and you'll never lose any quality due to recompression—because there isn't any.

WHAT'S IN A CLIP NAME?

Ever wondered how the clips the camera creates are named?

The format of the clip name is **Camera Letter+Reel Number_Clip Number_Month_Day_XX.**

The *XX* part is two alphanumeric characters randomly generated by the camera for each file. So, for example, **C001_C009_1114F6.R3D** indicates this is a shot from the C camera, reel 1, clip 9, shot on November 14 with the two-digit code F6. Remember this, because it could save your life someday.

Working with Metadata

Metadata is a word you're going to hear a lot of when you work with the RED, but what does it mean? Metadata is data *about other data* in any media. For the RED, metadata refers to any information about a particular clip that isn't video or audio. This can include (but is not limited to) camera-specific setup information, project and clip management information, edge code, timecode, date, lens parameters, audio settings, and any video image-processing information. If you record audio with footage, it becomes part of the R3D file and will also play back from the proxies. **Table 2.2** lists the RED metadata available from a single shot.

How much you utilize metadata depends on two things: how important metadata is to you and how much RED metadata the software you're using actually supports. Some productions hardly use metadata at all; they shoot and go right into editing, discarding most metadata that isn't directly related to the image. Other productions may rely more heavily on metadata. For example, visual effects artists routinely use all the metadata they can get, especially technical lens data, to help them create realistic 3D animation that properly integrates with 2D footage.

How much metadata you can actually put to use depends on your editing, compositing, or color-correction software. As we explore postproduction in the second half of the book, you'll learn more details about which software supports which metadata. The RED's own applications support a lot of the camera's metadata and use it to good effect for color correction and preparation of footage for editorial (see Chapter 9 for more information).

TIP Cooke's S4/i lenses communicate detailed metadata to the RED, including lens setting, focusing distance, aperture, hyperfocal distance, lens type, and focal length. You'll learn more about these topics in Chapter 4.

TABLE 2.2 RED RAW METADATA FROM A SINGLE SHOT

FileName	ReelID	AltReelID	CamReelID	Camera
C001_C030_11146Q_001.R3D	C001_C030_11146Q	C001C030	C001	C
Reel	Clip	Date	TimeStamp	FrameWidth
1	30	20081114	50447	4096
FrameHeight	FPS	Total Frames	TOD TC Start	Edgecode Start
2304	23.976	449	05:04:44:07	01:14:56:07
TOD TC End	Edgecode End	ColorSpace	GammaSpace	Kelvin
05:05:02:23	01:15:14:23	11	14	5600
Tint	ISO	Exposure	Saturation	Contrast
0	320	0	1	0
Brightness	GainRed	GainGreen	GainBlue	Black X
0	0.9	1	1	0
Black Y	Toe X	Toe Y	Mid X	Mid Y
0	0.25	0.25	0.5	0.5
Knee X	Knee Y	White X	White Y	Shutter (ms)
0.75	0.75	1	1	20.8
Shutter (1/sec)	Shutter (deg)	Firmware	Audio Channels	File Segments
48	180	3.4.1#17	2	1

Upgrading Your Firmware

One more area of the RED workflow that you may find new and different is the download-able software upgrades. The RED camera has highly sophisticated internal hardware and cir-cuitry, as well as software called *firmware*. The firmware handles image capture, compresses images, drives the video displays, and enables user controls (among a lot of other functions).

Figure 2.9 The RED camera startup screen with the current build noted.

Every modern HD and video camera uses firmware, and some are more sophisticated than others. Otherwise, they'd have to completely reengineer the camera every time there was a minor fix. What's special about the RED is you can actually download new versions of the firmware and install them on the camera yourself. These new versions, called *builds* (**Figure 2.9**), typically enable new features and fix problems or bugs from earlier versions. Some other cameras must be sent to the manufacturer to have the firmware updated by technicians in order to maintain the camera's warranty. Downloadable firmware is becoming more popular, especially with digital still cameras.

When a new RED build is available, you can go to RED's Web site, download the file, copy it to a CompactFlash card, turn off your camera, place the CF card into your camera, and boot up. (New builds are announced on RED's sites as well as e-mailed to owners who have subscribed to the company's newsletter.) The new build automatically installs itself and upgrades your camera. The newest build as of this writing is build 20, which ought to give you a good sense of both the amount of work RED has on its plate and its commitment to supporting its users. To download the latest build, visit www.red.com/support.

That's a quick taste of the RED workflow. The rest of this book builds on the concepts introduced here. You'll get the most use out of this camera if you can wrap your head around the tapeless and RAW workflows. With tapeless, the main point to keep in mind is you must carefully manage footage and never lose a shot because of sloppy bookkeeping. For RAW, remember that you are seeing only one possible look, controlled by metadata, as you view your monitor during production. Your options are wide open to alter that footage to whatever degree you'd like once you get into postproduction.

Rodney Charters, ASC

CINEMATOGRAPHER, *24*

Rodney Charters, ASC, on location in Cape Town, South Africa, on the set of *24: Redemption*. (Photo by Michael Klick.)

Cinematographer Rodney Charters, ASC, grew up on the coast of New Zealand, where as a young boy he starred in several of his father's Bolex 16mm movies. Charters made his first short film at the University of Auckland, which played to acclaim at the Sydney Film Festival and earned him a place at the prestigious Royal College of Art in London. His fellow students included director Tony Scott (*True Romance, Man on Fire*), director Richard Loncraine (*Richard III, Wimbledon*), and director of photography Stephen Goldblatt, ASC (*Lethal Weapon, Charlie Wilson's War*).

After several years of TV work in Toronto and Vancouver, Charters made the move to the United States to shoot the first season of Don Johnson's *Nash Bridges*. As a member of the Directors Guild of America, he has also directed several hours of episodic TV. Charters is currently the director of photography (DP) on the highly successful Fox series *24*, starring Kiefer Sutherland.

Charters was an early adopter of the RED camera and uses it mostly for personal projects. "Initially, I hadn't even seen the camera, but post–NAB 2007, my son Robin and I tested the same prototype units that Steven Soderbergh shot *Che* with," recalls Charters. "I stayed involved with early camera development, and we even tested shooting *24* with RED, outfitting it with our Panavision lenses and accessories. The lower light sensitivity of the RED and the limited camera supply at the time figured into the decision to hold off on switching over. We routinely shoot with up to eight cameras and often at low, moody, and contrasty light levels."

To keep his personal RED kit as portable as possible, Charters outfitted a Think Tank Airport Acceleration case to hold the RED body and a small set of Canon still lenses, along with Birger Engineering's Canon EOS mount. "I started out with just four lenses," says Charters. "They were all Canon zooms including a 16–35mm, 24–70mm, 70–200mm, and 100–400mm. Since one ARRI Master Prime is worth more than the RED body, I like taking the Canons around without having to spend an exorbitant amount. I also carry a really tiny tripod that barely gets me stable images when there's no wind. More than anything, it's to prove the portable workflow for myself."

Charters uses a fairly straightforward method to move into post on his way to a 1080p finish. "I use REDrushes to extract 1920 x 1080 ProRes clips, bring them into Final Cut Pro, and I'm editing. Sometimes I'll start cutting immediately with the small proxies. I think you'll eventually see CPUs continue to get faster and be able to handle the R3D files directly. There are also plenty of third-party developers on the verge of releasing intermediate codecs."

When Charters returned to his regular duties on 24, he passed his RED onto Robin. "It has become the workhorse for his own evolution as a DP," Charters proudly remarks. "I can never get my hands on the camera as it's always out on a job with him."

As a DP with many years of experience with 35mm film, Charters offers his quallity comparison. "I don't think there's a major difference anymore, especially if we're talking about a 35mm telecine transfer on a Spirit Datacine in 1920 x 1080 HD with 4:2:2 color compared to DPXs extracted from RED R3D files," notes Charters. "Film still has a wider dynamic range and more latitude, which you can really see in the telecine. RED's number-one limiting factor is the chip sensitivity, which is not as fast as 500 ASA film. The next generation's chip will be faster, and then it's a moot point. I can always bring in brighter lighting fixtures to compensate for the differences in sensitivity, especially given the price of shooting and processing film. On 24, we're shooting $4 million a year worth of stock, and Kodak loves us! When you throw in that money differential, you can see where a lot more shows will eventually switch over to RED."

Charters views archiving and asset management as other significant challenges for RED and for digital motion pictures in general. "To store all the assets of a major studio picture shot on film costs around $400/year for an air-conditioned, salt mine vault," he observes. "The equivalent in digital acquisition would cost around $12,000 to 15,000 per year, because completion guarantors expect you to replicate the data files every six months for safety. Still, I expect there will be major advances in optical storage technology to achieve 100–500TB capacity discs that last for 100 years and can be reread at any time. Digital animation companies like Pixar have always kept their work on LTO-3 and LTO-4 tapes as files, and they're not complaining about it."

As a longtime owner and renter of cinema gear, Charters sees a benefit to the RED camera's compatibility with 35mm accessories. "My focus-puller on 24 uses a Preston Cinema Systems remote unit, which costs about $20,000," Charters says. "We're shooting handheld 90 percent of the time with remote focus and Iris (aperture control). Manufacturers like Preston build and price their gear for a very limited number of sales because there are only so many 35mm cameras in use. Five thousand RED bodies hitting the market in the first couple of years should help drive a lot of small, indie manufacturers to create mass-market accessories that are more affordable.

"I have to give the utmost respect to Jim Jannard for opening up a Pandora's box of new technology innovation," he continues. "Established vendors like O'Connor were obliged to create new product lines after Jim posted a picture of a RED ONE on one of their new tripod heads and orders went up astronomically. The biggest excitement is in the startup field, where companies are exploding with orders for tools we've always craved but were often in the financial realm of fantasy.

"I am standing beside my RED ONE, affectionately named KIWI after my homeland," adds Charters. "I've got a Viewfactor.net Bluetooth remote focus, iris, and zoom control, along with a Canon still lens on a Birger Engineering mount. I have complete wireless, repeatable control of the focus on any of my Canon lenses from up to 50 feet away. All of this costs a small portion of what an ARRI FTZ or a Preston controller would have set me back."

Reflecting on his experiences with the RED (**Figure 2.10**), Charters sees the camera as an intriguing corollary to his ongoing work with film. "In this industry it's an unprecedented and historic technological development," he says. "It's intoxicating to be somewhere in the world, alone in a forest, and shooting 35mm quality files of whatever you choose to point your camera at. I did 20 years of documentary work in the field, and the best I ever got was 16mm/16:9. Carrying all that film with me was a limitation and a considerable expense. So, to be able to go around the world and shoot four or five hours of material without even blinking in terms of cost is truly amazing. Thanks to Jim for igniting this revolution and keeping it going. Cheers, mate."

Rodney Charters's Web site is www.rodneycharters.com. ∎

Figure 2.10 Rodney Charters, ASC, shot this RED footage in Pyongyang, North Korea during some rare time off from *24*.

3 DEFINING YOUR PROJECT

Before we get into all the juicy details of using RED equipment and configuring setups, you need to figure out what your project is and how that will impact working with the camera and shooting footage. You also need to think about what's going to happen with your project once you enter postproduction.

You should consider attributes such as project length, editorial format, and final delivery format carefully before you shoot your first frame. Defining your completed project in as much detail as possible up front will save you a lot of time and effort when you put everything together later. It will also help guide your on-set workflow and equipment purchasing or rental decisions.

Project Length

The first question you should ask is, "What's the anticipated length and style of my project?" Is it a short film, a wildlife documentary, a 30-second commercial spot, a 4-minute music video, a 90-minute concert, a 2-hour narrative feature, or an ongoing reality TV series? Depending on the length of the production, you might start by looking at renting versus buying filmmaking equipment. If you buy a RED ONE camera for a long-form production, you can generally expect to get a reasonable return on the gear if you decide to sell it when the production wraps. This may have changed by the time you're reading this, so be sure to research the market a bit on your own before making your decision. I explore the different budgets and cost/benefits of renting versus owning in greater depth in Chapter 4.

The style of your project also plays a role in how you approach using the RED camera. Every project requires a slightly different setup. You're likely to be shooting very long takes for a documentary, for example. If so, consider getting a RED-DRIVE or RED-RAM unit rather than using CompactFlash (CF) cards for extended record times (see Chapter 4 for more details on CF cards). You'll also want to have a *zoom* lens in your kit rather than rely totally on *prime* lenses, because you can't change the focal length of a prime lens, and you may need to do so during certain shots. Zooms are also great for narrative work, but it all comes down to the quality of image you're trying to achieve and how much lighting equipment you want to haul around. For shorter, shot-by-shot scenes in a narrative feature, you can probably get by with CF cards alone and have a streamlined, lightweight camera package to run and gun with. You'll learn more about stripped-down configurations in Chapter 4.

FEATURE FILMS

Feature filmmaking is a dream pursuit for many RED owners, and the ability to create a real movie is no longer the exclusive privilege of Hollywood big-budget 35mm filmmakers. You really can make your own high-quality movie for the price of a RED camera purchase or rental (plus accessories, of course, and you also have to pay actors).

The challenge lies in creating a RED movie that will stand up to Hollywood-level expectations in all aspects. On the creative side, that means a great screenplay, solid direction, and well-cast actors. On the technical side, you can stack the deck in your favor. Nothing separates an obvious indie from a big-budget blockbuster quicker than compromised audio so spend time getting the audio right too (see Chapter 5 for more details).

Next, get the best possible set of prime lenses you can afford, especially if a 35mm theatrical release is at all possible. Zooms are useful for quickly changing the framing of a shot without having to move the camera, but they're also typically less sensitive to light and produce images that are not nearly as sharp (unless you rent the really high-end zooms such as the Optimo, shown in **Figure 3.1**). You can save money on prime lenses by using zooms, but you lose that advantage by having to rent more lighting to compensate and perhaps by hiring a more experienced camera assistant to pull focus (if you have the budget) and nail the shallower focus on slower zooms.

Figure 3.1 RED ONE fitted with an Angenieux Optimo 24–290 zoom lens.

You may be contemplating adding a *B camera* (a second shooting camera) to the production. In the proper hands, two cameras can help an indie production capture twice as much material on a tight schedule while providing the editor with more choices to present the best possible version of the story. But many directors find it difficult to efficiently block scenes for two cameras at once. Many directors of photography (DPs) say it's tough to create an ideal lighting setup for multiple cameras.

DOCUMENTARIES

Perhaps the most important documentary workflow consideration with regard to RED cameras is the length of takes (**Figure 3.2**). Documentaries are often based on in-depth interviews with subjects that can require an hour or more to yield story-critical pieces of dialogue. For those long takes, using CF cards doesn't give you enough recording time, especially at RED's maximum 4K resolution. For these kinds of documentaries, you'll almost certainly want to work with a RED-DRIVE (**Figure 3.3**), which allows a recording time of three hours or more.

Figure 3.2 Shooting documentaries with RED requires careful consideration of media storage for longer takes.

NOTE Sometimes you'll work with more than one camera, depending on the kind of documentary you're making, so consult the "Multiple RED cameras" section later in this chapter if necessary.

Figure 3.3 A 320 GB RED-DRIVE portable hard drive recording module.

As with any magnetic hard drive with moving parts, the RED-DRIVE is more susceptible to physical damage or disruption than a solid-state CF card. In other words, be careful if you want to interview a helicopter pilot in flight or a demolitions expert, for example. In general, the RED-DRIVE is quite tough, but you need to take extra precautions such as bracing the camera and padding the drive to protect against intense vibration or impact. Generally, the standard RED-DRIVE cradle is unfit for high vibration and loud audio situations. This goes double for concerts: even the shock mount for the RED-DRIVE can skip at a concert.

If vibration is going to be a real issue for your documentary, look into the RED-RAM drive, which uses solid-state memory like a CF card to deliver far greater durability and resistance to impact than the RED-DRIVE. By the time you're reading this, it's likely that CF cards and the RED-RAM will have increased in capacity while dropping in cost. Whichever option you choose, mapping out not only your recording medium but also an on-set data wrangling strategy will be critical for a documentary project.

EPISODIC TELEVISION

In general, episodic television shows work with DPs who have extensive TV production credits. Networks also exercise a lot of control over the content and technical aspects of their programming. So, be very mindful of network delivery specifications as you work, and carefully coordinate with the post-production team. Because most TV shows finish at 1080/24p (see the following sidebar, "The numbers: p's and i's of high definition"), you'll probably wind up with your footage in a high-definition (HD) tape-based workflow (see the "HD" section of Chapter 13 for more tips). The RAW workflow is sometimes considered overkill for television broadcast, at least as of this writing.

THE NUMBERS: P'S AND I'S OF HIGH DEFINITION

The abbreviations 1080p, 1080i, and 720p describe high-definition footage. The 1080 and 720 refer to the vertical resolution of the image, and the *i* and *p* refer to *interlaced* and *progressive*. A notation such as 1080/24p HD, therefore, is shorthand for 1080 progressive high-definition footage at 24 frames per second. This explanation also applies to standard definition: 480i is interlaced, standard-definition footage.

Speed is another important consideration for episodic television work. Most TV shows routinely shoot 7–10 pages of script a day in order to complete each episode within a week. The RED ONE camera has many possible configurations and accessories, and all that reconfiguration for different modes can sometimes slow down a TV production's "need for speed." Having multiple cameras can help, but sometimes it's still not enough.

One solution, employed by Arthur Albert, DP on the TV series *ER*, is to set up several RED packages, each preconfigured for a specific shooting mode. *ER* carried three different RED packages to enable the production to quickly switch from handheld to dolly to Steadicam without any downtime. With this method, the relatively low price of the RED body can enhance a TV production crew's ability to move briskly from setup to setup. (Read Albert's POV Interview after Chapter 6 for more details.)

Reality TV series are completely different from scripted dramas (most of the time). They require an approach more akin to documentary filmmaking, with the RED configured for ENG-style photography. (ENG stands for *electronic news gathering* and is how documentary or news crews often refer to their camera setups.) A lightweight, handheld RED configuration with a zoom lens and a RED-DRIVE for long takes is usually a safe bet. Reality TV shows are also often composed of multiple formats. The RED might be used to capture the beauty of remote locations or to conduct interviews with reality-series participants, while smaller POV and hidden HD cameras are used to capture candid action. Consult the sections "Documentaries" and "Multiple formats" for more ideas.

MUSIC VIDEOS

Music video production relies heavily on sound, though in a different way than narrative and documentary filmmaking. Most music videos feature at least some portion of the song being sung on-screen by the recording artist (**Figure 3.4**). Unless it's a live concert video, the performer lip-syncs to a recording of their song, and no on-set audio is recorded. Careful synchronization of the song's playback with the RED is critical.

Figure 3.4 Music videos typically involve syncing live performance to pre-recorded music.

On lower-budget music video shoots, the performer might lip-sync to a CD playing over loudspeakers. Though CDs are digital, they do not guarantee perfect playback sync with SMPTE timecode like professional audio gear does and may drift out of sync over time. This can be corrected in postproduction, but it adds to the workload. If you're going the CD audio route, go ahead and record audio on set into the RED for an easy additional sync reference.

> NOTE   SMPTE timecode is a set of standards to label individual frames of video or film with a timecode, as defined by the Society of Motion Picture and Television Engineers.

More lavishly budgeted productions use timecode sources such as Digital Audio Tape (DAT) recorders or solid-state recorders, connected to speakers in conjunction with a digital smart slate. This method helps the RED capture perfect sync between singer and song. See Chapter 5 for more details on audio gear recommendations and sync sound setup.

> NOTE   A *smart slate* is a small device with built-in timecode and a writing surface to help with recording sync sound.

Most music performers are naturally very interested in the finish or "look" of their music videos. Watch any leading music video channel or Web site today, and you'll see numerous examples of glossy, intensive color correction. You'll want to offer a music video client the widest possible latitude for post finessing. Finish the project using either the RED RAW workflow or a highly malleable format such as DPX. Be sure to have plenty of fast hard-drive storage for those larger, less compressed files. Refer to Chapter 13 to learn how to set everything up for high-end finishing in either mode.

COMMERCIALS

In the United States, the most expensive commercials traditionally appear during the Super Bowl. Advertising agencies routinely spend millions of dollars not just on purchasing the airtime but on producing the commercials themselves. Those are the ultimate forms of television advertising, but most commercial productions are more manageable and straightforward. Commercial directors are most concerned with presenting the product or service in the most attractive way possible.

In terms of how commercial work affects the RED workflow, it depends on the kind of commercial. For car commercials, food commercials, and other image-oriented commercials, the actors and sets sometimes take a backseat to presenting the product in the best possible light. This means taking extra time on every shot and carefully preparing the angle and lighting for maximum appeal. Bring properly calibrated, high-end HD production monitors both for composing shots and lighting and for presenting setups to the client (because they will often be on the set watching your every move). Working with a food or product stylist is frequently necessary (**Figure 3.5**). (Certain companies specialize solely in preparing and detailing vehicles for commercial cinematography.)

Figure 3.5
Commercials featuring food cinematography often demand complex lighting and speciality lenses.

For consumer product photography, consider close-focus prime and macro-capable lenses. You can use snorkel and periscope lens attachments to capture extremely tight close-ups and details. Luckily, commercials have been shot for many years using 35mm equipment, so all the special lenses and accessories you could ever need are readily available for rent and will fit the RED, often without any modification.

SHORT FILMS

Shorts (**Figure 3.6**) are often made with the least amount of resources but are considerable labors of love for all involved. As a RED owner, taking on a short may mean being less concerned about your day rate and more about an opportunity to network and bring an interesting script to life.

Figure 3.6 Short films are good opportunities to network and explore unconventional subjects.

An excellent short may be invited to screen at a prestigious film festival, providing exposure and possibly jump-starting your career in the movie industry. At the very least, you'll wind up with more material to add to your RED reel. You'll also discover opportunities to experiment with new techniques and create interesting cinematography. Luckily, short productions are usually quite brief, often taking up no more than a few weekends. So, you're not likely to starve by taking one on every once in a while.

Depending on the vision and expectations of the director, a zoom lens can be a lifesaver for quick setup changes, where ultimate image quality is less important than getting through a compressed schedule. As with the other narrative forms, getting good sound is important to the success of a short and its elevation above the level of "amateur" quality.

Because short films consist of only a few shooting days, usually with no opportunity or budget to reshoot, you should be especially mindful of data management. Insist on transferring your own footage or working closely with the digital imaging technician (DIT), or whoever from the production has been assigned to assist with footage offloading, in order to assure that every frame is properly backed up. Losing even one take can make a major difference to a short film's final edit, so be extra vigilant and consider using CF cards instead of a RED-DRIVE.

You'll be compelled to transfer and check footage in smaller batches, rather than betting a whole day's production on a single drive. For the offloaded footage hard drive, request that the production purchase a top-of-the-line external FireWire 800 or eSATA drive with RAID capability. Don't get stuck with a slower drive that's not intended for video editing, because it will waste time and put the crew's hard work at risk of data failure.

Finally, although having an understanding and gentle heart is central to working on a short, as a responsible RED owner you must also insist that the production insures your equipment. If you have your own production equipment insurance, make sure to have it extended to the short, and request that the producers cover that expense if necessary. Short projects are something of a gamble and you should plan to risk only your time—not your valuable gear.

Production Mode

Once you determine the length of your project, the next question to consider is that of production mode. Will you be shooting with a single RED camera or going multi-camera? For the latter, make sure all cameras have synced timecode so you aren't spending half your life in postproduction, manually syncing takes. You'll learn more about audio and timecode setups in the "Timecode" section of Chapter 5.

Will you be mixing and matching RED footage with material from other cameras? Are those other cameras shooting standard definition or high definition in 1080p, 1080i, or 720p? Or are they shooting 35mm or 16mm film? Will that film be *telecined* (transferred to video) at 2K, 4K, or 1080p and into what format? This all sounds like a lot to consider now, but keep in mind it's much easier to get things clarified in preproduction—before serious money starts to be spent.

MULTIPLE RED CAMERAS

Concerts, sports, and theater events are routinely shot with multiple cameras to capture every potential angle of interest. TV series and films also often use multiple cameras to capture more footage and shave days off their production schedules. According to DP Rodney Charters, ASC, up to eight cameras are employed to cover a single take on the TV series 24. Once you get into postproduction, multiple angles on every take mean much easier cutting for continuity and a greater variety of creative options to tackle a scene.

Having multiple cameras involved does present challenges, both in production and in post. In production, ideal lighting is often difficult to achieve for more than one camera. For example, a nicely lit close-up may have to be somewhat compromised to make the wide-angle work at the same time, or vice versa. Experienced DPs sometimes dislike working with more than one camera for this reason, but they also understand the financial realities of production, and many have their own methods for achieving a solid image for more than one camera simultaneously.

When working with different cameras on the same shoot, make sure everyone is running the same RED firmware build so you get similar results in your on-set looks and in post. Use one camera as the master camera that all the others will match to. Make sure everyone is shooting the same frame rate, aspect ratio, compression settings, and resolution. Save the master camera's LOOK parameters to a Secure Digital (SD) card and then have each camera operator load those LOOK settings into their own camera (**Figure 3.7**). Finally, for the settings that are not included in the LOOK file, bring all the cameras together in a huddle and manually match things up.

Figure 3.7 The LOOK settings give you control over image attributes such as saturation—here set at normal, monochrome, and super color (top to bottom).

Having a nice set of production monitors equipped with waveforms and vectorscopes on set is also a big plus in assuring consistency from camera to camera. The closer you can get each camera to shooting a similar-looking picture, the less time you'll spend in post-production doing clean-up matching and the more time you'll have to creatively enhance your imagery. It goes without saying that using lenses of similar optical quality across the group helps maintain a consistent look.

In a multi-camera scenario, every camera may not be a RED. If RED cameras are being mixed with HD and/or film cameras, you most likely won't be able to match the look 100 percent. Ideally, the other camera formats were specifically chosen to present an aesthetic contrast to your RED footage. In any case, you'll want to work carefully to either attempt to match the camera's images as dictated by the DP or accentuate the differences.

Beyond the creative imaging aspects, the single most important technical consideration is audio sync. Typically in a multi-camera environment, sound is recorded separately either to a solid-state or to a DAT recorder. Sometimes the sound is fed to one of the cameras directly. Every other camera either is recording wild sound, typically unsuitable for use, or is running completely silent.

MORE ON THE LOOK MENU

The LOOK menu permits Video, Gain, and Tone values to be exported or imported to an SD card. As the name implies, the LOOK menu is a good way to set up a personalized look, or style, to your cinematography. But beware, these values are just a "grade" of what the camera is shooting; they're not the actual recorded image. Because the RED shoots RAW, the final image is infinitely alterable, and the LOOK settings are never baked into your footage. So, don't rely on this 100 percent, and don't be surprised when you open RAW files in post and find that they look completely different from what you saw in your viewfinder. In other words, learn how LOOK settings actually relate to your footage all the way through postproduction before relying on them extensively. Don't adjust these settings at all if you're not completely sure what you're doing.

Once you enter postproduction, you must have a reliable method for synchronizing all the angles not only to each other but also to the highest-quality sound you've recorded. Professionals use a smart slate to jam sync each camera along with a timecode-capable audio recorder. Doing so allows each camera to receive a common timecode that matches the audio and then allows you to sync sound and picture automatically in postproduction. Coordinate closely with your sound recordist to make sure everything is lining up. Cameras sometimes drift out of sync over time or when batteries are changed, so you should frequently check sync and re-jam all the cameras as the shoot day goes on. Getting all this to work reliably can be quite a challenge (and is tackled in more detail in the "Multi-camera audio" section in Chapter 5).

MULTIPLE FORMATS

Another scenario is the multiformat project. Let's say you want that Oliver Stone *Natural Born Killers* feeling, with a wild mixture of film and video formats for different textures. Or perhaps you're doing a feature documentary that gathers newly shot RED footage with archival 16mm, 35mm, and HD and SD video footage. In other words, you're mixing a bunch of different formats (**Figure 3.8**), with possibly different frame sizes, together into a single project.

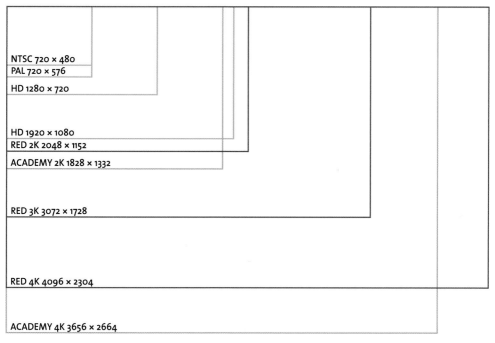

Figure 3.8 A variety of different formats and their relative frame sizes.

Your most important considerations will be related to postproduction. What is your editing format, and what is your delivery format? If it's an HD finish, then it's relatively straightforward. Any footage that's less than HD resolution needs to be up-converted to HD, and anything that's more than HD, such as your RED 4K and perhaps some 35mm scanned footage, should be down-converted. These days it's pretty easy to do a high-definition edit in most non-linear editing (NLE) programs.

So, it makes sense to simply create the whole project at full resolution in your NLE and then export the finished project directly once you're done (which I explore more in depth in Chapters 8–13). HD up-conversion can be done either within the NLE program, via hardware conversion at a postproduction house, or using a plugin such as Red Giant's Instant HD (www.redgiantsoftware.com).

Next, you'll want to pick a common frame rate. In general, more know-how and software exists to conform footage to 1080/24p as a common format, so I suggest picking that for simplicity's sake. A project that combines a multitude of acquisition formats into a common 1080p/24p sequence edit will have a relatively straightforward path to HD outputs and SD down-converts for tape and DVD.

> NOTE   In a country that uses the PAL system, make sure to choose frame rates that match the local electricity frequency when shooting under electric light. In PAL land, those are the 25, 50, 75, and 100 frame rates.

If your multiformat project is going to 35mm, things get a bit more complicated because in general you will be doing an offline version in your NLE program that will then be exported as an edit decision list (EDL) for creating a 35mm version on film. This is when it will be essential to work directly with a postproduction facility and film lab. For any footage that originated on film, you'll want to pull and cut that negative. Any footage that started digitally, such as your RED 4K footage and HD and SD video, needs to be printed to negative and cut in with any original film-derived negative. We'll get into the nitty-gritty of postproduction in Part II of this book.

The good news is that facilities and software exist to make all this possible. The bad news is that it can get expensive. But then again, if you have 35mm theatrical distribution, chances are you're doing a studio-financed or well-financed indie picture that has the budget. As with all the other scenarios examined in this chapter, the most important points to keep in mind with regard to RED are your shooting formats. Figure out what your final delivery format is likely to be first, and work your way backward. A 1.85 35mm print or a 16:9 1080p 23.98 HD master are both very common—which leads us right into the next section.

Delivery Format

The third and perhaps most important question for the RED workflow is, "What's my expected delivery format?" Will you be outputting the finished project onto 35mm film, HDCAM SR tape, standard-definition DVD, Blu-ray, H.264 QuickTime, DV, YouTube, or something else entirely? Maybe you're starting off on an indie feature that you're hoping will go to theaters on film, but you're not really sure you'll get distribution. It's okay if you don't know everything right now. Here are some different plans of attack and ways to keep your options as open as possible as you move into post.

DELIVERING IN HIGH DEFINITION

Let's begin with what is probably the most common final delivery scenario for RED projects: a high-definition 1080p, 1920 × 1080, 23.98 finish. You'll probably go out to high-definition tape at some point, most likely HDCAM or D5. You also want to create standard-definition 16:9 NTSC (or PAL) down-conversions for DVD and Digibeta. The good news is that outputting an HD 24p timeline onto a 29.97 NTSC tape is pretty easy with today's editing applications (see the "Converter cards" section in Chapter 8 for more details).

For an HD finish, one of your most important initial decisions is your production aspect ratio: 2:1, HD, or 16:9. Although 16:9 is the most proper match aspect ratio–wise, it's worth testing your postproduction performance. The 2:1 aspect ratio typically offers better playback performance in post, and because it was the first format enabled on the camera, it's somewhat better supported on third-party applications, at least at the time of this writing.

The drawback to 2:1 is you end up having to crop your image to fit a 16:9 frame, and you need to carefully use your frame guides in the viewfinder to see where your 16:9 crop will ultimately be. Make sure you keep any important visual elements framed within those 16:9 guidelines—otherwise you may need to reposition the frame in postproduction. Fortunately, repositioning 4K footage in an HD frame gives you a lot of leeway in terms of resolution and quality, which is another reason why 4K is the best resolution to shoot.

With the addition of the 4K HD mode, you have another option, which is a 3840 × 2160 frame that scales down by 50 percent perfectly to 1920 × 1080. You give up a bit of sensor resolution and field of view to your lenses in exchange for much faster decoding of images and a smoother postproduction workflow. If the HD format performs well with your NLE program and grading system, and you plan to do a 1080p HD 16:9 finish, select 4K HD for the smoothest workflow in postproduction. Otherwise, go 16:9 or 2:1 as your last resort for an HD finish. **Table 3.1** shows all the currently available resolutions on the RED camera.

TABLE 3.1   RED RESOLUTIONS

Frame Size	Resolution in Pixels	Frame Size	Resolution in Pixels
4K 2:1	4096 × 2048	3K 16:9	3072 × 1728
4K 16:9	4096 × 2304	3K ANA 1.2:1	2074 × 1728
4K HD	3840 × 2160	2K 2:1	2048 × 1024
4K ANA 1.2:1	2764 × 2304	2K 16:9	2048 × 1152
3K 2:1	3072 × 1536	2K ANA 1.2:1	1282 × 1152

WHY 2:1?

The 2:1 format was the first aspect ratio supported by the RED ONE camera and the only format it *could* shoot initially. Most modern movies are shot in 16:9 for high definition or 1.85 or 2.35 for film. The 2:1 format was chosen initially for its easy divisibility. REDCODE is a *wavelet*-based codec, which means it can be played back more efficiently by decoding only a fraction of the image. You get a half-resolution 2K frame by playing back at half resolution, and so on, down to $^{1}/_{2}$K. This is why the camera automatically generates *playback proxies* (low-resolution versions of the full 4K shots) as your shoot, and 2:1 makes that math work out more easily. Ultimately, 16:9 was enabled as a more common shooting format with firmware upgrade improvements to the camera.

Interestingly enough, there's also an aesthetic precedent for the 2:1 format. Famed cinematographer Vittorio Storaro, ASC (*Apocalyspe Now*, *The Last Emperor*), has proposed 2:1 as his Univisium format. He suggests 2:1 as the mathematical average of the 65mm 2.21:1 film and 1.78:1 HD aspect ratios to accommodate all possible movies into a single format. This approach has met with some resistance, especially from directors and DPs who prefer to maintain their own aspect ratio freedom of choice. At any rate, 2:1 as a shooting format is malleable to a wide variety of other aspect ratios in postproduction through cropping or matting. Reportedly, RED CEO Jim Jannard also appreciates the 2:1 format—another reason for its continued availability on the RED ONE camera.

It may look like a lot of choices, but there are really only three resolutions you'll spend most of your time with: 4K 2:1, 4K 16:9, and 4K HD. The 3K and 2K options are basically windowing off part of the sensor (**Figure 3.9**), so you're effectively getting a smaller frame by not using the whole sensor. That also means your optics are being cropped, so you'll see less image area on wide-angle lenses and telephoto lenses will seem longer.

RED 4K Full Optical Advantage

Diag "	RES	H	x	V	Units
1.18	FULL SENSOR	4900	x	2580	Pixel
		1.04	x	0.55	Inch
		26.46	x	13.93	MM
1.02	4K 1.66 (16:9)	4096	x	2467	Pixel
		0.87	x	0.52	Inch
		22.12	x	13.32	MM
1.00	4K 1.77 (16:9)	4096	x	2304	Pixel
		0.87	x	0.49	Inch
		22.12	x	12.44	MM
0.99	4K 1.85 (16:9)	4096	x	2214	Pixel
		0.87	x	0.47	Inch
	post crop 1.77:1	22.12	x	11.96	MM
0.97	4K 2:1	4096	x	2048	Pixel
		0.87	x	0.44	Inch
		22.12	x	11.06	MM
0.95	*4K 2.35:1	4096	x	1743	Pixel
		0.87	x	0.37	Inch
	post crop 2:1	22.12	x	9.41	MM
0.77	4K ANA 1.2:1	2764	x	2304	Pixel
		0.59	x	0.49	Inch
		14.93	x	12.44	MM

3K Horizontal

Diag "	RES	H	x	V	Units
0.75	3K 1.77 (16:9)	3072	x	1728	Pixel
		0.65	x	0.37	Inch
		16.59	x	9.3313	MM
0.73	3K 2:1	3072	x	1536	Pixel
		0.65	x	0.33	Inch
		16.59	x	8.2945	MM
0.57	3K ANA 1.2:1	2074	x	1728	Pixel
		0.44	x	0.37	Inch
		11.20	x	9.3313	MM

2K Horizontal

Diag "	RES	H	x	V	Units
0.50	2K 1.77 (16:9)	2048	x	1152	Pixel
		0.44	x	0.24	Inch
		11.06	x	6.2208	MM
0.49	2K 2:1	2048	x	1024	Pixel
		0.44	x	0.22	Inch
		11.06	x	5.5296	MM
0.37	2K ANA 1.2:1	1282	x	1152	Pixel
		0.27	x	0.24	Inch
		6.92	x	6.2208	MM

Figure 3.9 RED sensor formats compared.

Now, of course, not too many folks are actually completing projects at 4K resolution at this point. By acquiring in 4K, however, you get the highest possible source quality, and it looks great down-converted to 2K, HD, and SD. In addition to lowered bitrates and longer recording times, the primary utility of the 2K and 3K resolutions are their higher frame rates, which can go up to 120 frames per second (fps) at 2K 2:1 with a RED-DRIVE. That speed makes excellent slow-motion photography possible, and you can easily combine 2K and 4K footage on an HD timeline. Just make sure you're shooting in the same aspect ratio as your primary production resolution. If for some reason that's just not possible, make note of the cropping on your electronic viewfinder (EVF) or monitor so you get the framing correct when you convert aspect ratios in post.

DELIVERING FOR A FILM FINISH

From the earliest days of RED's development, the concept of the camera offering a viable and affordable alternative to 35mm film acquisition has been one of its strongest appeals. The basic idea is that you are capturing digitally to 4K, likely finishing up in post in 2K or 4K, and then exporting your final project to be digitally recorded frame by frame to 35mm film negative. From there it can be exhibited in a conventional film-projecting movie theater. More and more theaters are being equipped with digital projectors, but film projectors are still more prevalent worldwide. So, a film print gives you the maximum possible potential for theatrical distribution.

FOR EXPERIENCED FILM DPS

Conceptually, shooting with the RED is like shooting with a 35mm film camera with a stock balanced for 5000-degree Kelvin 320 ASA for daylight-lit scenes and 200 ASA for tungsten-lit scenes. Think of the monitor as your framing guide instead of as the final word in exposure. Meter and light like you're used to, and you'll be good to go.

Figure 3.10 ARRI prime lenses ready for action.

The production workflow for a film finish isn't quite as critical as the postproduction side, but there are some important considerations. Make sure to shoot in 4K at REDCODE 36 for the highest possible quality when going to 35mm. Film negative will absorb all the resolution you can throw at it, so go for the most the RED can offer. You should also select the highest possible optics, such as Cooke S4s or ARRI Ultra Primes (**Figure 3.10**).

It's also important to consider the frame rate: 24 fps goes 1:1 with a film or digital cinema projection (DCP) output. This rate, however, can give you some headaches if you plan to derive your HD and SD masters directly from the digital edit, rather than doing a telecine from the 35mm negative print. Your audio will need to be slightly pulled down to match the 24 fps footage. But that's not impossible, and most sound editors can handle this.

The 23.98 frame rate gives you a simpler workflow in postproduction and is well known as a source format by most film-out service bureaus, so you shouldn't have any insurmountable issues there either. The best bet is to closely consult with your audio production and postproduction crew as well as the lab doing your film outputs when making the final call between 23.98 or 24 exact.

Next, choose your aspect ratio. The two most common 35mm theatrical aspect ratios in the United States are 1.85 and 2.35. The 1.85 ratio is the simplest to derive, because it's simply a matter of masking off a portion of the frame, so start with 16:9 and make sure to use the viewfinder markings to get a rough concept of where the 1.85 frame will be (**Figure 3.11**).

Figure 3.11 RED display with 16:9 frame guides in red and action and title TV-safe markings in yellow.

Going 2.35 is another option, but there are some different ways to achieve it. The simplest and most common is to shoot 16:9 with conventional 35mm lenses and simply mask the frame off even further to derive the 2.35 frame in postproduction. You'll be throwing away a good portion of your original frame's vertical resolution, and you'll need to pay close attention to the frame guides on your viewfinder and monitor—but you'll end up with the classic wide-screen image beloved for its epic visual quality.

The other way to derive a 2.35 image is to actually rent 35mm anamorphic lenses and shoot a true anamorphic, optically squeezed image. This is exactly what Steven Soderbergh did on the second half of his *Che* epic. The 35mm anamorphic lenses require more light to achieve a given exposure. Therefore, in addition to the extra costs of the lenses, you need to beef up your lighting package to compensate. You'll use the camera's special ANA mode, which is around 1.20:1 with a 2X optical squeeze. It's a fair amount of extra work, especially in post, but it's one way to go if you are striving for the closest possible optical match for 2.35.

Ultimately the workflow for a film finish is more complex in postproduction because you'll be creating 2K (or possibly 4K) frames for recording directly onto 35mm film. That means you want to preserve as much of the original frame detail as possible, so working in a film recorder-friendly format such as DPX is a must. You'll see how each of the more popular NLE programs and color correction suites handle a potential film finish workflow in Chapters 10–13. The most important considerations are shooting in the highest possible resolution and bitrates and then picking your aspect ratio—16:9 for a cropped 1.85 or cropped 2.35 finish or 2:1/ANA for an anamorphic 2.35 finish.

DELIVERING FOR THE INTERNET

The Internet has developed into a showcase for footage from every corner of the globe. Video-sharing sites such as Vimeo and YouTube support HD resolutions at somewhat reduced bitrates, whereas trailer sites such as Apple's and Yahoo Movie's QuickTime galleries offer up to 1080p H.264 downloads at relatively high bitrates.

Delivering for the Internet is somewhat easier than a theatrical or high-definition finish because you can work with smaller file sizes and resolutions. For example, let's say you want to deliver a project at 1080p QuickTime H.264. You could convert all your 4K original R3D files to ProRes 1080p. You might even convert everything to uncompressed 1080p if you are working with an AJA Kona or Blackmagic high-definition output card and a nice RAID setup. Once in a while you might want to return to your original 4K files to zoom into a shot or reframe a shot for creative or technical reasons. Or if you're working with an NLE program that directly supports R3D, you can simply put the original files into a 1080p timeline and scale and re-crop as you desire.

Your final edit will be exported into a format that will either be uploaded and automatically transcoded into a proprietary format, in the case of sites such as Vimeo and YouTube, or be played out directly from a Web server as a QuickTime .mov, Flash, or Windows .wmv file.

This allows you to get your frame exactly as you want it and also set your color correction. Each video-sharing site has its own set of specs to work with, and some allow you to encode directly into their playback format, such as Flash, which gives you more control over how the final image will look.

Keep in mind that every computer monitor is slightly different, and Macs and PCs have a difference in gamma. Macs have a system display gamma of 1.8 (up to OS 10.6), whereas Linux and Windows PCs are set at 2.2. So, something that looks just right on a Mac may end up looking darker on a PC. On both platforms, gamma can be reset specifically to match the other (**Figure 3.12**), and it's very easy for your eyes to adjust to either setting. Therefore, be sure to be aware of which gamma your system is using.

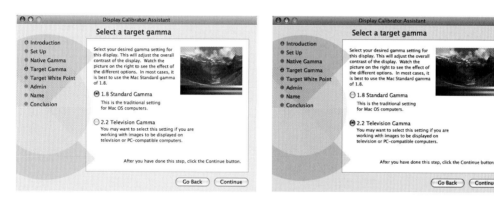

Figure 3.12 Setting gamma display preferences on a Mac.

Always check the finished output on a variety of computers. Upload the video to a private directory on the Web and then check it out on different computers at a school computer lab, a local Internet café, your friend's house, the library, the copy shop computer center—you get the idea—to make sure it looks good on a variety of systems.

The key to outputting RED footage for the Internet is keeping your final aspect ratio in mind. In general, a 16:9 aspect ratio is a solid bet for Internet distribution, and as with most other scenarios, sticking with 4K at the highest quality settings is prudent. You never know when a project will go from being a Web series to a broadcast TV show, such as the SciFi Channel's RED-shot series *Sanctuary*. Or, perhaps, a commercial will end up playing on both the Web and broadcast TV.

Following are some places where you can see what RED footage looks like encoded for the Web. The footage typically doesn't look anywhere near as good as the original 4K camera originals, of course, but online codecs are constantly improving in their trade-off between file size and image quality:

- www.red.com/shot_on_red
- www.vimeo.com/channel17650
- www.redrelay.net

Organizing Your Workflow

In **Figure 3.13** you'll find a handy project worksheet featuring the most common options you can use to help define your project in terms of its shooting format, editing workflow, and final delivery format. So, follow along with that as we explore the options. There's a downloadable version on the book's companion Web site at www.peachpit.com/red you can print, so you don't have to tear this one out of the book.

RED Project Worksheet

Project Title_____ Project Shoot Dates_____ - _____
Type   Narrative__ Documentary__ Other_____
Length   Feature__ Short__ Commercial__ Music Video__ Series__ Other_____

Production Format

Aspect Ratio	16:9___ 2:1___ Anamorphic___ HD___
Resolution	4K___ 3K___ 2K___
Bitrate	Redcode 28___ Redcode 36___
Frame Rate	23.98___ 24___ 25___ 29.97___ 30___

Post-Production Editorial Format

Aspect Ratio	16:9___ 2:1___ ANA___ 4:3 Letterbox___ 4:3 Pan/Scan___
Resolution	4K___ 3K___ 2K___ HD720___ HD1080___ SD___
Offline/Online	Offline___ Online___
Sequence Codec	R3D___ QT Proxy___ ProRes HQ___ DV___ Uncompressed___
NLE	FCP___ Avid___ Adobe___ Other___

Final Delivery Format - Video Finish

Aspect Ratio	16:9___ 4:3 Letterbox___ 4:3 Pan/Scan___
Resolution	HD1080___ HD720___ SD___
Digital Format	DVD___ Blu-Ray___ Web___ Uncompressed HD___
Tape Format	HDCAM SR___ D5___ DigiBeta___ BetaSP___

Final Delivery Format - Film Finish

Aspect Ratio	1.85___ 1.78(16:9)___ 2.35___ 1.33___
Film Gauge	16mm___ 35mm___
Scan Resolution	1/2K___ 1K___ 2K___ 4K___
Frame Format	DPX___ TIF___ Cineon___

Figure 3.13 RED project worksheet.

Even if you don't see the exact type of production you have in mind discussed in this chapter, you should find something similar enough to point you in the right direction. The most important concept to keep in mind is knowing as much as possible about the finishing format of your project before you start. Figure out your aspect ratio and your frame and bitrate and then be consistent throughout the shoot. If you don't have a clue, aim for 1080p as your mastering format, because it's really the most common format and can be used to derive just about any deliverable you're likely to need. Be prepared up front, and you'll save tons of time in post, avoid needless transcodes and format conversions, save yourself money, and ultimately end up with a higher-quality final project.

Albert Hughes (right) codirects with his brother Allen.

Albert Hughes

DIRECTOR, *THE BOOK OF ELI*

Writer/director Albert Hughes burst onto the international film scene in 1993 with *Menace II Society*, an intense urban drama he codirected with his fraternal twin brother, Allen. The duo followed up with *Dead Presidents* starring Larenz Tate, the documentary *American Pimp*, and *From Hell* starring Johnny Depp and Heather Graham, along with scores of music videos and other short-form projects. The Hughes brothers often codirect, with Albert focusing on technical aspects and Allen working with the actors.

The team recently wrapped the sci-fi/action feature *The Book of Eli*, starring Denzel Washington and Gary Oldman. Albert Hughes chose to shoot *Eli* with the RED ONE after extensive testing both on his own and with director of photography Don Burgess, ASC (*Forrest Gump*, *Spider-Man*). "Don's an old-school, textbook kind of cinematographer, but he also likes to keep current and try out new technologies," recalls Hughes. "We shot a series of 35mm film and RED side-by-side comparison tests with every possible lighting situation we would need for this project. We did daytime exteriors/interiors, nighttime interiors/exteriors, and makeup tests with men and women. Then we brought in our whole team, including producer Joel Silver (*The Matrix*, *Lethal Weapon*), to view the projected results on film and pick out the film-originated footage. Nine out of ten people in the room picked the RED footage as the best, which surpassed even my own hopes."

The initial impulse to shoot on the RED came out of Hughes' desire to capture a specific action sequence of *Eli* with a highly mobile camera. "It was a huge gun battle in a house where Gary Oldman's character finally catches up with Denzel's," says Hughes. "I planned it as one continuous take with the camera going inside and outside through windows and following characters as they take cover in different perspectives. I'd never seen a lightweight camera with a large enough film magazine to cover that long a scene.

"I also wanted to shoot the sequence high-speed to heighten the emotion, which would have burned through film even faster. I'd looked at Panavision's Genesis, but I didn't really like some of what I saw there, and I've always been more of an ARRI guy anyway. My friend and coworker Charlie Parish introduced me to the RED, and the size of the body looked like the camera I'd always dreamed of having. Of course, I didn't realize at the time it was a full-blown studio camera once you attached all the accessories and gear, but we made it work."

Hughes found the camera allowed him to alter his directing style to be looser than he was accustomed to working on film. "We did a lot of long takes," he says. "When you're running a series of takes without cutting on film, you feel that expensive stock running through the camera, and you get antsy and nervous. We used 16GB cards on the RED and never had a scene run longer than we had space for. It also takes more time to reload a film camera compared to RED. They were able to swap out and reformat a new card in the time it took hair and makeup to do their touchups before a new take started."

Though the majority of *Eli* was shot on the RED, the production switched to film cameras for high-speed shots. "We were doing a high-speed take of Denzel, where he's wearing a set of silver-rimmed sunglasses, with the RED," recalls Hughes. "We were getting these staccato, blurry sort of motion artifacts off the rims that didn't look right. I also noted that with high-speed shots we'd have to switch to 3K or 2K to get the higher frame rates, losing resolution. So Don suggested we switch to film cameras for anything over 30 frames per second. [RED CEO] Jim Jannard happened to be on the set that day with a prototype of the EPIC camera, and he agreed that we were making the right move. The thing with digital is people are looking for all the answers right away, while film has had more than 100 years to get its act right."

Eli was edited primarily on Avid with some initial sequences cut together by Hughes on his laptop using Final Cut Pro. "For me, the look of what you can do with any editing program is ultimately the same," says Hughes. "No one is watching a movie in the theater and spotting a great Avid or a great Final Cut Pro edit. And that goes for the image as well, regarding film versus digital. A few years ago, a similar sort of debate was happening over Super 35mm and anamorphic among directors of photography (because of the generational loss involved in making release prints from Super 35 compared to anamorphic). My feeling is that if the audience can't tell the difference, then it really doesn't matter. If the image is pristine when I look at my footage, I'm happy."

When asked what's next in the movie industry, Hughes believes increased image quality and resolution will be the most important innovations to come. "Everyone seems to be pushing 3D right now, but I think it's never going to take over as the primary image capture method," he says. "It's great for family entertainment and adult action movies, and RED has its own prototypes for 3D in the works. But I just don't see how people are going to want to shoot their small indie movies and dramas in 3D. So for me, I look at a camera like EPIC as the next big thing. I want to be able to shoot higher frame rates and maintain resolution and also reposition shots vertically, which is easier to do on film right now."

Hughes continues, "I also want to see the cameras get smaller and less bulky. I look at the film and high-end HD cameras of today, and we still have these huge pieces of equipment compared to my little handheld Sony HDV camera that I can jump around and quickly grab shots with. As they create new cameras and technologies, I'm willing to be the guinea pig. The closer we can get to that firsthand experience, the better for cinema." ∎

4 BUILDING A RED PACKAGE

Configuring a RED ONE camera package can be a challenging prospect because of the sheer variety of choices. Hundreds of accessories are available from a number of manufacturers, including RED, such as batteries, mounting hardware, onboard monitors, an electronic viewfinder (EVF), and two sizes of camera-mountable LCD monitors. RED also offers its own branded set of prime and zoom lenses designed for the camera. The camera is also compatible with many preexisting 35mm optics and accessories as well as new products designed by third-party manufacturers especially for the camera system.

So, what do you really need in a RED package—and what's nice to have if you can afford it? In this chapter, we'll look at the major categories of equipment and accessories and I'll offer my own personal recommendations. Then you'll learn about assembling RED packages at specific price points and for specific purposes.

The RED ONE Camera Body

The most important item to purchase is, of course, the RED ONE camera body (currently $17,500). The body is a very sophisticated digital camera and user-upgradeable computer surrounding a CMOS image sensor (see the "What's a CMOS?" sidebar). It's also a highly customizable platform for connecting video and audio input and output devices, and it accepts lenses and many photographic accessories needed to effectively capture motion pictures. Just about

Figure 4.1 The RED ONE camera body is the heart of the RED system.

every piece of equipment I covered in this chapter mounts directly onto the body (**Figure 4.1**)—and of course you'll need a lot more than just the body to shoot footage.

I recommend the base production pack ($1,250) for a starter kit. This set includes handles and rod mounts for use with a tripod as well as a battery cradle. You may choose to forgo the base production pack and purchase these necessary pieces, such as the ARRI Base, from manufacturers such as Element Technica.

WHAT'S A CMOS?

The RED ONE's MYSTERIUM image sensor is a 12-megapixel CMOS Bayer image pattern chip. (CMOS stands for complementary metal-oxide semiconductor.) Bayer chips record a single color (red, green, or blue) per pixel and require a sophisticated decoding algorithm to reproduce a full-color image.

Many previous HD and SD video cameras used charge-coupled device (CCD) chips. CCD chips have traditionally offered higher image quality than CMOS, but at a cost of higher power requirements, increased manufacturing complexity, and expense. RED pulled off many engineering feats to create a CMOS sensor with low noise and very high resolution that could be reliably manufactured in large quantities at an affordable price.

The MYSTERIUM measures 24.4mm x 13.7mm and has 4520 x 2540 active pixels. This gives the camera its 4K image resolution. Because the chip is similar in size than a 35mm film frame, it also offers 35mm depth-of-field characteristics and utilizes 35mm cinema lenses.

Optics

Figure 4.2 RED's PL mount. You can also see the MYSTERIUM sensor.

What gets cinematographers most excited about working with RED is its ability to work with their very familiar motion-picture lenses in both 35mm and 16mm PL-mount cinema lenses (**Figure 4.2**). The new and used market for these lenses is large. You can easily spend anywhere from less than $1,000 (for a used 16mm) to upwards of $100,000 (for a new 35mm zoom) on a single PL-mount lens. (Note that 16mm lenses cannot be used to shoot 4K because of their smaller image size.)

NOTE Positive lock (PL) is a lens-mounting system invented in 1980 by ARRI, the motion-picture camera and lens company. PL is a very simple, four-prong mechanical mount with a friction lock that makes lenses easy to attach and very secure once mounted.

Because every project is different and every shot has different technical and aesthetic requirements, you need a variety of lenses to complete your package. Having the flexibility of a zoom lens combined with the sharpness and sensitivity of prime lenses is ideal—if you can afford to have both. For my tastes, the ultimate RED optics kit includes a full-range zoom lens along with primes covering wide angles down to, say, 14mm and up to at least 85mm or more on the telephoto end (**Figure 4.3**).

Figure 4.3 A RED lens kit featuring a combination of prime and zoom lenses.

Many filmmakers use Canon and Nikon still camera lenses for their packages. Still lenses are a good way to save a lot of money on optics, but you might find a still lens to be too limited for extensive motion-picture work. Focusing in the middle of a take with a still lens can be very difficult because they are typically not well geared or marked for this purpose. Also, most still lenses exhibit visible *breathing* (where the image wobbles on the edges) when focusing during a shot. For that reason, we'll look at cinema lenses first.

Figure 4.4 Lenses from RED's Pro Prime Set.

RED LENSES

RED offers very reasonably priced zoom and prime lenses specifically designed for the RED ONE. The zoom lenses include an 18–85mm T2.9 ($9,975) and an 18–50mm T3 ($6,500—see **Figure 4.4**). RED's Pro Prime Set consists of five lenses ranging from 25mm to 100mm, all at a highly sensitive T1.8 stop and at a package price of around $19,000 (or the cost of a single lens from some of the other brands). The Pro Prime Set is also optically optimized for 5K imagery, meaning you can migrate to an EPIC kit down the road.

NOTE *T-stop* refers to the aperture setting of a lens—that is, the amount of light coming into the lens. It's the same concept as an f-stop on a still camera, just a different term.

THIRD-PARTY PRIME LENSES: ARRI AND COOKE

For third-party lenses, many major cinema lens makers have honed their glass throughout the long history of cinema. My personal favorites include ARRI and Cooke, which both manufacture PL-mount prime lenses. Neither is cheap, but the optical quality and sensitivity are unmatched, and I can almost guarantee you've already watched many 35mm Hollywood features shot on

ARRI and Cooke lenses. Cooke even offers a combo prime/zoom kit specially selected for the RED, though any of its regular 35mm PL lenses will do the trick.

The Cooke S4/i kit I personally use includes 14mm, 21mm, 25mm, 32mm, 50mm, and 75 mm primes, all at T2. The lenses aren't cheap at about $18,000–20,000 each but these are flawless pieces of glass that reproduce perfect colors and razor-sharp images on-screen.

On the ARRI side, I like to shoot with a similarly outfitted kit of ARRI Ultra Primes at T1.9. The set includes 16mm, 20mm, 24mm, 32mm, 50mm, and 85mm primes. As with the Cookes, these are expensive and very high end in terms of performance. You're paying for speed, smooth focusing throughout the focal range, and freedom from image artifacts (**Figure 4.5**) such as *chromatic aberration* (when the colors of the spectrum don't quite align in a lens, producing what appears to be soft rainbows) and *vignetting* (dark edges around the edges of the frame).

Figure 4.5 Some artifacts like lens flare can add desirable effects to your shots.

TIP One way to defray the costs of a very high-end prime kit is to consign it out to a local camera rental house. They will list your kit in their rental inventory and share the rental profits with you whenever your kit goes out—and you retain access to the lenses whenever they aren't rented. Alternatively, as with anything else, you can also rent a high-end set when you really need it and rely on lower-cost optics for day-to-day shooting.

ZOOM LENSES

The optical quality of a zoom lens is critically important because a low-quality zoom can cause so much softness in an image that it can visually offset the benefits of the RED's 4K frame resolution. In other words, your final image taken with a low-quality zoom may look no sharper than a regular high-definition or even standard-definition image, depending on the lens.

> NOTE Some lower-cost cinema lenses are still camera lenses rehoused in cinema mechanics, which means they can have issues with distortion and breathing like still lenses. You can usually find out from the manufacturer whether this is the case.

The zoom lens I recommend and use is an Angenieux Optimo T2.8 24–290mm. This lens is pretty fast for a zoom, and its focal range is quite staggering, especially on the telephoto end. Lots of sports networks use this lens for its long reach. Again, at almost $100,000 this is not an inexpensive lens, but it is amazing to shoot with, which is a reason why it can be found on many big movie sets.. The Optimo is not lightweight either, weighing in at 25 pounds. It needs extra support just to keep it steady in the mount, and you need to be pretty strong to consider handheld shooting with it. Remember, this lens is at the very high end of optics; don't feel like you must have this sort expensive gear to make pretty pictures with your RED. Angeniuex and other companies such as Cooke make nice zooms at much lower price points.

16MM LENSES

16mm lenses are often higher quality than still camera lenses, more suitable for production, and also less expensive than 35mm lenses. You should have no problem finding new, used, and rental 16mm PL-mount lenses.

The chief drawback to 16mm lenses is that they cannot be used to shoot in full 4K resolution because the images they generate don't fill the whole image sensor. The image size for most 16mm lenses, depending on focal length, is more likely to work for 2K or possibly 3K resolution. By checking the amount of coverage on a monitor, you'll quickly see vignetting on the edges of your frame once you've chosen a resolution that's too big for the lens (**Figure 4.6**). That said, even at 2K you're shooting at a much higher resolution than standard definition and with more control over your depth of field.

> NOTE Lens vignetting is also called *portholing* because the image cropping effect is similar to peering through a porthole window on a ship.

Figure 4.6 Lens vignetting appears as dark edges of the frame where the sensor's image area is larger than the lens can cover.

Figure 4.7 A Zeiss 9.5mm focal length T1.3 16mm Arriflex lens.

Some good 16mm lens brands to look at include Angenieux, Zeiss (**Figure 4.7**), Century, and Nikkor. 16mm lenses offer a good compromise between 35mm cinema lenses and still camera lenses.

STILL LENSES

Still optics are typically not as sensitive to light as their cinema cousins and, because their focusing mechanics are optimized for still work, can exhibit noticeable breathing. That said, real bargains exist in the still lens market, if you understand the potential limitations. I happen to be a huge fan of Nikon and Canon 35mm still lenses

Figure 4.8 Canon still lenses work pretty well and cost a lot less than cinematic lenses.

(**Figure 4.8**). They look great and are certainly affordable compared to cinema lenses. They're also readily available in sufficient quantity worldwide.

One caveat is that they don't just work out of the box with the RED. You need a lens adaptor to convert the RED's native PL-mount lens to the mount of your Canon or Nikon (covered next).

TIP Watch out for still lenses billed as "digital-only," such as the Nikon DX series and the Canon EF-S lenses. These are optimized for smaller-sensor digital SLR cameras and thus offer less coverage on the RED than true 35mm SLR lenses.

LENS MOUNT ADAPTORS

Many third-party lens mount adaptors are available for the RED because making them is a matter of traditional machining and engineering without a lot of electronics or software development necessary. Birger Engineering (www.birger.com) offers a $1,300 lens adaptor mount for use with Canon EOS still lenses (**Figure 4.9**). Birger entered into a special arrangement with RED to ensure that the modifications to the camera required by the mount retain RED's full factory warranty. So, you can use this product without any fear of damaging your camera.

Nikon mounts are a little more complicated. RED offers a $500 Nikon adaptor mount on its online store (www.red.com/store). This mount is optimized primarily for Nikon lenses with manual aperture control. On newer DX-series and G-series Nikon lenses, the mount can't alter the aperture settings. For more control, you can send the mount to be modified by Long Valley Equipment (www.longvalleyequip.com), makers of the original mount later adopted for sale by RED. For $295 you get a Nikon GDX mount with full aperture control for G and DX series lenses (**Figure 4.10**).

Figure 4.9 The Birger Engineering mount with a 50mm Canon EOS still lens.

Figure 4.10 Long Valley Equipment's Nikon GDX mount pictured with a lightweight rod support.

Storage Options

Storage is a critical concern for your RED ONE camera. You have three basic options: RED CF cards, RED-DRIVE, and RED-RAM. All of these items are available directly from RED.

RED CF CARDS

The RED CF cards are currently available in 8 GB ($165) and 16 GB ($495) capacities. You need the REDFLASH CF Module ($500) in order to use the cards. Record times are modest, because of the high data rate of REDCODE. You can expect about 4 minutes of 4K, 16:9 REDCODE 36 at 24 frames per second on an 8 GB CF, and about 8 minutes of the same settings on an 8 GB card.

Commercial shooters are likely to be fine with these record times. For many situations requiring long record times, such as unscripted interviews, they are too limiting, which means moving up to the drive units.

> NOTE You can try third-party CF cards instead of the RED CF cards, but they have not been tested with the high data rates RED uses. I've personally not had good luck testing third-party CF cards—the results include dropped frames. You don't want that on your shoot, so use RED CF cards if you can.

RED-DRIVE AND RED-RAM

The RED-DRIVE ($900) and RED-RAM ($4,500) are your options for longer record times. Both drives offer FireWire 800 and USB 2.0 connections for downloading footage to your editorial and postproduction system.

The RED-DRIVE provides 320 GB of storage space on a RAID 0 hard drive that connects directly to the camera and can be mounted with the RED cradle (also included with the base production pack). The drive gives you almost 3 hours of recording time in 4K, 16:9 REDCODE 36 at 24 frames per second. You also need a special RED cable for either drive unit, sold separately.

Figure 4.11 The iSee4K application for iPhone helps make RED calculations easier.

TIP If you happen to have an iPhone, grab the iSee4K application (www.isee4k.com). It offers several useful calculations for RED users, including lens field of view, maximum frame rate, and maximum available recording time per media type (**Figure 4.11**).

I recommend getting *two* RED-DRIVEs per camera body if you can afford them. That way, you can download from one drive while continuing to shoot with the other. Also, if you happen to be in a remote location and your RED-DRIVE is damaged or fails, you always have a backup ready to go. If you can't budget for two RED-DRIVEs, grab one drive and a couple of 8 GB or 16 GB CF cards. You'll be able to download footage off the RED-DRIVE and continue to shoot on the CF cards until the drive is ready to shoot again. Keep in mind that the RED-DRIVEs is sensitive to vibration, so having CF cards and a RED-RAM is wise if you're planning a shoot with lots of vibration. You can only get these custom drive cables directly from RED, so stock up on a few spares just in case.

The RED-RAM unit is approximately four times as expensive as the RED-DRIVE, but it brings some nice benefits. With no internal moving parts, the RED-RAM is nearly impervious to moderate vibration and impact. So if you're shooting a concert or an action film, you don't have to worry (in contrast to the RED-DRIVE) about the drive skipping and dropping frames.

The capacity of the RED-RAM is currently limited to 128GB because of the internal solid-state drive (SSD) used in the unit. This works out to a little more than an hour of 4K, 16:9 REDCODE 36 at 24 frames per second. The ultimate decision between the RED-DRIVE and RED-RAM should be determined by the types of projects you're doing. Of course, you can always get both for more flexibility.

Matte Boxes

If you've ever watched behind-the-scenes footage from a Hollywood film, you've probably seen a camera with an elaborate matte box mounted on it. The *matte box* is an important tool for creative control over your imagery. It protects your lens and shields it, to a certain extent, from sunlight and reflected light that can cause undesired flaring on your image.

A matte box also offers customizable trays for all your lens filters, which are essential; the RED camera has no built-in neutral-density filter wheel, so you must use glass filters to control exposure and depth of field. Those accustomed to working with traditional video cameras must be prepared for the extra time required to change filters. The filters must be removed, inspected, cleaned if necessary, and then inserted in the matte box, which any experienced cinematographer will tell you is essential. Even if you want to save creative color effects until post, you'll almost certainly need to work with basic neutral-density (ND) and polarizing filters to control light (you'll learn more about filters later in the "Filters" section).

Figure 4.12 ARRI MB-20 compact matte box with 4 x 5.65 mm filter trays.

Which matte box to get depends on your needs and budget. I use an ARRI MB-20 II compact matte box with 4 x 5.65mm filter trays (see **Figure 4.12**). You can also add trays and lighting shades as needed. By the time you read this, ARRI will also have an MB-28 model that looks like a great match for the RED.

The Vocas (www.vocas.com) MB-450 and the Chrosziel (www.chrosziel.com) 840 (both about $3,000) are other good potential options for the RED. Matte boxes come with a variety of accessories—such as support rods, swing-away brackets, and bellows rings—to fit onto the camera body and work with a variety of prime and zoom lenses. A dealer can help you select the best parts to work with the lenses you plan to use.

TIP Make sure the matte box size you select is big enough to fit over the largest lens you have—without blocking the image.

Filters

Filters have always been important to photographers and cinematographers. They can be used both for creative effects and technical control over exposure (**Figure 4.13**). Filters are available for every conceivable effect, and experimenting with them is a lot of fun.

Figure 4.13
Use infrared filters to handle scenes like this with extensive sunlight.

I believe there are only a few filters that you *must* have to work with RED: neutral-density filters, an infrared filter (**Figure 4.14**), and a polarizer. The brand I like best is Tiffen (www.tiffen.com); I use 5 x 5-inch and 6 x 6-inch sizes to cover a variety of lens types. Schneider (www.schneideroptics.com) and Formatt (www.formatt.co.uk) are also excellent filter brands.

Figure 4.14 The Schneider TRU-Cut IR filter gets rid of infrared light.

ND FILTERS

If you're coming from a DV or HD camera background, you're accustomed to the idea of an f-stop being important mainly for setting the correct exposure. You typically have so much depth of field with a small-sensor camera that it really doesn't matter where the f-stop is, because the depth of field will be similar. But with the RED's 35mm-sized sensor, you can profoundly affect the depth or shallowness of field via ND filters.

An ND filter simply blocks visible wavelengths of light by a very specific amount, forcing you to open up the aperture to another setting and giving a different depth-of-field characteristic. The more you open the aperture, the shallower the depth of field becomes. ND filters are typically notated as .3, .6, and .9, or as 2, 4, 6. With either counting method, you are usually decreasing one stop for each step. So, an ND .3 (or 2) is one stop, a .6 (or 4) is two stops, and so on. You can also get graduated ND filters in which only a portion of the filter halts light. Those can be very useful for balancing landscape shots where you want to reduce the exposure of a bright sky while maintaining the exposure of the foreground and below the horizon. A set of three ND filters will get you through just about any possible lighting situation, because they can be combined for greater strength as needed (**Figure 4.15**).

Figure 4.15
You can achieve shallow depth of field in bright lighting conditions with ND filters, allowing this shot to be exposed at T2.0.

AN ND FILTER EXAMPLE

Let's say you're outdoors using a 75mm T2 prime lens at noon, shooting at 320 ASA. Your metering might give you a T-stop of somewhere around T8 to T11. That's more than enough light to get a good shot, but you'll also have very wide depth of field. You want to knock that aperture down a couple of stops to T4 or T2.8 so you have nice, shallow depth of field for a pleasing portrait shot. That's a situation where the ND filters come into play.

IR AND POLARIZING FILTERS

Because of its CMOS chip, the RED camera has increased sensitivity to infrared light. This can cause unexpected color rendition, especially when shooting outdoors in strong direct sunlight with ND filters. The effect is something like a black light, except in this case colors that should read as black turn magenta. Infrared (IR) and Hot Mirror filters correct for this issue by reflecting away infrared light, while allowing visible light to pass through unaffected. For best results with the RED, use Tiffen or Schneider Hot Mirror IR filters with their stronger *dichroic* (layer of light-absorbing film) coatings.

Polarizing filters (**Figure 4.16**) are also very important for dealing with skies and reflections. In general, polarizers work to enhance contrast and reduce reflections, depending on your camera angle. You can rotate a polarizer to dial in the effect's strength. If the polarizer doesn't seem to be doing anything, try changing your camera position slightly.

Figure 4.16 The left side of this frame is with a polarizer and the right side is without.

DIFFUSION, SOFTENING, AND COLOR-CORRECTION FILTERS

Diffusion and softening filters are designed to soften harsh edges and enhance beauty. However, I think these are effects better left to post, because they decrease apparent resolution and take away from the advantage of shooting 4K in the first place. The same goes for special effects such as star filters that produce flaring around bright objects. These are easy filters to emulate in postproduction, but once you shoot with them, you're locked into that look.

Color-correction filters are not a 100 percent necessity either, because the RED's RAW sensor has no *native* color mode. It's technically balanced to daylight, but you can easily alter this in the RAW files. This doesn't mean you won't have to worry about color temperature. For example, if you're shooting indoors with windows looking outside, you'll have mixed color temperatures. To make that scene look natural, you'll need to either gel your lights for daylight balance or gel your windows for tungsten (artificial lighting) balance.

> TIP   The bottom line on filters is that if you shoot relatively "clean" except for NDs, polarizers, and IR filtration, you'll preserve all of your creative options as you shape your project in postproduction.

Follow Focus and Remote Control

If you're accustomed to working in the video world with autofocus-assisted cameras and their deeper depth of field, optics operation on the RED will be a big change. Focusing on the RED is completely manual, as it is on all professional film cameras. Manual focus means total creative control, but it also presents the challenge of keeping the image you want to see in focus. A lens is pretty difficult to manually operate, which is why all professional lenses have geared teeth along their diameters (**Figure 4.17**) to enable the attachment of manual and motorized follow-focus kits and whips. In this section, we'll start with the simplest, least expensive types and work upward.

Figure 4.17   A close-up of the gears on a 35mm prime lens.

The basic *follow-focus* kit consists of a gear that connects to the lens and a set of interconnecting hardware to control everything with a focus wheel. I use an ARRI FF4 double-sided follow-focus kit (about $3,000) with a 19mm rod adapter (about $500). It's nice and lightweight while offering precise control for most lenses. Sometimes it's not comfortable or physically possible to focus from directly alongside the camera—say, from a dolly or fast-moving handheld shot. Adding a nice flexible focus whip like the ARRI 13.5-inch can help alleviate this limitation. A *focus whip* is a mechanical cable that connects to the focus gears of a lens, allowing you to operate it from a distance (usually a couple of feet).

Figure 4.18 The Keson 50-foot fiberglass tape measure is perfect for measuring focus.

Figure 4.19 The Preston FI+Z remote wireless follow-focus controller.

TIP A tape measure is an important tool for pulling focus. You can quickly measure the distance to a subject and make corresponding marks on your camera's lens. I like the Keson 50-foot fiberglass tape measure (about $15—see **Figure 4.18**). It has a hook to mount to the camera and a roller to reel in the line.

Sometimes even a focus whip doesn't have sufficient physical reach to permit focusing, such as when the camera is mounted on a remote head high up on a crane. It's difficult to get anywhere near the lens to focus. For those situations, you need a *remote focus* (**Figure 4.19**). These can be wired or wireless, with the wireless usually being more expensive. The pros use gear such as the Preston FI+Z wireless system (www.prestoncinema.com), which can go for upward of $14,000 depending on the options you pick, but is worth every penny (Rodney Charters, ASC, uses these on *24*). C-Motion (www.cmotion.eu) offers an even more elegant and sophisticated wireless system called the C3 for higher-end budgets.

Moving down a few dollars but retaining plenty of functionality and quality is the Bartech (www.bartechengineering.com) BFD wireless focus unit for about $2,100. Bartech also offers wired units that are even cheaper. ARRI offers a simple wired remote follow-focus system. Whether you decide to include a remote focus system or not, you'll definitely want at least a regular mechanical follow-focus system to pull focus properly with cinema style lenses on the RED.

Tripods and Camera Support

A tripod is another must-have, because it's hard to imagine a project where you won't want the camera to be nice and steady at least some of the time. It's also a good way to keep the camera safe and protected as you mount accessories and change lenses. Compared to high-end HD and 35mm film cameras, the RED is about on par for weight, but next to DV and prosumer HD cameras it's quite heavy. The body alone weighs 10 pounds, and completely loaded with a big zoom lens, matte box, follow focus, LCD, EVF, battery, and drive, the RED can tip the scales at a hefty 50 pounds or so. That means you need more than a standard-issue video tripod to support it, especially when you're adding a heavy-duty zoom lens, matte box, batteries, monitors, and so on.

Figure 4.20 O'Connor's 2575D fluid tripod head is ready for heavy-duty use.

I use an O'Connor (www.ocon.com) Heavy Duty 150mm tripod with an Ultimate 2060 head and a Mitchell base mount. This is a very stable and fluid platform for the RED. You can find a complete 2060 package including case for just less than $10,000. That may sound like a lot for just a tripod if you're coming from the video world, but it makes all the difference in the world. If you splurge on the tripod now, you'll thank me every day you shoot with it.

The O'Connor 2575 is also a good choice (**Figure 4.20**), though it's a bit heavier than the 2060. O'Connor is very popular these days, but if I wanted another tripod brand for less money, I'd look into

Sachtler (www.sachtler.us) or Ronford Baker (www.ronfordbaker.co.uk). They all make tripods for much less than $10,000; just make sure to get one rated to hold the weight of your intended package. More examples are the Miller Arrow 55 System 1726 (about $6,000). You can also scan eBay for a used tripod, because they can last for decades with good care.

> TIP Another useful item to have is the Element Technica hybrid bridge plate ($1,200), which makes the RED ONE compatible with all the standard ARRI accessories that many film operators and camera assistants are familiar with.

Batteries and Power

I'll get right to the point on batteries: You can never have too many. On a typical shoot day, I turn on the RED at 7 in the morning and turn it off when the sun goes down. That can mean anywhere from three to five battery changes per day. When a battery comes off the camera, it immediately joins its brothers on a plugged-in charger when we're in the studio or a location that offers AC power, which isn't always the case. Don't wind up having your shoot day curtailed by the last battery going out.

I suggest getting at least two, if not four, RED Brick batteries ($450) per camera body. Or grab a RED Power Pack ($1,450), which is great because it includes two batteries and simultaneous charging capability for both. With two RED Power Packs and a RED cradle ($750) to mount onto the camera, you'll be all set.

If you happen to have a stock of Anton Bauer camcorder Hytron 140 batteries (www.antonbauer.com), you'll want to get its special adapter that fits onto the RED. RED also offers a 12V DC charger ($85) to connect to a car or boat DC power outlet. It can come in handy if you expect to be away from available AC power for most of the shoot.

Cases and Carts

There are a zillion equipment cases out there, and you can mix and match types and configurations to your heart's content. I prefer to have the camera body and a few accessories in one case, the tripod in another, lenses in a third, and so on. If you go that way, RED's custom camera case ($600) is a solid investment (**Figure 4.21**). It's an off-the-shelf Pelican 1620, which already is one of my favorite cases, and it features a laser-cut foam insert designed to hold the RED ONE and a good number of accessories.

Figure 4.21 Getting my RED 1620 case custom-branded in person at RED HQ.

If you prefer a soft case, try the Petrol (www.petrolbags.com) PRB-15 ($499), which is designed to hold the camera, viewfinder, and handheld-mode accessories (**Figure 4.22**).

I use Tuffpack (www.tuffpak.com) cases for my tripods, which go for less than $500 and can be configured with or without wheels. For optics and other accessories, I use A&J DI (www.ajcases.com) cases, which can be custom-fitted for specific accessories. They are designed to meet or exceed the Air Transportation Association specification 300, Category 1 requirements (meaning they will likely survive an overzealous baggage handler).

Figure 4.22 Petrol PRB-15 RED soft case.

I also like Anvil ATA (www.anvilcase.com) cases, which meet the airline standards and can be custom-fitted as well.

The RED Cart ($1,290) features a standard tripod ball base so you can mount your tripod head directly on it. It's very durable and yet collapses to a compact size for shipping. It weighs a lot (about 70 pounds), but you want something built tough to hold your camera while you mount optics and all the necessary accessories. This is a lot better than just having it on the floor or perched on a case. (The RED cart also has wheels, so you can even use it as a dolly in an extreme pinch, but I wouldn't recommend this.)

Monitoring

You have two primary reasons to monitor your RED footage while on a shoot: operating the camera and critically evaluating images, including for exposure, color balance, and focus. With onboard HDMI and a 4:4:4 playback signal, you have a lot of potential for high-quality viewing. You typically use a smaller monitor and/or the EVF for framing and operating the camera during a take. Then you can use a higher-quality and typically larger outboard monitor for evaluating exposure, focus, and color temperature. I think it's important to have all three kinds: EVF, onboard, and studio (production) monitor. That way, you really have a good idea what you're shooting on the set rather than waiting for surprises when you get into postproduction.

Figure 4.23 RED's electronic viewfinder is a must-have for confident shooting.

ELECTRONIC VIEWFINDER (EVF)

RED's EVF ($2,950—see **Figure 4.23**) should be another must-have on your list. It has a very sharp 720p (1280 x 720 lines progressive, high-definition resolution) display and offers user-programmable camera control buttons. The EVF also has a diopter adjustment to accommodate variations in operator eyesight.

The EVF comes with a customizable mount. However, you might want more flexibility to place your viewfinder. I recommend the Element Technica (www.elementtechnica.com) EVF mount ($1,190—see **Figure 4.24**), which lets you position the EVF in a wider variety of places on the camera and virtually eliminates the risk of damage that can occur if the standard mount loosens.

Figure 4.24 The Element Technica EVF mount kit.

NOTE David Macintosh, designer of RED's EVF, also created the AccuScene viewfinder. It was considered one of the finest HD/electronic viewfinders ever made and costs more than $10,000. The RED EVF is a bargain by comparison.

ONBOARD MONITORS

The EVF is excellent for the person operating the camera, but a second onboard monitor is also critical. This lets the director and the camera assistant see what's being photographed as they stand next to the camera, and it can be used to communicate framing intentions (**Figure 4.25**). RED makes two models: a 5.6-inch LCD ($1,700) and a 7-inch Pro LCD ($2,500). They're lightweight, affordable, and perfectly matched to the camera.

Figure 4.25 Using the EVF and monitor simultaneously enables the crew to see what the operator is shooting.

Other nice onboard production monitors you can try include the Panasonic (www.pana-sonic.com) BT-LH900A (about $4,000) and LS Designs' Carrion (about $2,000). Just don't get completely lulled into using an onboard monitor to gauge exposure and color balance. These monitors can give you a rough indication, but you're better off leaving the really critical image judgment to a larger and higher-quality production monitor.

STUDIO MONITORS

Usually when you set up a scene, you place the camera and then run the cabling and power off to the side where you can mount your studio (or production) monitor out of the way. A large studio monitor can be very helpful for judging image quality details and can also serve as a client monitor (a viewing monitor a production client can watch from). Also, if you're using a remote camera and a wireless follow-focus system, the camera assistant might use the studio monitor to gauge focus as the shot is made.

I use the Panasonic BT-LH1760 17-inch LCD monitor (less than $4,000) as the main studio monitor. It's big enough to show what you're shooting clearly, with lots of definition, but it's not so heavy as to prevent it from being carried into the field. The BT-LH1760 includes a Histogram and waveform monitor for more accurate evaluation of a shot. You can also power it via stan-dard Anton Bauer camcorder batteries for use in remote locations. I also recommend the hood accessory to shield the monitor for easier viewing outdoors. Some other suggestions for studio monitors are Tamuz (www.tamuz.tv), Cinetal (www.cine-tal.com), JVC, and Sony.

> NOTE   Even though the RED has a built-in exposure meter, a handheld cinematog-rapher's light meter to set exposure can be a huge help. For more details, refer to Chapter 6.

ROUTING

Depending on which monitors and accessories you get, you'll need cabling to route those signals. I recommend having both short and long cables to allow you to connect to monitors right next to the camera or a good distance away. The RED ONE camera uses mini-coaxial connectors, for which you need special cables to connect to most third-party monitors. Most of the cables you need are available through RED's Web site.

Alternatively, you can get the Element Technica RED Video Break Out Box ($580) to convert the onboard connectors to standard HD-SDI BNC connectors. This gives you more flexibility and ease of use with outboard monitoring, and I highly recommend this accessory (**Figure 4.26**).

Figure 4.26 Element Technica's RED Video Break Out Box.

Transfer Equipment

Along with all the camera accessories, you also need some peripheral gear to download footage from the camera. This is a job your digital imaging technician (DIT) or (possibly you) might do, depending on the size of the crew. (We'll look at on-set data management in more depth in Chapters 9 and 14.)

You will use a computer to transfer footage from CF cards or RED-DRIVEs. Try to match the transfer computer type to your editing system. If you're working on a Mac editing system, for example, use a Mac to transfer footage; conversely, if you're cutting on a Windows machine, transfer with a Windows machine. This saves you some initial challenges involved in transferring from Mac to Windows systems. I like to carry a 17-inch MacBook Pro with a FireWire 800 port. When I know there will be available AC power, I use a MacPro desktop with an eSATA card and eSATA drive.

You need sufficient hard drive space to hold all the footage you intend to shoot, along with enough for a backup, too. If you're shooting CF cards, you also need a card reader. (For more workflow details, see the section "Archiving in the Field" in Chapter 14.)

NOTE Sound equipment is also a very important part of your RED package—so important that it gets its own chapter (Chapter 5).

Working Within a Budget

Now that you've been introduced to the major kinds of gear, you're probably asking, "But what do I *really* need?" Ultimately, that depends on two factors: how much you have to spend and what kinds of projects you want to do with your camera.

If you're simply buying the RED for personal projects that may not see a major release, you can get away with a very minimal package. You need the body and an EVF or a monitor (you can get away with having one or the other). You could hook up an inexpensive HDMI-equipped prosumer HD monitor for your viewing—of course, you'll give up accuracy, but it's better than nothing. You can find less expensive tripods, but be certain they are rated for at least 40 pounds so you don't have problems balancing the RED. For optics, try the RED zooms and/or primes. Or grab the Canon or Nikon mount, and go with still lenses. You need a set of batteries, a charger, and either CF cards or a RED-DRIVE to record to. You could be set up for less than $30,000, excluding a postproduction/editorial system.

Moving up a few notches, I'd first look at monitors. Spring for the secondary onboard monitor and then grab a good studio monitor with waveform and vectorscope, which are useful for getting a proper exposure (covered in more detail in Chapter 6). Next, upgrade your tripod and work in some focusing and mounting accessories.

Optics are probably the most expensive investment you can make. A complete set of professional cinema primes with a matching quality zoom can run you upwards of $200,000. Remember, you can always rent lenses on a per-job basis. If you're not using your camera regularly on paid jobs, the price of cinema lenses may be too great to ever recoup. As with everything, plan and look before you leap into a full RED package.

> TIP   Try renting a RED package for a weekend before you make any purchases. You'll get hands-on experience and learn which accessories you truly need.

Scarlet and EPIC

Although the RED ONE is the focus of this book, the company has announced that more cameras are on the way. These include the prosumer-leaning Scarlet and the high-end EPIC. The Scarlet is aimed at the under-$10,000 market, where prosumer high-definition cameras such as the Panasonic HVX200 and Sony EX1 and EX3 have become very popular. The EPIC is intended as a high-end cinema replacement for the RED ONE, with 5K resolution. Here I take a quick look at each of these cameras with a reminder of RED's unofficial motto, "Everything in life changes... including our camera specs and delivery dates."

NOTE Check the companion Web site at www.peachpit.com/RED for updates on Scarlet and EPIC.

The Scarlet (**Figure 4.27**) takes the RED's modular design concept and runs with it. To put together a Scarlet system, you first start with a brain unit (same concept as the RED's body) with a sensor size ranging from a standard 2/3-inch chip all the way up to full-frame 35mm. The rest of the modules give you battery power, monitoring and EVF, recording media, and I/O options. There's a nice wireless remote control unit as well. RED also plans to offer prime lenses designed for the 2/3-inch chip and for the full-frame 35mm camera. The Scarlet's entry-level price is planned to be about $3,000.

The EPIC (**Figure 4.28**) lies at the opposite end of the spectrum from the Scarlet. EPIC's sensor options start at Super 35mm size all the way up to a massive 168 x 56mm "Monstro" sensor, capable of shooting considerably more massive frame sizes than any other motion-picture camera ever released. Prices for the EPIC brain modules are expected to start at about $28,000 (or about 40 percent more than the original RED ONE). RED plans to extend a full-price trade-in credit to RED ONE owners who want to upgrade to the EPIC, which should make the transition easier. Many of the original RED ONE accessories are expected to work with the EPIC as well.

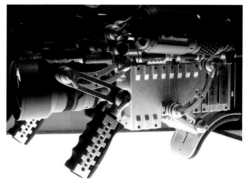

Figure 4.27 The Scarlet prototype on display.   **Figure 4.28** The EPIC prototype on display.

NOTE   RED envisions a 3D configuration for the EPIC, enabling moviemakers to create new forms of digital content.

Both the Scarlet and EPIC are intended as part of RED's Digital Stills and Motion Camera (DSMC) concept. Though both are designed primarily as digital motion-picture cameras, RED hopes they will be accepted as digital still cameras as well, because of their very high resolution. This reasoning makes a lot of sense, because the digital still and motion-picture camera worlds have been rapidly converging ever since the release of DSLRs such as the Canon EOS 5D Mark II and the Nikon D90, which offered HD video modes in addition to standard still-photography capabilities.

Mark L. Pederson preps for a shot in New York City with RED #6.

Mark L. Pederson
COFOUNDER, OFFHOLLYWOOD

As the owner of RED ONE serial numbers 6 and 7, Mark L. Pederson is one of the most knowledgeable people about the camera outside of RED staff. Pederson runs the New York–based production and postproduction company Offhollywood. He cofounded the company with Aldey Sanchez in 2003 using one Mac and one license of Final Cut Pro. "We didn't have a business model at first, but we knew technology was going to change the filmmaking process," Pederson recalls. "Production and post were merging together as we tracked a lot of technology and did desktop finishing. For a while we were the low-budget indie option for finishing projects shot with the Panasonic VariCam in New York."

"When we began, filmmakers were shooting indie features with the VariCam and the Sony F-900," Pederson continues. "The consensus was that you had to hire video engineers from post houses. As experts in HD and scopes, they saw a huge opportunity. Part of it was perpetuated by the fact that everyone wants to be an expert, but I didn't think it was rocket science. Today I don't know of any DP in New York City who doesn't know their way around the menu of a VariCam or an F-900."

As Pederson continued working with VariCam productions, Offhollywood also constructed a postproduction facility to support its high-definition features. "We built our company on AJA products, so we knew Ted Schilowitz [who later went on from AJA to RED]," Pederson reveals. "In 2006, Ted told me he was going to leave AJA and build a camera with Jim Jannard from Oakley. I didn't think they could do everything they planned, but if they did half, it would be good enough. I was invited to help out in the NAB booth in 2006 when RED decided to tell the world their plans and price point. During a conference call they decided they were going to take reservations at the next NAB, and I asked if anyone objected to my reserving the first two cameras, serial numbers 6 and 7 [the first five were slated for Jannard]. The ensuing hype astounded me, and a year and a half later, we got our cameras."

Pederson sees his work as not only technical but also educational, as the camera was initially met with skepticism. "Every week we're working with someone who's never shot with the RED before, but that's certainly changing," he observes. "I'm in this business because I like features, and we always try to have at least one indie going. We're making inroads into the ad market so we can earn our keep. We are also building a next-generation production and post-production facility in Manhattan based entirely on shooting and finishing with RED camera systems."

Offhollywood beta-tested early builds of the camera as it was being developed and provided constant feedback while utilizing it in daily production. "It feels like 20 years ago since we got the first cameras," says Pederson. "Now we have eight cameras, and this week we'll have all eight on seven different productions. It's completely changed our business model. At this point I think that RED delivers for the money—the picture is just much better than anything near its range, and Jim is just getting started."

One of the most important areas in which Pederson's techs help production crews is on-set data management. "We do it a couple of different ways, whether it's a small project or a feature," he says. "We try to use the CF cards as much as possible instead of the RED-DRIVEs because they are RAID 0. Someday one of them will fail, and all of the media could be lost. So, we always make productions take two drives and hot swap the drives as often as possible during a shoot day. That way, if one of those drives dies, there's only so much material at risk. That's going to change in the future with the solid-state RED-RAM drives."

Production on the East Coast has always shared a (mostly) friendly rivalry with Hollywood, and Pederson is quick to take note of the differences in approach with regard to RED. "L.A. is more of a tape-driven post market, while we want to push files because the future is tapeless," Pederson says. "It's kind of a joke to make tapes because they become digital files again once they get digitized into an Avid or other system. RED has accelerated things that were already happening with respect to tapeless workflows."

Pressed for more specifics, Pederson points to the world of digital intermediates. "Pre-DI you had your film printer lights. You could say cooler or warmer and push/pull process your developing, which sounds like a zillion years ago. Now there's barely a single feature that hasn't gone through a DI. This isn't just a RED-specific thing but definitely something RED is really accelerating."

Pederson also sees other parts of the production workflow with room for technological innovation. "RED has a whole bunch of metadata in every frame. I want to attach more to the media and really put it to work. Instead, you've got a $60 million dollar movie where the sound recordist and assistant camera technicians are still putting handwritten reports on carbon copy forms that get photocopied and eventually make their way into a binder. Then the editor picks up the binder and puts it up on a shelf. Well, there's no GUI [graphical user interface] for a 5-inch binder.

"We will see, in the 'never-near' future, new ways of collecting that metadata on set and using it throughout the postproduction process," he adds. "Adobe now has speech-to-text translation in CS4, which lets you search your media for a word or phrase, and Avid has a script-based editing tool. The media with the most tags wins. Google is looking in your e-mail and serving you ads based on personal keywords, and sites like YouTube and Netflix have search engines that display media based on tags."

With RED cameras now much easier to acquire than in the early days of the company, Pederson believes optics will be the next area of major activity. "The real war is going to be over glass—there aren't enough high-quality cinema lenses in existence," he observes. "Jim's making new high-end glass, but he can't make it fast enough. The demand is tremendous. Making good glass at a low price point appears to be harder than making the camera itself."

Surveying the impact of the first few years of RED in the industry, Pederson believes change is just getting started. "RED's technology has completely transformed our business," he says. "Our early adoption of the camera system allowed us to leap our company forward. We are anxiously awaiting the new DSMC camera systems from RED to take everything up to the next level."

Mark Pederson's Web site is www.OffhollywoodNY.com. ∎

5 WORKING WITH SOUND

Sound is a crucial part of any filmmaking endeavor nowadays. As George Lucas once said, "Filmmakers should focus on making sure the soundtracks are really the best they can possibly be, because in terms of an investment, sound is where you get the most bang for your buck."

Audio is an aspect of moviemaking that everyone is aware of, but not everyone completely understands or appreciates. Some directors concentrate primarily on their images and leave audio as something to be finessed in post. Ask any successful filmmaker how important it is to get good production sound and then complete a professional mix in postproduction. You will likely receive an overwhelming affirmative.

Why You Need Good Sound

Let's do a little mental exercise: Imagine you're seated in a movie theater with a packed house of non-movie-business people. These are folks who know nothing about the RED camera or its technical capabilities; they just like to go to the movies. We're going to project two different clips for this group. One clip is gorgeous RED 4K footage color-corrected to perfection but with a poorly mixed soundtrack featuring barely audible, scratchy dialogue. The other clip is basic, flat-looking standard-definition DV footage but with a perfect audio mix and natural, well-recorded dialogue.

After the lights come up, I can almost guarantee you the DV footage will be better received, and the RED footage will be criticized by this audience. Good production sound and mixing is expected by today's audiences. Do a less than stellar job, and poor sound will stick out like a sore thumb, ruining the experience of watching your movie no matter how well it's shot.

Quality audio is not that easy. You can't just hang a couple of microphones on your RED camera, ENG-style, and expect professional sound. (Later in this chapter you'll learn that doing this *can* be useful as a sync reference, however.) In fact, you need to carefully select not only the equipment you use to record sound but also the personnel who operate it. Having a dedicated, experienced sound recordist/mixer and boom operator is key, if you can afford it; running and gunning both camera and sound all by yourself should be an absolute last resort.

In this chapter, you'll learn how to follow through on these goals in more detail.

Double-System Sound

In the film world, it's a given that sound and picture will be captured separately, because a 35mm camera negative has no provision for sound. Sound is added only for the final release print. Most motion-picture cameras aren't even equipped to record sound. The film camera captures the picture, and sound is recorded by another piece of gear, typically a Digital Audio Tape (DAT) recorder or a solid-state digital recorder. Occasionally an analog tape recorder such as a Nagra 4.2 (**Figure 5.1**) is used, though analog is getting pretty rare in the production audio world. Nagra (www.nagraaudio.com) doesn't even manufacture analog recorders anymore and has replaced the 4.2 with its digital VI recorder (**Figure 5.2**).

Figure 5.1 Nagra 4.2 analog audio recorder.

Figure 5.2 Nagra VI digital audio recorder.

Why not just connect up a mic and mixer, you may be wondering, and use the RED's onboard audio? For one thing, the ideal camera and microphone placement location don't always match, and you want some flexibility without having to always run long cables from the mic into the camera. Running a wireless mic into the camera isn't always going to give you top quality either, because of possible radio interference and noise. The camera's onboard menus for audio can also be challenging to set levels and mix with, compared to an outboard hardware mixer. Or you may want a higher bitrate or more channels than the RED's 4-channel 24-bit/48 kHz specs. Most professional sound recordists believe the best option is *double-system sound*, which means using an external recording device, mixer, and the necessary mics and cables.

With double-system sound in mind, a critical aspect of recording sound and picture separately is maintaining a reliable method of synchronization. The RED offers *time-of-day* timecode, with an internal clock that continues to tick away accurately when the camera is not actually recording. Whenever you shoot a take, each frame is marked with timecode derived from that exact time of day. Most modern audio recorders designed for film-style production can synchronize with this timecode (see the "Digital Recorders" section later in this chapter). The RED can be *jam synced* (meaning electronic synchronization of timecode) to an external timecode source with a five-pin LEMO timecode cable connected between the two. You'll learn more about audio sync later in this chapter.

Audio Equipment Shopping List

This section recommends audio gear that will provide the maximum possible sound quality for your production. Some of this equipment can get quite expensive, so consider hiring a sound recordist who has his or her own gear. You can also rent as needed if buying this gear puts you over budget.

MICROPHONES

A high-quality microphone is a critical piece of your production audio package. One solid, hyper-cardioid or shotgun mic and a boom pole can capture the vast majority of the production dialogue for an entire show. Some good shotgun mics are the Shure SM89 (**Figure 5.3**) and the Sennheiser MKH-416, MKH-60, and MKH-70. Omni-directional microphones, such as the Shure VP88 (**Figure 5.4**), are excellent for recording ambience and sound effects, but in general their pickup pattern is too broad for clean dialogue. Avoid stereo mics except for sound effects, because they can make dialogue mixing very difficult in post.

Figure 5.3 The Shure SM89 microphone is a good shotgun mic.

You can use a lavaliere, or *lav*, mic (a small mic you can clip onto a tie or shirt lapel), combined with a wireless transmitter, in situations where it's impractical to use a shotgun mic on a boom pole. Take great care in selecting a lav mic, because they can be somewhat limited in their dynamic range and produce a thinner vocal quality compared to a hyper-cardioid. Some nice choices for lav microphones are the Sony ECM88, TRAM TR-50, and Sennhesier MKE2 (**Figure 5.5**).

Figure 5.4 The Shure VP88 microphone is omni-directional.

Figure 5.5 The Sennheiser MKE2 lav mic clips onto actors.

HEADPHONES

Get yourself a nice set of personal headphones. All the great audio in the world doesn't do you much good if you can't listen as you record it. Having your own set of headphones rather than relying on rentals or borrowing from the sound crew is wise. You'll get used to how they sound from production to production and learn to spot issues. (Besides, you'll look cool in your official director's photo with your headphones on.)

Figure 5.6 Sony MDR series headphones are a bargain.

Avoid fancy noise-canceling headphones, which are great for listening to music on an airplane but add acoustical artifacts that interfere with accurate live dialogue monitoring. The Sony MDR series headphones (**Figure 5.6**) have long been a favorite of sound professionals because they're reasonably flat sounding, inexpensive, compact, and they can take a lot of punishment. Sennheiser, Audio-Technica, and Beyer also make excellent headphones for production use.

RECORD SOME ROOM TONE

Make a habit of recording at least 30 seconds of room tone or ambience on every scene and major location change. It can save your life in postproduction. Often you'll find that the recorded sound quality is pretty solid in post, but you'll notice gaps in your audio edit whenever there are long pauses between pieces of dialogue. You'll hear the change in audio level between the natural background ambience present in a scene and anywhere there's no sound at all on your editing sequence. Having room tone at your disposal will allow you or your sound editor to fill in those gaps with the matching ambience and make everything sound smooth and continuous. Every location sounds slightly different too, so taking the time during production to insist that cast and crew cooperate for those 30 seconds of "silence recording" will pay off once you get into post.

MIC ACCESSORIES

Another key to good sound is proper mic placement. That means recording as close as possible to the actors' mouths without dipping the mic into the frame. Setting up the RED in such a way that the boom operator can see the picture whenever they want can be very helpful. Mount the onboard monitor on a quick-release swivel so you can show the boom operator or mount a secondary monitor at your video playback cart or area. If you really want to go the extra mile, provide the sound recordist with a small monitor for their equipment cart so they can communicate your framing directly with their boom operator.

Figure 5.7 Field audio recordist Matthew Sheldon balances a boom pole.

Get a lightweight carbon-fiber boom pole (or *fishpole*) that extends out to at least 8 or 9 feet (**Figure 5.7**). Use a longer one if you're working in expansive locations or doing a ton of outdoor work on wider lenses. A shock mount that fits the microphone snugly is also essential. A *zeppelin* (**Figure 5.8**) protects the mic from impact, light wind, and miscellaneous noise. For very windy locations, a furry wind sock (called a *wind jammer*) can do an amazing job of damping the mic against big gusts. Rycote (www.rycote.com) makes excellent zeppelins and wind jammers, some of which you can slip on quickly for immediate use.

Figure 5.8 Rycote Windshield kit with shock mount, wind jammer, and zeppelin.

DIGITAL RECORDERS

Digital is the recording format of choice for sound professionals. DAT recorders were the most popular devices for recording, but they have been largely supplanted by solid-state memory devices. These record to CompactFlash cards or built-on hard drives. The advantage of quick access to recorded audio through inexpensive media such as CF and SD cards has assured the rise of solid-state audio recorders.

Zaxcom, Sound Devices, and Aaton make some of the more popular devices. With these recorders you can count on high-quality analog-to-digital (A/D) converters, very low noise/distortion, and audiophile bitrates of up to 24-bit/192 kHz for high-quality recordings with up to 16 separate channels. Any of these devices would pair nicely with the RED for double-system sound.

DEVA

Zaxcom's Deva (www.zaxcom.com) was one of the first units specifically designed for hard drive–based digital recording. The Deva 16 features 16 tracks of 24-bit audio at up to a 192 kHz sampling rates with eight hardware faders for precise mixing. With an internal DVD-RAM burner, the Deva offers an end-to-end solution for capturing audio and delivering it ready to go for postproduction.

SOUND DEVICES

Sound Devices (www.sounddevices.com) offers a number of different digital audio recorders, from very compact 2-channel units all the way up to 12-track recorders. The 744T is a compact recorder with full timecode support and four channels of 24-bit/192 kHz audio. The 744T can record to its own 40GB internal hard drive as well as CF cards. This is great because CF cards are reasonably inexpensive and can be easily found at electronics and photo stores—heck, probably even at your local grocery store.

> TIP Clearly label and differentiate CF cards used for audio and those used for RED footage. Make sure they never get mixed up.

CANTAR

Aaton's Cantar X2 (**Figure 5.9**) is an elegant recorder with features best suited to a large ensemble cast, where you want to capture several discrete tracks and have maximum control over each. Like the Sound Devices equipment, the Cantar (www.aaton.com) records either to its own internal drive or to removable CF cards. It creates Broadcast Wave Format (.bwf) files at 24-bit/96 kHz with up to eight channels. Aaton has always been at the forefront of audio and video synchronization, going back to its film camera days, and the X2 comes with extensive software support. This includes automatically detecting where the clapper slate has closed, along with timecode stamping and automated sound report generation as a PDF file. The Cantar is expensive, but it looks and sounds top-notch.

Figure 5.9 Aaton's Cantar X2 digital audio recorder is not cheap, but provides great quality.

MIXERS

The digital recorders in the preceding section include some form of either hardware or software faders (for volume level adjustment), but sometimes you'll want to separate the recording device from the mixing controls. For example, let's say the recordist has the audio recorder on a sound cart far from the set, whereas the boom operator is right next to the actors. The boom operator is in a much better position to be ready for sudden changes in volume level, such as an actor who's getting worked up in a dramatic scene and is about to yell the next line. If the boom operator has a compact mixer such as a Shure FP33 (**Figure 5.10**) with volume controls, that can make a big difference in getting more accurate sound levels for your project.

Figure 5.10 Shure FP33 field audio mixer gives you flexibility on the shoot.

Working with Timecode

Once you select a double-system recording device, you need to assure synchronization with the RED. This is relatively straightforward on a single camera shoot—you'll see a more complex multi-camera scenario later in this chapter. As mentioned earlier, you need the special LEMO timecode cable to connect to the RED. In order to jam sync the timecode of your RED to the audio recorder, connect both of them with the timecode cable, and choose the JAM SYNC option (**Figure 5.11**) in the timecode menu. The RED will reset its timecode to exactly match the incoming timecode of the recorder. The RED always acts as the slave to whatever source you feed it, so make sure the audio recorder is set up for the desired initial timecode first. Setting it to the current time of day on a 24-hour clock is a reasonably safe bet. (Refer to the "Set Clock" section of RED's Operations Guide for details.)

Figure 5.11 Setting the JAM SYNC option in the RED timecode menu.

23.98 VS. 29.97

Choosing the proper timecode base to use is a subject of some debate among sound record-ists. Most commonly you'll be running the RED at 23.98 (or 25 in PAL territories), so it logically follows that you'd want to record audio at 23.98 (or 25) as well. This doesn't always end up being the case, and sometimes audio gets recorded at 29.97 NDF (non-drop frame) instead. This isn't a major issue in postproduction, but be consistent and aware of it. Sound is always being recorded at the same speed; it's a question of how timecode is being measured. If you do go with 29.97 on the audio recorder, choose the CROSS option in the RED's timecode menu (**Figure 5.12**). Doing so makes the camera jam sync the equivalent 23.98 timecode from a 29.97 NDF source.

Figure 5.12 Selecting the CROSS option in the RED timecode menu.

> TIP Every once in a while, ask the sound recordist if you can listen to the playback of a recent take. You might hear something you didn't notice when you heard it live, and be able to request a correction. The sound recordist will (ideally) also appreciate your taking the time to listen to their work. Let them know they're doing a good job.

MULTI-CAMERA AUDIO

Things get trickier when you use more than one RED camera. It goes without saying that you want to jam sync each camera to the timecode source and make sure they all stay jammed to each other throughout the day. You can easily verify this by having the camera operators call out their timecodes by the second every hour or so, and having the sound operator confirm they are all on the same mark. Usually when sync drifts, it goes off by more than a second, so it's easily spotted this way. A couple of pieces of gear can make the synchronization process even easier.

A *smart slate*, such as the Denecke TS-C (**Figure 5.13**), is a clapper board with a built-in digital counter that can be synced up to audio gear and the RED. The camera sees and records the slate's visual timecode, which should precisely match the timecode it's recording to the

Figure 5.13 Denecke TS-C smart slate.

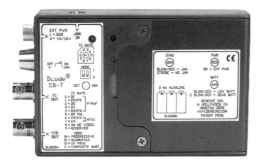

Figure 5.14 Denecke's D-Code SBT sync box is easy to use.

R3D files. A smart slate can act as the master timecode source, from which the audio recorder and any number of RED cameras derive their own matching timecode.

Another handy device when working with multiple cameras is a *timecode generator*. Denecke's (www.denecke.com) D-Code SBT sync box (**Figure 5.14**) is a good example of a lightweight, easy-to-use timecode generator. It has very low power consumption and, unlike a smart slate, is able to easily last throughout a long production day without needing its batteries replaced. If you use a timecode generator as your master timecode source, you'll never have to worry about losing sync when you run out of batteries on a slate or camera. You can use a timecode generator as the timecode master source for everything, including the smart slate, your audio recorder, and the camera.

The actual action of the clapper sticks closing serves as another method of manual sync in post should timecodes fail to match. If everything works properly with the timecode, the takes can be synced without ever looking at the sticks. However, it's good to have for redundancy, and psychologically speaking, there is something special about the slate clapping shut that gets the crew and actors a little more focused on making a movie.

PROPER SLATE ETIQUETTE

As a DP or director, you're probably not going to run your own slate. But it might fall to someone who's never done it before, like a production assistant. So, here are some tips for doing the job right.

Make sure the slate is accurately marked for each scene number and take using a dry-erase marker or pieces of removable gaffer's tape and a Sharpie. Keep the sticks open before marking so the editor can easily tell the moments before they come together when *scrubbing* (quickly playing backward and forward) through a take. Shoot the slate well lit, in focus, and as close to full frame as possible (**Figure 5.15a**)—focus the lens onto it (if the focus is initially set on a different subject). A slate that's out of focus, out of frame, or unlit is not very useful to an editor (**Figure 5.15b**). Call out the scene/take as listed on the slate clearly after sound and camera are rolling, and say "marker" to cue the closing.

Figure 5.15a A well-framed and focused slate.

Figure 5.15b This slate is out of focus and not close enough to the camera.

Clap the sticks together swiftly. Or if it's MOS (a silent take), keep the slate closed entirely. Clapping doesn't have to be especially loud. As a courtesy in an actor's close-up, keep it particularly quiet. The clapper sticks make an audio spike that's very easy to spot on a waveform in postproduction (more on that later). Hold the clapper still for a second after closing, and then quickly exit the frame. Make sure to have a good exit route planned before the roll is called. There's nothing more embarrassing than being trapped holding a slate in frame while the director is waiting to call action. Call out "second sticks" if for whatever reason the camera didn't catch the first marker.

You can also slate at the end of a shot—say if the camera came down from a high crane shot or it was otherwise impractical to shoot the slate until the end of the take. Hold it upside down to signify tail slate, and call out "tail slate." These procedures might all sound like overkill, but when audio and picture are separated, you'll want all the clues you can get to merge them back together.

THE LEGEND OF MOS

Most film crews just *know* that MOS means a take without recorded sound, but no one really knows where the term came from. One story goes that early Hollywood directors who emigrated from Germany had trouble pronouncing the word *with*. So, instead of saying "We're recording this without sound," they would say, "We're recording this '*mit* out' sound." The true origin of MOS may never be fully known.

As with everything else you do on a production, taking careful notes about your sound recordings is an excellent way to prepare for postproduction. Some of the recorders mentioned earlier, such as the Aaton Cantar, can be set up to take notes automatically. Otherwise, you'll want to do it with a spreadsheet on a laptop or simply with pen and paper. Location Sound Corporation (www.locationsound.com) makes a nice form (**Figure 5.16**) complete with carbon copies so every department that needs a copy can receive one.

LOCATION SOUND CORP **PRODUCTION SOUND REPORT** LOCATION SOUND CORP

TITLE:		PRODUCTION CO:	**DISC/ROLL #:**
SOUND MIXER:			**DATE:**
PHONE:	MEDIA:	❑ MASTER ❑ COPY	PAGE _____ OF _____
RECORDER:	SAMPLE FREQ:	BITS:	BWF FILE TYPE: ❑ MONO ❑ POLY
TIME CODE:	TONE:	MONO MIX ON CH# _____	FORMAT: ❑ UDF ❑ FAT16 ❑ FAT32
DAILY INSTRUCTIONS:			

	SCENE	TAKE	SEGMENT/ FILE #	#OF PRINTS	NOTES	1	2	3	4	5	6	7	8	9	10
1															
2															
3															
4															
5															
6															
7															
8															
9															
10															
11															
12															
13															
14															
15															
16															
17															
18															
19															
20															
21															
22															
23															
24															
25															

This 4-part form is available through Location Sound Corporation • 10639 Riverside Dr. North Hollywood, CA 91602 (818) 980-9891 or outside CA at (800) 228-4429 • www.locationsound.com

Figure 5.16 Location Sound's Production Sound Report.

Using the Onboard Audio

So, you've read everything here regarding double-system sound, but you still prefer to use the RED onboard audio instead. Or perhaps you're on a run-and-gun shoot that can't accommodate or doesn't have the budget for full double-system sound equipment and personnel. For these cases, this section covers the RED's onboard audio.

You should at least consider running the mic through an outboard mixer before going into the camera. The RED has no hardware audio-level volume controls, which means you have to set audio levels via the on-screen menu. This is fairly tricky to do for general levels, because you have to adjust the input and then switch back to the main display to see its effects on the meters. Making these adjustments is even more challenging to pull off during an actual take. As a bonus, external amplified mixers usually come with headphone outputs, so you don't have to tether your headphones directly to the RED.

CONNECTIONS

The RED direct audio setup is fairly straightforward. One of the most important aspects is making sure you have the right cables. Just about every professional microphone uses a standard XLR connector, whereas the RED uses Mini XLR connectors (also known as TA3M). It's important to know this up front because the Mini XLR cable is not common and will not come in the box with most microphones. Coffey Sound (www.coffeysound.com) makes a 5-pin adaptor cable specifically designed for RED. Coffey also offers a special mini 5-pin to standard ⅛-inch mini jack so you can monitor audio outboard without connecting directly to the camera's onboard headphone jack.

MENUS AND OPERATION

Next, from the Audio/Video menu, select the appropriate channel, power, and level settings for your mic. (Review the "Audio" and "Sound Menu" sections of RED's Operations Guide for details on this.) You have four channels of audio and four connectors on the RED to connect to. Typically you would use the mic setting if the microphone is connected directly and you're using the camera as a mixer. If you're connecting the mic first to an outboard mixer and then routing to the camera, choose the line level input (**Figure 5.17**). Consult your microphone's instruction manual to determine whether it requires 48-volt *phantom power* (the technical term used for microphones that don't use batteries and draw power directly from the recording device they're plugged into). The RED can supply this through the Audio/Video menu

(**Figure 5.18**), but make absolutely certain first. Sending phantom power to a mic that doesn't require it can damage the mic.

> NOTE   If you're renting a camera, inquire whether it's had the audio hardware updated by RED. The initial versions of the camera had audio hardware with lower-fidelity and nonstandard wiring for phantom power. So, make sure you're getting an upgraded camera.

Figure 5.17 Channels 1 and 2 are set to mic; 3 and 4 are set for line level input.

Figure 5.18 Switching on 48V phantom power.

Use the audio-level meters to adjust the sound level. You want to set it so that your levels peak past the first hash mark just out of the green (**Figure 5.19**). As levels on the meters get higher and higher, they begin to show as yellow, orange, and finally solid red when levels have overloaded (**Figure 5.20**). In digital audio recording, once a sound is recorded over-loaded, the sound is distorted and cannot be recovered. So if you want to err on the side of caution, keep the levels in the green but just a little low. It's a lot easier to boost levels and perform noise reduction in post than try to recover badly distorted audio. You can set up an outboard mixer with an electronic limiter to keep any loud sounds from peaking, which is another reason I recommended that you use one.

Figure 5.19 Normal audio levels just reach out of the green.

Figure 5.20 Overloaded audio levels display as red.

Postproduction Audio Tips

Let's assume all went well in production and you're ready to start working with your audio in postproduction. If you shot with audio going directly into the camera, your setup work is going to be relatively easy. All you have to do is ingest your R3D footage into your non-linear editing system (NLE), and the audio will come along already synced up. The QuickTime proxies files will also contain the onboard audio. Check the first few takes to make sure everything is in sync.

Figure 5.21 Manually syncing sound and picture using Final Cut Pro.

You shouldn't have any issues—but just in case, you'll want to learn about any as soon as possible so you can troubleshoot. An out-of-sync take with a current build of the camera is pretty rare and can indicate a need to update your operating system or NLE software. Or perhaps your hard drives need to be replaced. You can always unlink audio from video in your editing program and then slide them back into sync manually (**Figure 5.21**). This should not be happening in the first place, but keep an eye and ear out for it.

If you shot double-system sound, you need to get the audio resynced. Most of the recorders discussed in this chapter can record in WAV or BWF format. The BWF format is nice because it lends itself to automatic sync, especially when combined with the XML files that some of the recorders such as Sound Devices will create to ease syncing in post. BWF is supported in most NLE programs including Final Cut Pro, Avid, and Premiere Pro.

Depending on your editing software, the sync between BWF and your RED clips can be done automatically according to timecode. In Final Cut Pro, you'll want an excellent third-party tool called BWF2XML from Spherico (www.spherico.com), which takes the XML and BWF and sorts everything into bins ready to auto-sync in Final Cut Pro (**Figure 5.22**).

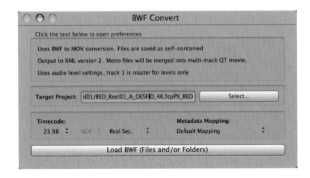

Figure 5.22 Sending BWF to Final Cut Pro with BWF2XML.

If you're unable to sync automatically via timecode, you can also do it manually by visually spotting the moment where the clapper comes together in the picture and aligning this with the frame of audio spiking in your waveform. Look for the very first frame after the clapper sticks are closing. When the sticks are still moving, they will be blurry, making them easy to spot. Next, search for the spike in the audio waveform (**Figure 5.23**), which is typically very easy to hear and spot. Line up the audio and video in your NLE software (**Figure 5.24**). Typically the audio will run slightly longer than the picture, so you can trim the audio to match exactly if you want to be really careful. Listen toward the middle and end of the take to make sure there's no sync drift. If all is well, keep doing this with each take until you have everything synced up.

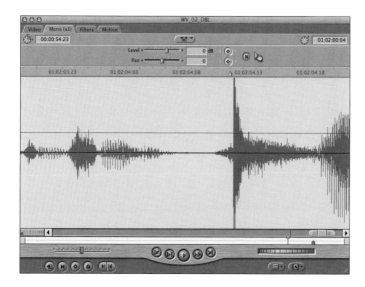

Figure 5.23 The clapper slate makes a tall waveform spike.

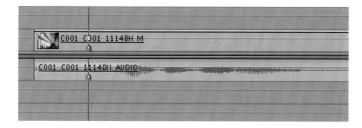

Figure 5.24 Audio and video lined up.

TIP Try putting a small mic on the camera just to capture one channel of internal audio as a reference. This is audio that will not really be usable quality-wise because of the mic placement, but it can be an invaluable secondary check on sync by comparing it to the dual-system audio in your NLE software. Out-of-phase sync is very easy to spot because it sounds like an echo until the sync is perfect. Then, you can mute or delete the internal audio and keep the synced dual-system audio. Of course, this works best in quieter locations, where the actors are closer to mic. If the location is loud or the actors are far away from the onboard mic, you might not hear them well enough to take advantage of this tip.

If your production audio is simply too noisy, is too low quality, or just didn't get recorded properly, you can always do what's called *dubbing*, *looping*, or *automated dialogue replacement* (ADR) in post. I recommend avoiding ADR as much as possible. It *can* be a lifesaver, but it can be difficult on a budget to make ADR sound natural and properly integrated with the original production audio. Also, not all actors are skilled at perfectly repeating their dialogue and matching their original performance and timing. And for some projects, such as documentaries, it isn't completely ethical to ADR original dialogue.

Good noise-reduction programs are readily available, some of which are included with affordable postproduction audio suites such as ProTools, SoundTrack Pro, and Adobe Soundbooth that can rescue relatively noisy production sound.

NOTE If you have a noisy sound clip that's irreplaceable, you can have it reclaimed by a professional sound studio using a high-end tool such as the CEDAR audio restoration system. CEDAR is expensive, of course, but can work minor miracles on noisy audio.

Do your absolute best to get great audio to match your 4K imagery. A high-quality soundtrack is an audience expectation, and if done well, it will simply slip into the background of your audience's enjoyment of the story. Work hard on your soundtrack, and you'll end up with a higher-quality final project.

Dean Georgopoulos

DIGITAL IMAGING TECHNICIAN, KOSMOS INNERTAINMENT GROUP

Dean Georgopoulos poses next to a RED, customized with AJA and Element Technica hardware.

Dean Georgopoulos owns RED camera serial number 31 but came into the RED world almost by accident. He'd worked for more than 20 years as a producer and post-production supervisor in Hollywood. One of his highest-profile jobs before the RED was overseeing the Digital Entertainment Network (DEN). Founded at the height of the late 1990s Internet boom, DEN was a multimillion-dollar startup producing 26 original series for the Web.

"I was running DEN as an Avid editorial operation with 30 editors on staff cutting 24 hours a day in two shifts," recalls Georgopoulos. "I built a post facility in Los Angeles at the corner of Olympic and Barrington, and I became good friends with Peter Fasciano of Avid. He had modified a BetaSP camera to be able to shoot directly to a 9 GB hard drive. It cost him millions to develop the technology, but you could pull it directly off the camera and start cutting. In a way, RED is a manifestation of that dream."

Today, Georgopoulos's daily work typically finds him as a DIT on commercials and features in Hollywood. "I was working with CamTec camera rentals, teaching everybody about the RED camera when it was brand new, and that just snowballed for me," he says. "Fifty percent of every job I've done since then is with a first-timer on a RED. They've told their producer, 'We want to use the camera, and we want to work with Dino.' I've developed relationships with directors of photography, producers, directors, and major clients like Mattel, Nike, and HBO."

Though Georgopoulos rents his camera and services as a package, he leaves certain accessories such as optics up to the client. "Within 50 miles of L.A. there are tens of thousands of lenses," he observes. "I don't have $100,000 sitting around to buy glass, and I don't know anything about taking lenses apart to maintain them either. Rental houses like CamTec, Abel Cine Tech, and Birns and Sawyer employ full-time technicians for their lenses. I simply own the 18–50mm RED lens, which none of my clients really use, but it's enough to see an image and test the camera. From there they can order the glass they really want."

Georgopoulos's primary duties are data management and camera operations. "I bring three separate Mac systems to the set," he explains. "This has evolved over time, starting with just my laptop. Then I added a 24-inch iMac and finally an eight-core Mac Pro into the mix. The laptop transfers files via FireWire 800 to G-RAID G21 TB hard drives. Then I'll run another transfer on the iMac. We work with whatever media they're shooting to: CF cards with FireWire 800 readers or FireWire direct from a RED-DRIVE. It's drag and drop off one box and then over to the next one. I wind up with four copies from two CPUs, all copying the original data. If there's a hiccup, it won't be on both machines.

"Depending on the postproduction path the client wants, I'm often making ProRes 1K files from every shot on the Mac Pro via REDrushes on set," Georgopoulos continues. "My work is a combination of keeping a log of what's come off the camera and literally looking at a drive to see how shots are transferring. I'll also create a REDCINE and a Final Cut Pro project for every show while on the set. I can just scrub through a shot on the iMac while I'm tweaking the color in REDCINE. On commercials and music videos, I've actually cut part of the project together when there's downtime. On a lot of the early jobs, the clients were just stunned when they saw 4K on the Cinema Display."

As a production day continues, Georgopoulos prepares deliverables for his clients. "If they want tape masters, I prep R3D files for PlasterCITY Digital Post," he explains. "They take my drives and run layoffs to HDCAM tape in real time. When the shoot wraps, I'm typically still working. But when I'm finished transferring for the day, I'm usually done with the project. Anybody can call me with questions afterwards, and I often act as a bridge between production and post, if needed."

Being in demand has permitted Georgopoulos to work with a wide variety of high-profile filmmakers, including a recent job with renowned director Terrence Malick (*Days of Heaven, The Thin Red Line*), cinematographer Emmanuel "Chivo" Lubezki, ASC (*Children of Men, Burn After Reading*), and Oscar-winner Sean Penn. "I got that job through RED," says Georgopoulos. "Chivo contacted RED and said he wanted to rent a camera and shoot tests for an upcoming project. RED referred him to me, and I ended up flying out to Texas to work with the crew.

"They wanted to use RED in a compact mode for some very specific shots from late in the day, dusk to actual nighttime," Georgopoulos says. "I spent about seven days shooting with Malick and Chivo. Terrence Malick is a genius filmmaker and very spontaneous. He decides what he wants to shoot and where he wants to do it in natural lighting situations and with very small crews. We got to do a scene with Sean Penn where he was driving. I was tucked in the back of a BMW SUV, and it was just awesome. We were driving around Houston, Texas, at 1 in the morning, and Sean got a green light to do whatever he wanted. It was like being with a 15-year-old who'd just stolen his dad's Porsche."

Dean Georgopoulos's Web site is www.red31.com. ∎

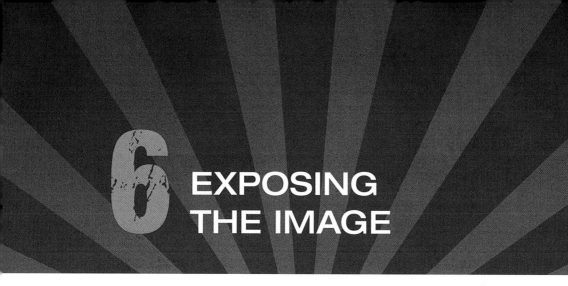

6 EXPOSING THE IMAGE

Once you have all the gear you need and you're ready to start shooting, you still need to learn to set the best possible exposure for your images. I could write another book devoted just to cinematography and lighting, but in this chapter you'll learn how to achieve the optimal exposure using the RED ONE's onboard tools and some external gear as well. Getting a proper exposure with the RED can be challenging, but it's something you'll get a feel for with some practice.

First, we'll look at some basic concepts from photography that go into making a correct exposure. Then, you'll get some specifics on RED ONE operations and tools you can use to achieve an optimal exposure. This is one subject for which you'll also want to carefully study RED's own camera manual, which goes into extensive detail on camera exposure and operation. You can download the latest version of the manual at www.red.com/support.

Exposure Concepts

Before getting into the menus and technical functions of the camera, let's look at some cinematography basics. It's useful to study still photography because the more you understand about concepts such as aperture, shutter speeds, and filters, the better your shots will look. As with everything else, the more you practice, the more your work will improve.

WORKING RAW

For every lighting situation, there's an optimal exposure (or T-stop setting on your lens) that will give you the best possible image. An important concept to keep in mind is that the RED shoots to a RAW file format, which can be extensively manipulated after production is completed. This safety net doesn't free you from the need to carefully expose your shots and avoid under- or overexposure. But you'd be surprised how the RED ONE lets you take shots that have slightly incorrect exposures and bring them back into proper ranges when compared to most other HD and video cameras. The latitude is more akin to working with 35mm negative, where you can "print" shots with a high degree of flexibility. Avoid the temptation to rely too heavily on the corrections RAW allows. The further exposure is from optimum, the less color correction is possible and the more likely noise will be difficult to conceal. As with standard HD formats, detail lost to extreme over- and underexposure cannot be recovered.

THE ASA SYSTEM

The American Standards Association (ASA) has created a specific exposure index measurement system used to classify film stocks' sensitivity to lighting—the higher the ASA number, the more sensitive the film. Some common film stock speeds include 500 ASA, which is considered a fast stock, suitable for indoor and nighttime filming, and 100 ASA, which is considered a slow, fine-grain stock best used for outdoor, daylight work.

There has always been a trade-off between sensitivity, noise, and contrast. The faster stocks can be used with less light but often exhibit increased grain and reduced image contrast. If possible, most experienced cinematographers would not want to shoot film much faster than 500 ASA because of the high amount of grain and generally reduced image quality. Indeed, very few motion-picture stocks higher than 500 ASA exist.

The RED ONE also uses the ASA system to classify its sensitivity to light, though of course because it is a digital camera, the RED's ASA is a variable control. You can set the sensitivity of the camera anywhere from 50 to 2,000 ASA, but the camera's optimum setting is 320 ASA.

As with film, when you dial in the faster ASA settings on the RED, you get increased grain (technically called *image sensor noise*). In my opinion, the image starts looking unacceptably noisy above 500 ASA. And unlike slow film emulsions, there doesn't seem to be much benefit to shooting a slower ASA even when there is ample exposure to do so. My advice is to always keep the ASA set at 320 ASA. If you need more light, increase your illumination; if you need less light for your desired exposure, use neutral density (ND) filters.

APERTURE

The T-stop, or aperture, setting of your lens (**Figure 6.1**) is the most critical control you have over your exposure. If you're from a video background, you may be tempted to aim the camera at a

given scene and simply adjust the aperture until your onboard light meters report the correct exposure. You'll get better shot-to-shot consistency, however, if you work the other way around: Choose a specific T-stop on a per-scene basis, and then do your best to light each shot in the sequence to that stop.

Figure 6.1 The aperture (or T-stop) of a lens is controlled by a mechanical iris ring.

Aperture is also a way to creatively control depth of field. The more open the aperture setting, the shallower your depth of field. For example, if you are shooting a portrait at T1.8, you can expect to have a very shallow depth of field (**Figure 6.2**). Set up the same shot at T16, and you'll get much deeper depth of field, with less visual separation between the foreground and background (**Figure 6.3**). If you take control of your aperture with lighting and ND filters, you'll be able to use depth of field creatively to focus the viewer's eye rather than simply having it as a random function of your cinematography.

Figure 6.2 An aperture setting of T1.8 gives you a shallow depth of field.

Figure 6.3 The same shot at T16 exhibits a deep depth of field.

SHUTTER SPEED/ANGLE

Shutter speed is another concept that's carried over from film cameras. In a film camera, the shutter speed is typically a mechanical blade that determines how long each frame is receiving light—as opposed to the aperture, which controls the intensity of the light and depth of field. The faster the shutter speed, the sharper motion will appear in a given frame (**Figure 6.4**).

Figure 6.4 Shots with fast-moving elements such as water require careful selection of shutter speed.

But a faster shutter also means less light and thus a lower exposure. For example, at 24 frames per second, a $1/48$ second shutter will give a pleasing motion blur and a reasonable exposure. Move the shutter speed up to $1/96$, and you'll be losing one stop of light, but the motion will become more staccato and sharper (e.g., the *Saving Private Ryan* effect).

The default setting automatically adjusts the shutter speed to a standard setting across any given frame rate. This is the RELATIVE mode of the camera's SHUTTER MODE menu. I recommend keeping the shutter in the RELATIVE mode unless you are going for a specific motion effect or unless it's an emergency where you need more exposure by going to a slower shutter speed such as $1/24$. Keep in mind that a slower shutter speed will give you more light, but the image motion will begin to smear and look more like 60i video than 24p footage.

You can also use the shutter to synchronize the camera to an external monitor. Say, for example, you want to shoot something off a television screen or computer monitor. Those black bars moving up the screen are due to a mismatch in the refresh rate of the screen and the shutter speed of the RED. The SYNCRO setting in the SHUTTER MODE menu allows you to make very precise changes to the shutter speed. You can dial in the exact scanning rate of the monitor and achieve a distortion-free shot. Typically you make this adjustment while looking in the viewfinder and adjusting until the screen distortion disappears.

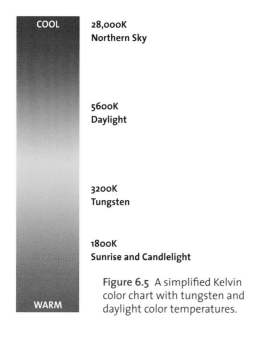

Figure 6.5 A simplified Kelvin color chart with tungsten and daylight color temperatures.

COLOR TEMPERATURE

Color temperature is another subject that could fill an entire book. In a nutshell, it's a characteristic of visible light that associates its color to a specific temperature scale measure in Kelvin, or K (**Figure 6.5**). Sunlight is often simplified to be around 5,600 K and is a bluer color when compared to artificial lighting. Indoor incandescent light sources like standard household tungsten such as bulbs are typically generalized as 3,200 K, which has more of an orange hue.

Color temperature is important for two main reasons with regard to the RED. First you have to tell the camera which color temperature to balance for. If you're going to be outdoors primarily, you want to balance closer to 5,600 K, and when you're indoors with mostly tungsten lights, you'll dial down toward 3,200 K. The camera has presets for these temperatures, which you'll find in the COLOR TEMP menu as options for DAYLIGHT and TUNGSTEN, respectively.

The second reason is that because you're shooting RAW, color temperature is not as critical as it would be on a non-RAW camera. If you miss the ideal color temperature setting when you shoot, you can easily compensate for it during postproduction on the R3D files. What you can't easily do is rebalance the actual lighting sources within the image.

For example, if you're shooting indoors with tungsten light during daytime and you're also seeing daylight outside through windows, you'll need to do some balancing work (**Figure 6.6**). You'll want to gel your lighting with Color Temperature Blue (CTB) filters so they match the outside light. Or use lights that are not incandescent such as Hydrargyrum Medium-arc Iodide (HMI) units. Alternatively, you could gel the windows with Color Temperature Orange (CTO) filters to alter the outside sunlight to match the tungsten sources (**Figure 6.7**). Always be mindful of color temperature because your eyes automatically adjust and make lighting sources look balanced, but the camera actually captures something very different.

Figure 6.6 A tungsten-lit indoor shot with unbalanced outdoor windows using the TUNGSTEN preset.

Figure 6.7 The same shot using CTO gels on the windows to balance out the indoor lighting.

THE BLUE WORLD

Many cinematographers, such as Nancy Schreiber, ASC (who calls the RED a *blue world camera*), have reported that the RED produces less noisy results under daylight-balanced lighting versus tungsten lighting. This is because the RED's image sensor is biased toward daylight sensitivity. It's not a major issue for most types of shooting, except in greenscreen keying where the amount of noise created by tungsten sources can cause issues in pulling successful composites. So if you have a choice between tungsten and HMI lighting for green screen shots, go for HMI whenever possible.

External Exposure Tools

Now that you've learned some general theory about exposure, let's get into specifics. First we'll look at some equipment and techniques for obtaining the right exposure, and then you'll learn about RED's onboard camera tools.

LIGHT METERS

Light meters (**Figure 6.8**) have been around since the early days of motion-picture cinematography. As their name implies, they measure the amount of light in a given scene to help

determine the best possible exposure. Light meters take into account your camera's current ASA, shutter speed, and frame rate in order to suggest proper exposure with great accuracy.

Since the RED uses industry standards, you can use just about any light meter with the camera. Light meters are much more necessary with film cameras because you have no other way of knowing whether you've set the right exposure until the negative is developed, and by then it's too late to fix any mistakes. With a digital camera such as the RED, you can see the image on a monitor right away and easily tell whether a shot is not being exposed properly.

Working with a digital camera doesn't completely do away with the usefulness of a light meter, however. It's true that the RED has very accurate built-in light metering, but it measures only the exact frame the camera is pointed at. You can measure all the lighting around a set with a handheld light meter. This gives more thorough readings for all the potential lighting changes within a moving shot than you could get with just the onboard camera metering. You can also use a light meter to

Figure 6.8 The Sekonic L-558 digital light meter offers a highly accurate measurement of lighting for optimum exposure.

measure the output of specific lighting instruments for much finer control over the look of a scene. I recommend using a light meter, especially if you're doing commercials or green-screen cinematography, where lighting ratios and levels are critical.

WAVEFORMS AND VECTORSCOPES

Many high-end production monitors, such as the Panasonic BT-LH1760 mentioned in Chapter 4, have a built-in waveform monitor and vectorscope. Standalone units also exist (**Figure 6.9**). The waveform monitor is used for measuring overall levels of brightness, or *luminance*, in a video signal, whereas the vectorscope is for measuring levels of *chrominance* (color values).

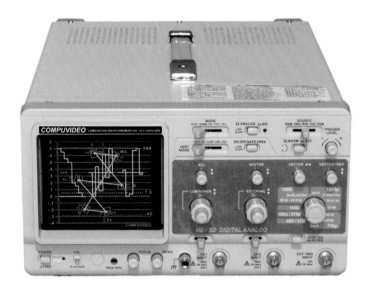

Figure 6.9 A waveform monitor with a built-in vectorscope.

I mention waveforms and vectorscopes because using them with the RED differs from using them with a non-RAW camera. When you connect a monitor to the RED's outputs, you are actually measuring a video signal with a specific color and gamma profile already applied. Although you can make use of these tools in determining broadcast-safe colors and maintaining a specific range of brightness in your shot, be aware that you are measuring one possible interpretation of your imagery—not the actual RAW signal. You need to use the onboard tools for a more accurate reading, which we'll look at later in this chapter. (For more on the camera's color and gamma settings, turn to the "Color and Gamma Space" section of Chapter 9.)

USING A COLOR CHART

Sometimes you want to achieve very specific color values, but these can be difficult to calibrate for in postproduction. Maybe you're shooting with a highly tinted colored gel on your lights, but you still want to get accurate skin tones. Shooting a color chart (**Figure 6.10**) can be helpful because you'll have a standard reference that you can color correct to, no matter what the on-set color temperature was. I recommend carrying a ChromaDuMonde (www.dsclabs.com) or a Macbeth color chart and shooting a few seconds of it under any special lighting setups. This gives you a standard reference you can compare in every shot for which you shoot a chart. You can also use a color chart or gray card with the onboard spot meter to achieve a more accurate exposure (you'll learn more about that in the "Spot meter" section later in this chapter).

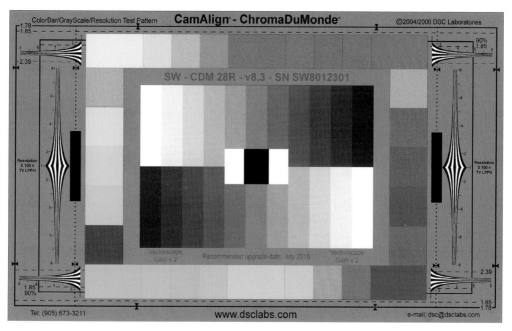

Figure 6.10 A color chart helps ensure color calibration and accuracy.

Onboard Exposure Tools

The RED ONE is about as far from a point-and-shoot camera as you can get. There's no single setting on the camera that will give you a proper exposure. You achieve the best exposure through a careful combination of the meters and tools the camera offers, and each lighting situation is a little different, so take the time to do the job right.

LOOK SETTINGS

Before getting into the specifics of the onboard exposure tools, I want to mention the LOOK menu. In general, I recommend *not* using the LOOK settings because you can easily fool yourself into exposing for a completely different look and color setting than the camera is actually recording. Remember, you're capturing a RAW image, which can be extensively manipulated in postproduction.

You can substantially change the look in the camera by altering settings such as SATURATION, EXPOSURE, and BRIGHTNESS within the LOOK menu. This can cause under- or over-exposure or inconsistent color because you've pushed the LOOK settings too far past an accurate display of what you're photographing. Keep these settings on the defaults, and you'll get a better sense of what you're actually capturing.

FALSE COLOR

The most powerful onboard exposure tool in my opinion is False Color. In False Color mode, the normal colors of the image are replaced by a color overlay representing the different exposure levels within the frame. Blue colors represent underexposed areas, green is 18 percent ND (or exact median exposure), and yellow and red colors indicate areas approaching overexposure. **Figure 6.11** shows a chart defining what each color on the scale stands for.

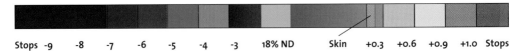

| Stops | -9 | -8 | -7 | -6 | -5 | -4 | -3 | 18% ND | Skin | +0.3 | +0.6 | +0.9 | +1.0 | Stops |

Figure 6.11 The False Color scale used by the RED indicates areas of the frame that are over and under the ideal exposure.

TIP   As with most digital cameras, the RED is more likely to clip highlights than shadows. *Clipping* is when a recorded luminance value goes beyond 100 percent, resulting in a pure white image with no detail. If you err on the side of slight underexposure and protect the brightest parts of the image from overexposure, you'll have more detail to work with in postproduction.

To access the camera's False Color mode, press the VIDEO button, and then access the VIEWFINDER menu. In the Color settings you'll then see the FALSE COLOR setting.

Point the camera at your subject, and adjust your aperture setting. You'll quickly see the effects as you get warmer colors (indicating overexposure) when you open up the lens aperture and you get cooler colors (indicating underexposure) as you stop down. This is when a color chart can come in handy, because you can expose the 18 percent gray on the chart to match the 18 percent gray on the camera's False Color scale and get a perfect exposure. **Figure 6.12** shows an example of a shot framing an 18 percent gray chart, and **Figure 6.13** shows the same thing without False Color.

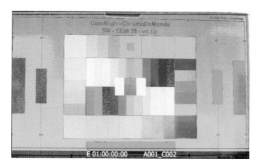

Figure 6.12 A color chart used to set exposure with False Color.

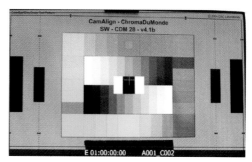

Figure 6.13 The same shot with False Color turned off.

Here are some more hints for getting the most out of False Color: Expose Caucasian flesh tones so that they fall in the pink zone. (Notice how this particular chart also features color chips for other skin tones as well. For those, use the IRE indicator as described in the "Spot Meter" section instead of using the pink False Color method.) Avoid excessive amounts of red (overexposure) or purple (underexposure) on anything you want to expose as your main subject. Be mindful of overexposure on highlights and skies. It's best to use False Color in conjunction with the other onboard tools to ascertain the proper exposure.

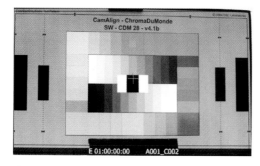

Figure 6.14 The same shot in Monochrome mode.

MONOCHROME

Monochrome completely removes the color from the image, displaying in grayscale (**Figure 6.14**). This can be useful for spotting specific areas of high contrast in an image for fine-tuned lighting, because seeing everything in full color can sometimes confuse the eye. You access MONOCROME in the same VIEWFINDER menu as FALSE COLOR.

SPOT METER

The camera's spot meter is a carryover from still cameras, in which you can focus the camera's exposure metering on a very small and specific portion of the frame. The spot meter is in the ANALYSIS menu on the ANALYSIS METER toggle—simply switch it to SPOT METER.

With the spot meter activated, you'll see a small rectangle in the frame along with a numerical display that indicates the IRE level within the rectangle. You can move this rectangle around with the camera's joystick, though you might find it easier to just pan or tilt the camera to put the item you want to measure under the rectangle. The spot meter can be useful for exposing skin tones when used in conjunction with False Color. Caucasian faces should generally fall between 50–70 IRE for proper exposure (**Figure 6.15**). For darker skin tones, expect to go down a few points on IRE, and for best results confirm the settings with an 18 percent gray card.

NOTE   *IRE* stands for Institute of Radio Engineers and is used to measure the amplitude of video signals. For *luma* (or brightness) values, 100 IRE indicates pure white, and 0 IRE indicates pure black.

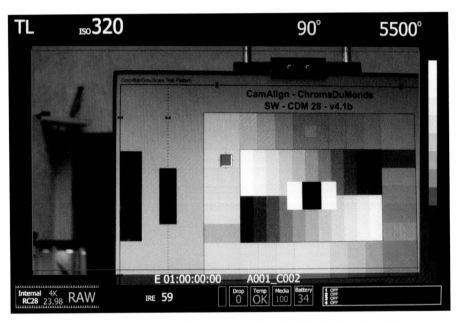

Figure 6.15 Exposing for skin tones using the spot meter with the IRE indicator at the bottom of the display.

TIP   The spot meter and many of the other analysis tools are affected by the current color and gamma space settings. Make sure you get to know their results well so you know what to expect from the onboard tools in different gamma and color spaces.

HISTOGRAM

Similar to still cameras, the RED also offers Histograms for exposure feedback. A *Histogram* is a graph of exposure values within the shot, showing where they peak. You have access to

two types of Histograms: Luma, for checking overall exposure levels within a shot, and RGB, for checking exposure levels in the three primary color channels.

You access both the Luma Histogram and the RGB Histogram from the same ANALYSIS METER menu as the spot meter.

Notice how the Histogram changes rapidly as exposure is changed. As we close the aperture down, the peaks begin to appear toward the left edge of the Histogram, indicating growing underexposure within the frame (**Figure 6.16**).

Figure 6.16 This RGB Histogram indicates an underexposed shot.

As you open the aperture up, you start to see the peaks appearing on the right side of the Histogram. Once those peaks begin to flatten, you're getting into heavy overexposure (**Figure 6.17**).

The ideal Histogram is highest in the middle, indicating a good medium exposure that is protected against severe underexposure and overexposure (**Figure 6.18**). This gives you maximum flexibility in postproduction. A few spikes on the edges are not a big issue—you might have something within the frame like a bright light source or normal shadow areas.

Figure 6.17 This RGB Histogram indicates overexposure.

Figure 6.18 An ideal RGB Histogram is center-weighted, indicating a more balanced exposure.

ZEBRAS

If you have a DV or HD video camera background, you may be familiar with Zebras. A *Zebra* is a striped pattern overlaid onto any areas of the frame that read within a certain range of exposure. You'll find the ZEBRAS setting in the VIDEO > VIEWFINDER menu.

On the RED you have two sets of Zebras that you can customize to indicate specific LOW and HI IRE levels. Zebra 1's default settings are for highlight indication, with LOW IRE at 90 and HI IRE at 108. Zebra 2's default setting is for 18 percent gray with LOW IRE at 44 and HI IRE at 47. You'll see crosshatched overlays on areas of the image when one or both Zebras are activated. Zebra 1's pattern is oriented northwest to southeast, and Zebra 2 goes northeast to southwest. (Note that when both Zebra areas overlap, Zebra 1 has priority.)

With the default Zebras activated, you can quickly determine where your highlights are and where 18 percent gray is reading at any given exposure. For example, you could drop an 18 percent gray card into a frame where your main subject is, adjust your exposure until you see Zebra 2 around the card, and then check for Zebra 1's highlights (**Figure 6.19**). If the highlights are excessive, you need to bring in more light on the gray card/subject area in order to reduce the aperture and balance out the highlights (**Figure 6.20**).

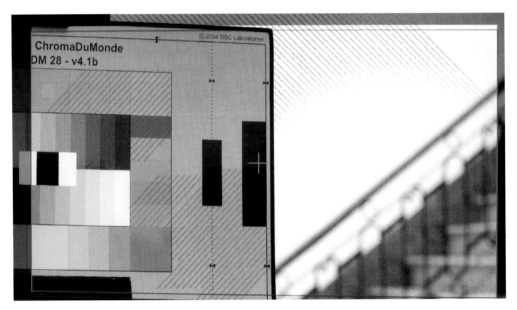

Figure 6.19 Using a gray card and the Zebra indicators, you can see the subject is underlit because Zebra 1 shows blown highlights when exposing for the card with Zebra 2.

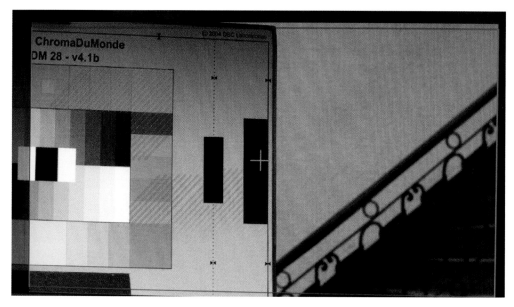

Figure 6.20 With added lighting, this card is now properly exposed, and the highlights are now more balanced according to the Zebras.

This chapter covers only a handful of the more useful tools the camera has to help you with exposure. I recommend reading the official RED manual and practicing with your camera. If you can master the use of the False Color mode and Zebras, you'll be well on your way to good exposure in most lighting scenarios.

The most important goal—beyond avoiding over- and underexposure—is avoiding extreme contrast. You have about 11 stops of latitude on the RED, which sounds like a lot. But remember that's really only about 5 ½ stops above and below the set exposure. You could easily end up with a frame showing 15–20 stops of latitude between dark shadows to bright sunlit sky (**Figure 6.21**). To control that, you'll need to bring in extra lighting and work with filters. Cinematography is a whole other art form and there is much you can learn. Practice the techniques covered in this chapter and you'll be able to analyze and understand the exposure of whatever winds up in front of your lens.

Figure 6.21 Shooting indoors with visible outdoor windows is a challenge of balancing both exposure and color temperature.

Arthur Albert, with the RED ONE on the set of *ER*.

Arthur Albert
DIRECTOR OF PHOTOGRAPHY, *ER*

The NBC medical drama *ER* consistently scored in the Nielsen ratings for the top 20 television shows since it debuted in 1994. During almost the entirety of the show's 15-year run, it was shot on 35mm film using Panavision cameras and lenses. Director of photography Arthur Albert (*Happy Gilmore, The District*) shot *ER* for eight seasons, beginning in 2001. For the final seven episodes of the series, the producers decided to completely switch to the RED ONE, making *ER* one of the highest-profile shows to shoot with the RED to date.

Albert had grown accustomed to working with film on the *ER* set but was prepared to move to the RED when the decision was made. "It came down from [executive producers] John Wells and Chris Chulack," Albert says. "We shot a test with the Panavision Genesis about a year ago. It had a good look, but at the time the camera was too heavy for our Steadicam setup, which we shoot about 60 percent of the show with. So, the producers put in an order to buy RED cameras and planned to make the transition to digital. They envisioned *ER* as a test bed for their future shows. They've also shot a pilot called *Southland* with RED, which was picked up by NBC."

The switchover from film to digital required primarily technical and workflow changes—Albert found that his creative techniques could be mostly transferred. "First we switched our lenses over from Panavision to ARRI," notes Albert. "They were exactly the same kinds of lenses I'd have used in 35mm had we not been shooting Panavision. We ended up adding diffusion filters to knock back some of the RED's sharpness. Film grain has a noticeable softening effect, but with RED you can see every hair on an actor's beard and every imperfection."

Albert also made some adjustments to the lighting of the show's standing sets. (Though set in Chicago, the majority of *ER* was photographed on a soundstage in Burbank, California). "Before RED, I was rating 500 ASA–speed Kodak 35mm film at 1000 ASA, and I could get away with underexposing another stop down when I needed to," says Albert. "The RED ONE is more like ASA 250 to my eye. You can shoot it at 500 ASA, but then you're pushing into video noise. I've effectively lost two stops, or four times the amount of light. The solution was to trade out lighting instruments for bigger and more powerful units and boost overall lighting by one stop.

"We've had to readjust our eyes a bit and rely more on the monitor and waveform," he continues. "It's a tricky balance because so much of the show plays on the drama of medical displays and machines, and we wanted to make sure those read clearly without washing out. So, we underexposed the RED just a little and evened things out in color correction. I'm very happy with the general look and how the camera handles color."

ER was well known for its fast-moving handheld and Steadicam aesthetic. This dictated a rapid pace for Albert and his crew. To keep things moving on the set, he prepared three different RED configurations that could be quickly swapped during a day's production. "We have three RED bodies because the camera just has a ton of add-ons," he explains. "We can quickly reconfigure from handheld to Steadicam to dolly. And because the camera is basically a computer, having a backup is always a good idea. We usually work with a single production unit shooting a single camera, rather than multiple camera coverage of the same scene."

In terms of on-set data management, Albert chose to go with RED CompactFlash cards instead of hard drives. "Flash cards make for a lighter camera and less potential dropouts [glitches or lost frames]," he says. "It's the same time limitation as a 1,000-foot magazine of 35mm film. The difference is if you shoot ten takes, it doesn't cost you anything extra, except the time."

Albert guesses the average viewer was completely unaware of the switch to RED. "Our colorist, who has been on the show for 15 years, has been instructed to make it look like *ER*, says Albert. "To my eyes it already looks fairly close. RED records a look that's more saturated than film, but it's easy to curl it back off in post."

When asked whether he prefers film or digital, Albert professes a desire for maximum flexibility and creative choice. "You really need to know how to do both, and each has its advantages," he notes. "Film handles extremes of bright and dark really well, while video struggles. RED is great that way, but it's still not as sensitive as film. You can also work faster with film and have less of a struggle to maintain a specific lighting ratio. The claim of other digital cameras is that you can work at really low light levels, but then you give up detail and latitude on the high end.

"Ultimately I think film is in trouble due to the costs," Albert adds. "The cheaper it gets to store archives and deal with post issues, the more the equation shifts to digital. It also comes down to the project. Some lend themselves to digital. If you shoot a lot of takes or improvise a lot, digital can save you money on film costs; but if you're shooting in a jungle, you don't want a bunch of electronic gear that goes down in heat or water. Film cameras are relatively bulletproof.

"I was involved with the original Sony Portapack videotape recorder 30 years ago, and a video tech predicted film would be dead in three years. If someone said that again today, I wouldn't necessarily argue with them, but I'm personally hoping film sticks around. It's like the difference between painting with oil and painting with watercolor. They each have their merits." ∎

7 EXPLORING SHOOTING FORMATS

Now that you're up to speed on the equipment and using the camera, let's take a closer look at the camera's different formats so you can best understand when to use which format and why. In this chapter, we'll go over recording-quality settings and the different resolutions available for shooting. You'll learn when to use specific aspect ratios. Then, you'll learn about some special in-camera effects you can do, such as slow motion and time-lapse.

Recording Quality

The RED has two recording quality settings: REDCODE 28 and REDCODE 36. REDCODE 28 records at 28 MB/second, and REDCODE 36 records at 36 MB/second. I recommend recording in REDCODE 36 for the maximum possible image quality, though it can be hard to tell the difference between the two resolutions on anything less than a 35mm blowup or a very high-resolution monitor.

I think it's much wiser to go with the best possible image quality and bank on it rather than save a little space with the lower-quality setting and find yourself in postproduction with an issue and wishing you hadn't cut corners. The one caveat is that if you're shooting REDCODE 36 to Compact Flash (CF) cards, you'll be limited to certain frame rates and resolutions because the data rate exceeds what the card can achieve. **Table 7.1** shows the maximum possible frame rate, resolution, and recording quality combinations for each type of media. (The iPhone application iSee4K I mentioned in Chapter 4 can also be a big help in reviewing the different settings.)

TABLE 7.1   MAXIMUM FRAME RATES AT EACH RESOLUTION FOR DIFFERENT RECORDING MEDIA (REDCODE 28)

REDCODE 28	RED 8GB CF	RED 16GB CF	RED DRIVE	RED RAM
2K 2:1	100 fps	120 fps	120 fps	120 fps
2K ANA	120 fps	120 fps	120 fps	120 fps
2K 16:9	100 fps	100 fps	100 fps	100 fps
3K 2:1	50 fps	60 fps	60 fps	60 fps
3K ANA	60 fps	60 fps	60 fps	60 fps
3K 16:9	30 fps	50 fps	60 fps	60 fps
4K 2:1	25 fps	30 fps	30 fps	30 fps
4K ANA	30 fps	30 fps	30 fps	30 fps
4K HD	25 fps	30 fps	30 fps	30 fps
4K 16:9	25 fps	30 fps	30 fps	30 fps

TABLE 7.1, continued MAXIMUM FRAME RATES AT EACH
RESOLUTION FOR DIFFERENT RECORDING MEDIA (REDCODE 36)

REDCODE 36	RED 8GB CF	RED 16GB CF	RED DRIVE	RED RAM
2K 2:1	75 fps	100 fps	120 fps	120 fps
2K ANA	100 fps	120 fps	120 fps	120 fps
2K 16:9	75 fps	75 fps	100 fps	100 fps
3K 2:1	30 fps	30 fps	50 fps	60 fps
3K ANA	50 fps	60 fps	60 fps	60 fps
3K 16:9	30 fps	30 fps	50 fps	60 fps
4K 2:1	25 fps	30 fps	30 fps	30 fps
4K ANA	25 fps	30 fps	30 fps	30 fps
4K HD	N/A	25 fps	30 fps	30 fps
4K 16:9	N/A	25 fps	25 fps	30 fps

TIP I recommend confirming these maximum frame rates with your camera. Some users report they are unable to achieve them on certain CF cards or drives.

To set the recording quality, follow these steps:

1. Press the SYSTEM button on the back of the camera, and then select PROJECT with the camera's control stick to see the PROJECT menu (**Figure 7.1**).

Figure 7.1 The PROJECT menu.

2. Next go to the CONFIGURE menu, and then select the QUALITY button. You'll then be able to toggle between the two REDCODE quality settings (**Figure 7.2**).

Figure 7.2 Choosing between REDCODE 28 and REDCODE 36.

Choosing Resolution

Though the RED is touted as a 4K camera, it is capable of shooting 3K and 2K resolutions as well. 4K offers the highest possible image quality, but 3K and 2K also have their uses (**Figure 7.3**).

Figure 7.3 Comparison of 16:9 frames at 4K, 3K, and 2K resolution.

4K

When in doubt, shoot 4K. It's the highest resolution on the camera, uses the largest number of pixels on the sensor, and can be easily reduced to 2K for film as well as to high definition (HD) and standard definition (SD). It's simple to go down from 4K to whatever resolution you want, but if you shoot a lower resolution and then try to scale it up, you end up with a notice-able degradation in image quality. No matter which resolution you eventually screen your project at, acquiring footage at 4K will give you the best-looking image because of oversam-pling. *Oversampling* simply means you capture an image at a higher resolution than you need to display it. When a higher resolution image is reduced, the resulting picture appears more detailed and sharper than one that began at the smaller size. There are more pixels to choose from as the image scales, and thus the image rendition is ultimately more accurate.

The 4K resolution does have a few limitations, and one of the main ones is frame rate. This isn't an issue if you don't plan to shoot at high speed (that is, for slow motion). You can still shoot from 1 to 30 frames per second in 4K, so sped-up effects are easily done without changing resolution. But if you're doing an action sequence or filming pyrotechnics and you want to crank up the frame rate, you'll be limited in 4K to 30 frames per second. To go higher, you'll need to gear down to 3K or 2K. The 3K resolution goes up to 60 frames per second, and 2K goes up to 120 fps. You'll learn about slow motion, or *Varispeed* as the camera refers to it, later in this chapter in the "Varispeed" section.

3K

The 3K resolution is primarily useful for shooting higher speeds than 4K while preserving reasonably high resolution. On the post end it means you'll still be spending some time doing down-converts, though not as much as with 4K. Record times are slightly longer than 4K, too: At 3K 16:9 REDCODE36, you have about 16 minutes on a 16 GB CF card.

> NOTE Be sure to test 3K with your editing application before committing to it, as it's the least-supported frame size in most 3rd-party software.

2K

One question that comes up often among RED users is, if I'm finishing on HD or film, why not shoot a resolution that's closer to my finishing resolution so postproduction is more effi- cient? Although it is true you'll have smaller files and need less conversion time by shooting in 2K, in my opinion the quality trade-offs are too great. The main issue is that you're shooting a much smaller "slice" of the image sensor, and as a result, your lenses will have a narrower field of view. 2K is the format you want to use primarily for the highest possible frame rates, but other than that I'd stick with 4K.

> TIP If you're shooting with 16mm lenses, you need to shoot in 2K.

Some people like to shoot in 2K to save storage space. For example, on a 16 GB CF card, you get about 34 minutes of 2K, 16:9 REDCODE 36 at 24 fps footage, versus about 8 minutes at 4K. So, it's definitely something to think about if you're very limited in your available stor- age. 2K still looks great and is much sharper than most other HD cameras. Make sure you have some fairly wide lenses, because you'll be dealing with a significantly narrower field of view with 35mm lenses compared to 4K or 3K. See the sidebar "Lens perspectives change with resolution" for more information.

LENS PERSPECTIVES CHANGE WITH RESOLUTION

In a 35mm camera, you would expect the standard point-of-view lens to be around 50mm. That is a lens that gives a perspective similar to what the human eye sees. With the RED, the standard lens is different for each resolution because of the recording area of the sensor. These numbers are subjective as well, but figure something around a 35mm lens for 4K, a 25mm for 3K, and a 16mm for 2K for standard perspective. Before purchasing a lens, try renting a set so you can get a good look at what different focal lengths look like at different resolutions.

Here's how to select resolution on the camera:

1. Start in the PROJECT menu.
2. Select the RESOLUTION button. You'll see the 4K, 3K, and 2K options (**Figure 7.4**).

Figure 7.4 Selecting resolution options.

3. Select the resolution you want with the joystick. (Notice that you have aspect ratio choices for each resolution—you'll learn more about that in the next section.)

WARNING   If you ever see a crossed-out VALID SETTINGS warning appear in the menu, you've selected a combination of resolution, time base, or recording quality that won't work with your current media type. You need to change settings to resolve this.

Working with Aspect Ratios

You learned about aspect ratios in the "Delivery Format" section in Chapter 3. The basic concept is that you should shoot an aspect ratio that is most useful to your intended final output. Your aspect ratio choices with the RED are 2:1, 16:9, HD, and Anamorphic. You select an aspect ratio in the PROJECT menu under RESOLUTION. The 2:1 and 16:9 modes are intended for working with film-destined projects (**Figure 7.5**). The HD mode is best suited for projects that are intended only for high-definition and standard-definition television. The Anamorphic mode is designed specifically for use with 2:1 anamorphic lenses. So, use this mode only when you're absolutely certain you have the proper lenses.

Figure 7.5　A 2:1 frame (left) compared to a 16:9/HD aspect ratio frame (right); the 2:1 has slightly less horizontal image area than the 16:9 aspect ratio.

2:1

Productions often shoot 2:1 for movies destined for theatrical release, where the image is likely to be further cropped for a different aspect ratio. For example, Simon Duggan, ACS, shot *Knowing* in 2:1 for an eventual 2.40:1 release. Out of the box, 2:1 footage, played back in an HD timeline, will exhibit a small amount of letterboxing at the top and bottom. The camera has built-in frame guides so you can shoot 2:1 and see where the eventual 16:9, 1.85, or 2.40:1 cropping could be (**Figure 7.6**). This makes it much easier to compose a shot. You'll find these options in the FRAME GUIDE section of the MONITOR menu.

A HISTORY OF CROPPING

It might seem counterintuitive to photograph a frame that you know will be cropped into another aspect ratio in postproduction, but this is exactly how film cameras have always worked. All 35mm movies are shot on a piece of film with an aspect ratio of approximately 1.37:1. The cropping to 1.85 or 2.35 or 2.40 is done as a matting effect in postproduction (or by masking the image during projection). I've even seen monitors cropped off with gaffers tape to approximate the desired aspect ratio. It's not the most elegant method, but it does the trick.

Figure 7.6 1.85 frame guides activated for composing shots that will be further cropped in postproduction.

16:9

The 16:9 format is the native format of HD TV. At 4096 x 2304 (4K), this mode also happens to be the highest possible image resolution you can shoot with the RED at this time. However, the mathematics don't quite work out because to get from 4096 x 2304 to 1920 x 1080 for HD, you are not dividing by an even number. So, you end up dealing with longer processing, and your proxies will not scale exactly 1:1 when you drop them into an HD edit. And that leads us right into the next format: HD.

HD

The HD resolution is related to working with high-definition TV. This format sacrifices some resolution in the interest of a smoother postproduction workflow for productions destined only for video release. At 4K HD, the resolution is 3840 x 2160, so you're losing almost 10 percent of your resolution compared to 4096 x 2304 for 4K 16:9. However, a 10 percent loss going from 4K to HD is still a lot of resolution once you've downscaled. 3840 x 2160 divides mathematically exactly by 2, which achieves 1920 x 1080—the resolution of HD at 1080p.

As a result, not only are exports from R3D files to other formats in HD faster, but you can also drop half-size proxies right into a 1080p timeline without any letterboxing or scaling required. It also produces better-looking conversions from HD to SD, especially in 16:9. This mode is the one to use if you're sure you *won't* be finishing on film. Confirm that everyone is on the same page from production and postproduction before committing to this format.

> NOTE   The 4K HD option was enabled fairly late in the RED's development; it first appeared in Build 17.

ANAMORPHIC

The anamorphic mode is specifically designed to work with special anamorphic lenses. Its aspect ratio is 1.2:1, with pixel dimensions of 2764 x 2304 in 4K. It may sound like a lower image resolution than, say, 2:1 4K (at 4096 x 2048), but remember that anamorphic lenses shoot an optically compressed image. When the final output is created from this mode, it will be unsqueezed and appear much closer to the 4K resolution (with an aspect ratio of 2.40:1). We don't get into anamorphic mode too much in this book, because, to be honest, the lenses are very expensive and not used much. In fact, many movies shot on film these days are shot with standard spherical lenses and cropped to 2.40 in postproduction (for that epic movie feel).

Choosing Time Base

You also need to choose your shooting frame rate, or TIME BASE as it's called in the camera. The standard frame rates are 24p, 24.00, 25, and 29.97 (with 50 and 59.94 in 2K and 3K). Essentially this is the playback frame rate and the shooting frame rate as well. Unless you're shooting Varispeed, then it's only the playback frame rate; you'll learn more about Varispeed later in this chapter.

24P

The 24p frame rate, or 23.98 as it's more technically referred to, is generally what you want to use. This is the classic "film look" setting that gives you the most aesthetically cinematic motion (**Figure 7.7**). At 23.98, you're also perfectly set up to work with most editing and finishing applications, which have long been designed to work with 23.98 projects.

Figure 7.7 Footage shot at 24p exhibits the classic film look.

24.00

There's a school of thought that says you should shoot exactly 24 frames per second to have a perfect 1:1 shooting ratio when you output 24 frames of video to 24 frames of film. In the abstract, this makes sense, but you might find that most existing editorial workflows are best designed for 23.98 rather than 24.00 exactly. Also, a 24-frame project is more difficult to work with for a video-only finish. So, unless everyone in the postproduction department is completely in agreement that you should be shooting 24.00 instead of 23.98, I recommend sticking with 23.98.

25

If you're working in a country that uses the PAL TV standard instead of NTSC—such as the United Kingdom, India, mainland China, and Australia—you might want to go with 25 frames per second. The PAL TV system uses 25 frames per second, and as a result, many film-based productions shoot at 25 to make transfers to video more straightforward. As with 24.00, you should consult carefully with your postproduction team to determine whether 25 frames per second is the right choice. It's fairly easy to convert 25 to 24 or 23.98 in software, so it's not the end of the world if you change your mind after production. There will be audio sync issues to be ironed out in the changeover, though. So have an agreement with production and post personnel before committing to 25 frames per second.

29.97

29.97 is the NTSC frame rate, used by countries such as the United States, Mexico, Japan, and Canada (see the map of world TV standards in **Figure 7.8**). Some people say you should shoot 29.97 for a 1:1 frame rate relationship when creating a project for TV in NTSC regions. If you do this, you won't have to add any sort of pulldown in your finished version for TV, which means essentially all frames are progressive. Many TV shows shot on film are shot at 29.97 to make things simpler in post.

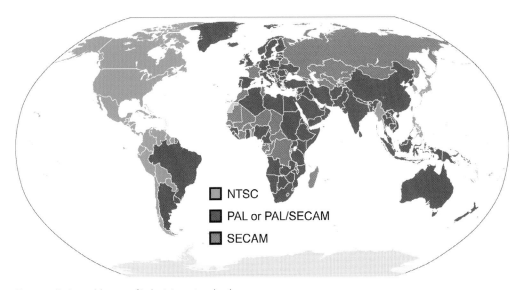

NTSC
PAL or PAL/SECAM
SECAM

Figure 7.8 A world map of television standards.

There's an aesthetic difference to footage shot at 29.97. I recommend a test for your own eye. The 23.98 to 29.97 workflow is so well established in postproduction these days that it's unnecessary to shoot 29.97 for a TV finish.

> TIP SECAM's a third international standard, is in limited use by some countries (such as France, Luxembourg, and some African and Asian countries). It shares the same frame rate as PAL: 25 frames per second. If you're shooting for SECAM, choose 25 as your time base.

To set up the time base, start in the PROJECT menu, and select the CONFIGURE button, as with the previous project options. Next, select the TIME BASE option. You can then select a frame rate with the joystick (**Figure 7.9**).

NEW PROJECT   E 01:00:00:00   A001   TIME BASE   23.98

RESOLUTION   TIME BASE   QUALITY   ✓ MAX   VALID SETTINGS

Figure 7.9 Selecting a frame rate from the TIME BASE menu.

When in doubt, shoot 24p. It's as close to a universal format as there is. It's easier to derive HD, film, and Internet conversions from a 24p master than from any other format.

In-Camera Effects

Though much of your work is likely to be at "normal" frame rates such as 24p and 29.97, you also have more creative options with the RED. You can use Varispeed to achieve slow-motion and sped-up frame rate effects along with special time-lapse effects.

VARISPEED

You achieve fast- and slow-motion effects in the same way you do with a film camera. You have a base frame rate, at which all footage is played back, and a shooting frame rate. Let's say your playback frame rate is 23.98 (24p). As long as you shoot at exactly 24p, everything will look normal, and events will occur at the same speeds they did on the set.

However, once you capture footage at a different speed than your playback frame rate, you get variable speed effects. For example, if you capture footage at 120 fps and play back at 24p, everything will appear to move slowly. An event that took 1 second to occur during shooting now takes 5 seconds to play back and appears to be slowed down by a factor of 5.

Conversely, if you shoot fewer frames per second than your playback frame rate, you get sped-up motion. If you shoot at 12 frames per second, then, and play it back at 24 frames, a 1-second action plays back in 1/2 a second. Action appears sped up by 2 times. In the RED camera, this is referred to as *Varispeed*.

What are some uses for slow and fast motion? Slow motion is typically used for explosions, fire, and glass breaking—basically any sort of motion that normally goes by quickly that you want to accentuate (**Figure 7.10**). Fast motion has some creative uses as well. For example, if you're shooting a landscape or other essentially unmoving object at night, switching to fast motion gives you additional exposure because each frame receives light for a longer period of time. Thus, you can get shots with much lower light than you could at standard frame rates. Of course, you want to keep the camera steady to avoid a jumpy shot. You'll also get streaks and blurs on objects at the slower frame rates, which can be used to creative effect, so experiment. Fast motion can also be used to speed up fights and stunts and, of course, to create comedic effects.

Figure 7.10 Use slow-motion to highlight motion-intensive subjects like fire.

You can also design very creative effects by ramping. *Ramping* is switching speeds during a shot, say from slow motion to regular speed to fast motion. I present some ways to achieve ramps in the upcoming "Ramping" section.

With the RED, an important consideration is figuring out your resolution; try to shoot at the highest possible resolution you can. If you can live with 60 frames or less, you can use 3K. For faster than 60 fps, you need to switch to 2K. For example, 60 fps played back at 24 fps can look slow enough for many desired shots. But maybe it's not quite slow enough to capture all the details you need. In that case, you could gear down to 2K and get up to 120 fps. My general advice on frame rate effects, as with most things on a movie set, is to do some tests.

RAMPING

Ramping, or speed changing in the middle of a shot, can be a very cool effect. You've seen it in movies such as *The Matrix* and *Gladiator*, where action goes from normal speed to slow motion and then back again. You can create a ramp in-camera or in postproduction. The postproduction method is simplest: You simply shoot at the maximum desired speed and then alter the playback speed as desired in postproduction. All editing applications have speed controls, so it's possible to have single frame accuracy.

The in-camera method is much more challenging because you have to trigger the change in speed very precisely. The advantage to the in-camera method is that you can change the shutter speed during the shoot. Say you have a very dark frame that's lit up by an explosion. You could get a much wider dynamic range by increasing the exposure for the dark part of the shot and then decreasing for the much brighter explosion.

Here's how to set up an in-camera ramp:

1. First go into the VARISPEED menu, and select the RAMP option.
2. Next, adjust the TRIGGER setting between ON-RECORD and ON-EVENT (**Figure 7.11**).

Figure 7.11 Choosing between ON-RECORD and ON-EVENT trigger types.

If you select ON-RECORD the ramp starts immediately as you begin recording. ON-EVENT will hold the ramp until an external trigger command is received (learn more about triggers in the "Using an external trigger" sidebar). Use ON-RECORD to ramp a continuous action that's ongoing such as people walking by in a crowd, for example. Use ON-EVENT to capture a specific moment of action such as a car crash or a punch, for example.

3. Finally, select END RATE. This is where you decide what frame speed to ramp to, either a faster speed than you've already picked with the VARISPEED menu's FRAMERATE option or a slower one (**Figure 7.12**).

Figure 7.12 Selecting an end rate for your ramp.

USING AN EXTERNAL TRIGGER

You can start and stop recording using the onboard RECORD button on the RED. You can also trigger recording via an external trigger connected to the GPI connector. GPI stands for General-Purpose Interface and is a fancy term for a generic interface. On the RED ONE, it enables external hardware to control certain functions of the camera. This control can be very useful if you don't want to press the button on the camera, either because it's not safe, because you can't reach it (the camera is high up on a crane), or because the camera is locked down and you don't want to nudge it.

POSTPRODUCTION RAMP

Doing a ramp in postproduction is easier than in-camera because you needn't worry about perfect timing on the set. Avid, Final Cut Pro, and Premiere Pro have speed controls specifically for this purpose. You take a shot that has been photographed at high speed into a 24 fps timeline (or whichever is your base frame rate) and then define specific frames for which you want the speed of the clip to change.

Figure 7.13 A speed ramp using the Time Remap controls in Premiere Pro.

For example, a shot taken at 48 fps, when sped up to 200 percent, will play at what appears to be a normal speed. You can then set another keyframe later at 100 percent speed, which will look like the clip went from regular motion back to slow motion all in a single shot (**Figure 7.13**).

TIME-LAPSE

Think of clouds billowing like steam and flowers opening magically. That's time-lapse cinematography, and it has been around since the late 1890s on film cameras. The technique is very simple; you shoot one frame at a time over a given interval, such as one frame per second (or minute or hour). When played back at 24 frames per second, action is greatly sped up (**Figure 7.14**).

Figure 7.14 Clouds are a favorite subject for time-lapse cinematographers.

Typically a time-lapse shot is made from a tripod—otherwise movement between frames would be distracting and spoil the effect. For more expressive camera moves, you can combine time-lapse cinematography with a motion-control rig, which uses a computer and servo motors to accurately move a camera across a predefined path over a set period of time. A notable example is the movie *Baraka*, which features moving dolly shots over great lengths of time as clouds burst by, stars shoot overhead, and people dart by like race cars.

With its 4K resolution and sturdy build, the RED is perfect for time-lapse work. Since there's no moving piece of film or film gate inside the camera, you don't have to worry about the frame shifting over time. There are different ways to capture frames in the TIMELAPSE mode. You can either set up the camera to control the entire process or use an external triggering device. I think setting it up with the camera is best because it's simple. However, there are lots of existing triggers and intervalometer devices that some shooters may be more accustomed to using.

> NOTE   An *intervalometer* is a mechanical or digital timer that can be set to trigger frame recording on a camera at set intervals. The TIMELAPSE mode on the RED is essentially a digital intervalometer programmed into the camera's software.

On the TIMELAPSE menu, your options include SPEED, STEP PRINT, INTERVAL, and BURST TYPE. SPEED gives you access to longer shutter speeds (**Figure 7.15**). Because you're photographing only a few frames per second, you can use longer shutter times of up to a half second. The slowest shutter will cause moving objects to streak but will also give you a much brighter exposure at night.

Figure 7.15 Choose a long shutter speed in the SPEED options to get streaks on moving objects.

STEP PRINT is a term held over from film cameras. It essentially means you repeat each frame up to 10 times. This can help to smooth out motion and make the frames take a little longer to play back (**Figure 7.16**).

Figure 7.16 The STEP PRINT options.

INTERVAL is the heart of the TIMELAPSE mode, where you set the delay between frame captures (**Figure 7.17**). You can set this between 1 to 1,024 seconds (approximately 17 minutes).

Figure 7.17 Selecting an INTERVAL option.

Time-lapse cinematography is a lot of fun, and you can create some amazing shots. The trick is figuring out the best combination of shutter, interval, and step print settings to achieve the effect you want. Experiment with different settings on the same shot. As with anything that takes a lot of time, patience is often rewarded with great results.

The RED can be deceptively complex with its variety of formats, but you'll probably shoot most projects on just a few of them:

- When in doubt, shoot 4K REDCODE 36 24p, because that's the best quality the camera can achieve and the most flexible to convert to other formats.

- For aspect ratio, shoot 2:1 or 16:9 for film-destined projects; or shoot the HD mode for projects designed for the small screen. That should get you through most of the projects you'll encounter. Try to shoot for the final aspect ratio of your project whenever possible because shot composition changes with different aspect ratios.

If the settings you shoot with aren't ultimately the same as the finished format of your project, with 4K worth of resolution you can still reformat and down-convert footage to whatever you really need.

Nancy Schreiber, ASC
CINEMATOGRAPHER, *EVERY DAY*

Cinematographer Nancy Schreiber, ASC, works with the RED ONE.

Cinematographer Nancy Schreiber, ASC, has brought her considerable skills to bear on many different film and digital camera formats throughout her career. Starting with Super 8mm cameras as a child, Schreiber eventually found her way into the world of independent films armed with ÉCLAIR NPR and AATON 16mm cameras. She quickly moved up to full-fledged high-definition and 35mm features, including *Your Friends and Neighbors* and *The Nines*, and has also shot hundreds of music videos and documentaries. In 2004, Schreiber shot one of the first high-profile digital features on the Panasonic DVX100 24p camera, *November,* starring Courteney Cox. Continuing her reputation for innovation and experimentation, Schreiber shot *Every Day* (directed by Richard Levine and starring Helen Hunt and Liev Schreiber) on the RED ONE.

"The production company, Ambush Entertainment, had recently completed another movie on the RED and was impressed," explains Schreiber. "Ambush ordered its own camera, and it arrived in time for *Every Day*. Taking advantage of tax incentives, we shot for 23 days on location in New York, mostly in Queens with a few days in Brooklyn and Manhattan. I had two days worth of testing, including night exterior and makeup tests. I wanted to see how much, if any, filtration I could use and also determine the ASA of the camera. Technicolor in New York had built up a lot of experience working on Steven Soderbergh's RED features. I was able to screen the test in their large DI suite and also record out a couple minutes of the test to film. We rented a second camera from Offhollywood Digital, who is incredibly RED-savvy; lenses from ARRI CSC; a 24-inch Sony monitor from Abel Cine Tech for me; and a 17-inch Panasonic for Video Village."

With an eye toward an eventual output to 35mm film for theatrical release, Schreiber shot *Every Day* at 4K resolution using REDCODE 36 in the 16:9 aspect ratio. "I have to say the camera is an engineering marvel, and I think it's amazing that for $17,500 such an impressive camera body exists," she observes. "It's also great to be able to use film lenses. Once you mount the matte box and all the accessories, it looks like a film camera, which puts actors at ease. It's just as big as well, though much lighter. In fact, the camera was so light our Steadicam operator, Jamie Silverstein, had to put an extra battery on to balance it properly. He never had to put the rig down, since it was so light."

Accustomed to working rapidly on documentaries, indie features, and music videos, Schreiber used a pared-down optics package. "I pretty much used short and long Optimo Zooms on most scenes," she says. "We couldn't afford Master Primes, so we used Cooke S4s and also a set of Zeiss Super Speeds for low-light scenes. I rated the camera at ASA 200-250 when I could. There were night scenes when I needed to see the lit-up Manhattan skylight through tinted windows. So, I used Super Speeds [lenses] and would have to rate the camera much higher than 250. The blacks held, but focus was challenging. If only those actors didn't move!"

The location was set in a loft on two floors of a hotel. "The set was all windows and had a great view of the skyline," Schreiber recalls. "But there were very few buildings lit up outside, and those that were turned off at midnight. I had to drop my lighting levels down to practically nothing so the buildings would read and work quickly before the city turned off their lights."

"It's difficult to shoot night interiors and exteriors on small movies when you're working in practical locations," Schreiber adds. "The camera performs best in daylight situations or in a 'blue-based world' [i.e., absence of warmer-colored tungsten lights]. HMIs are large and expensive, and if I tried to use small Fresnels with my low-ceilinged locations and gelled them blue, I would have no T-stop [lens exposure aperture] left. I do use Kino fluorescent lights and Litepanel LED lights, which are daylight-balanced but are often too large or nonfocusable for many situations. I found myself using tungsten light more. The images look natural and beautiful, but occasionally I did pick up a bit of noise."

Besides lighting sensitivity issues, Schreiber also found the camera's depth of field to be almost too shallow at times. "Maybe it's the CMOS chip, but you have very little depth of focus at low light levels," says Schreiber. "I like shallow depth of field, but this goes to an extreme. That makes it very tough on a quick shoot. You need to have an ace focus puller to get your shots."

Offhollywood handled dailies for *Every Day* by initially transcoding the incoming R3D files into Avid's DNxHD format. "Our editor in L.A. was using an early version of RED's integration with Avid," says Schreiber. "The editorial dailies were very low resolution, which was a bit of a drag. Part of this was the size of the files, our budget, and the quick turnaround the editorial crew needed, with dailies sent overnight to L.A.

"Fortunately, I had our wonderful RED tech, Eric Camp, download a set of dailies onto a hard drive at DNxHD75 so I could show them to our director, Richard, and assure him everything looked fine. Now we're color correcting on a large DI screen at PlasterCITY Digital in Los Angeles, and some focus issues have come up that we couldn't see during editing. If we can't find replacement takes that are as good for performance, we'll just have to live with it. Even sharpening plug-ins can only go so far. Otherwise, I'm very happy with the way the movie looks. PlasterCITY and our colorist Milton are so RED-savvy, and I know the actors will also be pleased."

Comparing RED's resolution to her previous digital feature shot on the DVX100, Schreiber noted the difference. "I had to suffer through seeing *November* on a huge screen at Sundance because it wasn't sharp," Schreiber says. "It has a look, but it was a DVX100 feature made for a very low budget ($300,000) even though we had an A-list cast, as on *Every Day*. You can't really make an image sharper, but you can make it softer through filtration. Cinematographers are always softening skin tones, and we want the freedom to have things sharp when we need them to be. So, the RED is an amazing step up from many digital cameras, but it still needs to improve its resolution."

When asked about her wish list for RED, Schreiber has some suggestions. "Initially my desire was for more speed," she says. "I begged RED to make it faster and sacrifice resolution if needed. Now, after going through color correction on a 27-foot screen, I think we need both resolution and speed. Resolution is a problem with most HD and video cameras where you lose a lot of detail in the wide shots that you'd still have on film. It's going to be tricky in terms of RED keeping their costs down, but I imagine Jim and gang will figure out a way. Generally I think the RED is a remarkable camera that is democratizing filmmaking and is a great tool for certain movies. We DPs like to have a choice and hopefully receive the respect to be consulted on which camera is appropriate for each new venture. Maybe the RED was intended for a niche market, but it's being used quite broadly now. It has caught on quickly in prime-time TV and Hollywood features, and that's incredibly amazing." ■

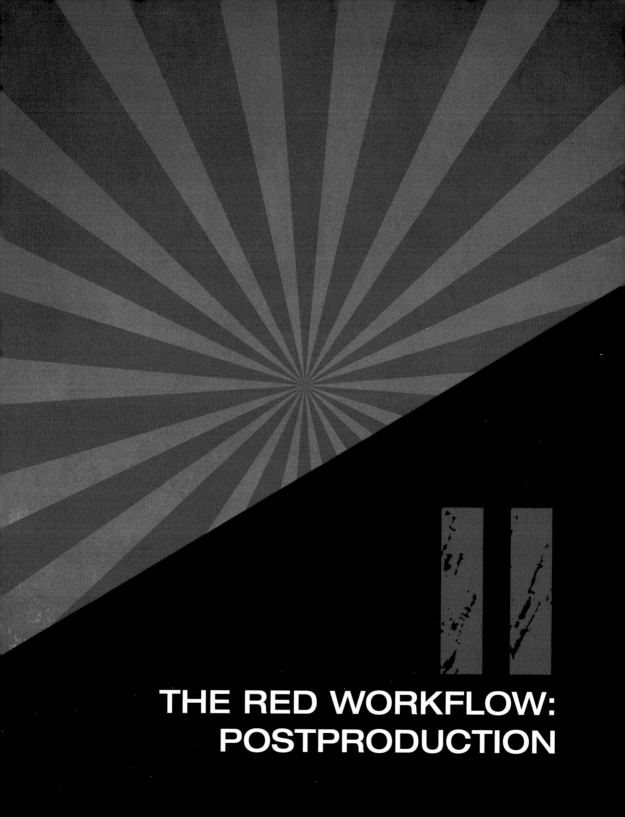

THE RED WORKFLOW:
POSTPRODUCTION

8

BUILDING A POSTPRODUCTION SYSTEM

Up to this point you've learned about equipment and accessories, as well as operating the camera and the basic workflow in the field. Starting with this chapter, we'll move from production to postproduction topics. Postproduction includes editing, color correction, effects work, and output to a variety of destinations such as film, TV, the Internet, and more.

Because the RED shoots 4K resolution, the system you choose for postproduction needs to be as powerful as you can afford. Though it is possible to edit and finish RED projects using a relatively modest system, it increases the time you have to wait for tasks such as rendering and debayering. (Debayering is the process of converting RAW R3D data into a video format you can play back directly. The faster your system, the quicker you can do the conversions.) In this chapter, I'll give you my recommendations for the best possible computer hardware and software to use for maximum efficiency and performance during postproduction.

In subsequent chapters, we'll get into more detail about manipulating RED footage using third-party utilities and common editing applications such as Apple Final Cut Pro, Adobe Premiere Pro, and Avid Media Composer. You'll learn different ways to edit and color correct footage, discover a variety of output formats, and learn how to archive your completed projects for safekeeping and future reuse.

Choosing a Platform

The first decision you need to make is which system platform you will use. Now, I know there are lots of nice Linux boxes and other platforms out there, but they enjoy little RED support. You're welcome to try one, but prepare to be in the wilderness as far as getting help and up-to-date tech support. The best option, as far as RED is concerned, is Macintosh or Windows. I know that brings us to an age-old debate, so let me just cut to the chase. I have to come down on a side, and that side is the Mac.

I have plenty of good reasons for recommending the Mac as a RED editing platform. Many of the staff and engineers at RED are unabashed in their support for Macintosh products. If you've ever visited RED or its booths at NAB, you'll see lots of Macs. As a result, some of RED's helper utilities—which you'll want to have the latest versions of—are developed first for the Mac and then later for Windows. Some applications—such as RED Alert!—don't even exist for Windows at the time of this writing. Also, the camera itself shoots its proxies to QuickTime, which is the Mac's native video format. The proxy files won't work on a Windows machine because RED's QuickTime proxy codec is Mac-only. So, you'll have to convert the R3D files in your editing application in Windows.

Many of the third-party applications and software you need to work with RED footage either are available exclusively for the Mac, such as Final Cut Pro, or are available for both platforms, such as Avid and Premiere Pro. ASSIMILATE SCRATCH stands out as one key application that's Windows-only, but that's a major investment which renders the platform itself somewhat immaterial (for more on SCRATCH see the "Desktop Color Correction" section of Chapter 13). In other words, the Mac currently offers more choices and support for third-party RED workflow software.

If you do go with the Windows platform, head over to the REDuser forum (www.reduser.net), and ask around to see what the hottest Windows systems are these days. Premiere Pro and Avid are cross-platform, so when we get into those workflows in the upcoming chapters, almost everything discussed regarding the Mac applies to Windows.

RECOMMENDED SYSTEMS

People often ask me, "What's the best machine to get?" That's easy: Get the most power-ful machine you can afford. Working with the RED, you'll never feel like you have a system that's too powerful. If you can afford an eight-core Mac Pro ($3,299 and up as of this writing), you'll be well on your way (**Figure 8.1**). You can use a MacBook Pro (about $1,999 and up) or even an iMac ($1,199 to $2,199), but your workflow will be slower. You need an Intel-based Mac because the RED applications won't run on older PowerPC machines such as Power-Books and G5s. Also, ProRes, which is key to many of these workflows, is for Intel-chipped machines. See the sidebar "Recommended RED Mac Systems" for what I consider minimum, optimum, and price-is-no-object-maximum RED Mac systems.

Figure 8.1 Apple Mac Pro desktop computer (Courtesy of Apple).

The faster the processor, of course, the faster you'll be able to convert files, process effects, output finished edits, and so forth. RAM (memory) allows you to run more programs simultaneously and more instances of the same program. For example, RED's command line footage processing soft-ware, REDLine, takes advantage of multiple processors and more RAM to convert R3D to other formats.

Hard drive space is another key feature, and more is always better. At 4K REDCODE 36, you're creating footage at 36 MB per second. That jumps way up once you start transcoding to formats such as DPX, uncompressed, and ProRes. You'll learn how to augment the internal storage space with outboard storage in the "Storage Options" section later in this chapter.

Higher-end Mac systems are expensive, but if you think about the difference of a few thou-sand dollars when you're already spending $17,500 for the camera body alone, it's a relatively small portion of your whole budget. Your work can only be as efficient and enjoyable as its weakest link, so I urge you to invest a little extra on a more powerful machine. I haven't had to pull an all-nighter because of a slow computer in a few years now, and that's a good thing.

RECOMMENDED RED MAC SYSTEMS

Minimum recommended system for RED $1,799

iMac, 24-inch, 2.93GHz, 2.93GHz Intel Core 2 Duo, 4 GB memory, 8x double-layer SuperDrive, NVIDIA GeForce GT 120 with 256 MB memory

Optimum recommended system for RED $3,299

Eight-core Mac Pro, two 2.26GHz Quad-Core Intel Xeon, 6 GB (six 1 GB) memory, 640 GB hard drive, 18x double-layer SuperDrive, NVIDIA GeForce GT 120 with 512 MB

Maximum recommended system for RED $6,199

Eight-core Mac Pro, two 2.93GHz Quad-Core Intel Xeon, 8 GB (4x2 GB), 640 GB hard drive, ATI Radeon HD 4870 512 MB, 18x SuperDrive

Postproduction Workflows

Once you decide on a platform, it's time to select the most important piece of software: your nonlinear editor. Before the advent of computer editing software, you were stuck cutting either directly on film or with videotape. Either way, you were cutting pictures with minimal sound editing. You did color correction and effects in a completely different step. With today's editing software, you can do almost every task within the editing application—sound and picture editing, transitions, effects, mixing, color correction, compositing, and more. Before getting into specific software recommendations, let's define a few key terms and workflows you should consider as you think about editing programs.

OFFLINE VS. ONLINE EDITING

Offline editing means that you are editing at a lower resolution and quality than your final output in exchange for better performance and efficiency. The first nonlinear editing programs were capable of editing offline only. You would digitize 35mm film or standard-definition video and compress it to a smaller file size. When you were done editing, the program would export either a negative cut list for film or an edit decision list (EDL) for video. You'd take that output and either conform film negative to it or online tape-to-tape edit the original format videotape from the EDL.

Modern editing programs offer some form of *online editing*, where the quality and format you are working with in your editing program is the same as the final finishing format. This is a lot simpler when you're coming from a relatively low-bandwidth format such as standard-definition DV or HD formats such as DVCPROHD, HDV, and AVCHD. It becomes more complex with RED footage because online resolution is harder to define. You can edit RED in high-definition—at the same resolution as you plan to finish—and this in a sense is online editing, because you don't need to convert to another format before finishing the edit. Some programs offer the ability to cut R3D files natively in 4K, which is closer to true online editing.

If you're planning to finish out to film at 4K, it makes sense to edit at a lower resolution, such as 1080p or 2K, and then conform the final edit to 4K. Otherwise, your editing software's performance on all but the most powerful hardware is going to lag (and some won't even support 4K editing). It's better to work quickly and more efficiently at a lower resolution and then conform everything to the online resolution when you're done editing.

If you intend to finish out to high-definition or even standard-definition video, then an online workflow at HD makes more sense. There are a number of different ways you can get RED footage into a high-definition edit; some are faster than others and they offer different levels of quality. Each editing program offers a different way of working as well.

FILE FORMATS

Depending on whether you want to work at online or offline resolution, you also need to consider the types of files you want to use. With the RED, you have three basic choices once you're done shooting: native, proxy, or transcode.

NATIVE

Native means you work directly with the R3D files in your timeline. At the time of this writing, only Premiere Pro supports a truly native editorial workflow with R3D. Even that is not completely native because there's no way to encode to the R3D format outside the camera. So, anything that's not a straight cut—such as filters, effects, color correction, and transitions—still has to be rendered in another format. Final Cut Pro offers a way to transfer R3D files into QuickTime that preserves the native metadata.

PROXY

Proxies are created right in the camera when you shoot and instantly become playable in QuickTime Player. They are immediately editable in any program that supports proxies, such as Final Cut Pro. That means you can conceivably go immediately from shooting to cutting simply by dragging and dropping the proxy files into your NLE. You need to figure out which size proxy to work with, which we'll look at later in the chapters on specific editing programs.

You could do an offline/online proxy workflow in which you edit with lower-resolution proxy files for speed and then conform to the higher-resolution versions when you're ready for output. If you're working in standard definition or HD, the proxy files have high enough image quality to make great-looking output. You can even instantly color-correct and change their look just by reprocessing via RED Alert! or REDCINE (learn more about these helper applications in Chapter 9).

TRANSCODING

A third file format workflow is *transcoding*, which is taking the R3D files and exporting them to a different format for editing and possible finishing. Transcoding can be done in different ways, but the two most common are transcoding within the computer or playing a RED clip out to a tape format and recording it.

For the computer method, you can use a number of applications, such as REDrushes. You can also use the import tools in some editing applications to do this. Both Avid and Final Cut Pro offer utilities to convert from R3D to other formats. In Final Cut Pro, the conversion is typically to ProRes, and for Avid it's to DNxHD. Both are optimized for smooth editorial work while maintaining very high image quality for final output. You can easily create an online version for an HD or SD workflow using transcoded files.

The one major downside to working with transcoded files is that because you are converting RAW sensor data from R3D files to an RGB file format, you're losing the ability to grade the original camera RAW metadata that you have with R3D files. Also, by exporting to a specific format, you're essentially locking in a resolution, be that high-definition, 2K, or whatever format you choose. You can always take an edit completed with transcoded files and conform it to proxies or another format. Utilities such as Crimson Workflow make this possible (you'll learn more about this in Chapter 9).

> TIP No matter what you do with your transcodes, try to maintain the original file-names created by the camera. It will leave your options open because you'll be able to more easily correlate an edit with transcoded files back to the original R3D files.

FINISHING RAW VS. 'BAKED IN'

Coming back to the RAW workflow for a moment, you should decide whether you want to preserve the capability to access the original RAW R3D files for grading after the edit is complete. Typically, if you work with transcoded files, you color correct those and don't go back to the RAW workflow. However, if you edit native or proxy, you have a simpler path to going back into RED Alert! or REDCINE and completing a color grade from the RAW files. Some third-party color-correction applications (such as Scratch) permit grading directly from R3D as well.

> NOTE   I call transcoded files *baked in* because the RAW metadata is no longer adjustable and your gamma and color settings at the moment of transcode are locked in.

For my taste, I prefer working with RAW versus transcoded files and their baked-in color. You can still do significant color correction from DNxHD or ProRes files, so you shouldn't feel like baked in means *locked in*. Sometimes the RAW workflow is overkill for a simple or rush project. However, if your project is destined for film output or has a lot of intensive effects or compositing, I'd be more inclined to finish RAW. That gives you maximum flexibility with the final look. It takes some doing but you can switch a project from baked-in transcoded files to RAW, or vice versa.

Editing Software

The next choice to make in your postproduction system is which editing program to use. In my opinion, the choice comes down to: Final Cut Pro, Premiere Pro, and Avid. Here are a few pros and cons to consider (we'll get into more detail in Chapters 10–12).

APPLE FINAL CUT PRO

Final Cut Pro (included in the Final Cut Studio package for $999—see **Figure 8.2**) happens to be my favorite editing application. As I mentioned earlier in this chapter, it's Mac-only. The current version of Final Cut Pro offers support for RED in a number of different workflows.

Figure 8.2 Edit your RED footage by transcoding to ProRes via the Log and Transfer window in FInal Cut Pro.

Apple has worked closely with the engineers at RED to provide broad support. You can edit footage by transcoding to ProRes using the Log and Transfer window within Final Cut Pro. This takes more time up front and moves you away from the ability to manipulate footage in RAW, but it does buy you a much more fluid edit and the ability to add more real-time filters and effects. You can also convert R3D files into special QuickTime files that can be graded with RED native metadata in Color, Final Cut Studio's color-correction application. (We'll look at the preferred workflows for different types of projects in Chapter 10.)

ADOBE PREMIERE PRO

Premiere Pro ($799 or $1,699 with Production Premium suite—see **Figure 8.3**) permits as much of a RAW editorial workflow as possible, at least in terms of the ability to drop R3D files directly onto a Timeline. Adobe has worked hard on its RED integration, and it shows in how much you can work natively. Premiere Pro is also cross-platform, so you can use it on Mac or Windows and easily exchange project and media files. This may be critical or not so critical, depending on your needs. If you're in an all-Mac or all-Windows shop, cross-platform capability is not that important. But if you're working with a lot of different editors or service bureaus with both Mac and Windows, a cross-platform application such as Premiere Pro is advantageous.

Figure 8.3 Adobe Premiere Pro offers a native RED workflow.

In the past, I used Premiere on Windows and found it to be a powerful application. It's also very well integrated with the rest of the Adobe applications such as After Effects for compositing, Encore for DVD and Blu-ray authoring, Photoshop for image editing, and more. The one downside to Premiere is it has probably the fewest number of users of the three editing applications surveyed in this chapter. You'll find it in lots of event and corporate video shops, but you'll be hard pressed to find Premiere used much in the TV or big-budget film worlds—they tend to use Final Cut Pro and Avid. That's not an issue if you're working on your own, but if you're planning to make a career in editing or want to be able to easily exchange projects with a wide user base, it's an important consideration to make. You'll see the Premiere Pro RED workflow in more detail in Chapter 11.

AVID

Avid has a number of editing products in its lineup, compared to the single versions of Final Cut Pro and Premiere Pro. Avid DS, Media Composer (**Figure 8.4**), and Symphony all work with the RED. Media Composer offers a complete editing solution for $2,499 while the other programs range in price and options. Avid uses a transcoding workflow, in which you convert R3D files to another format to edit.

Figure 8.4 Avid Media Composer offers a transcoding workflow with RED.

You transcode from R3D to DNxHD for editing using Avid's MetaFuze application (which currently runs on Windows only). You then edit with the DNxHD clips in Media Composer. When your edit is complete, you can export your sequence to DS for effects and finishing. DS allows the direct loading of R3D files, enabling a much higher level of control over the final output. Because Avid's original products were offline editors for film negative finishing, the two-step approach is in keeping with its established methodology.

NOTE   Read more about Avid and RED in Chapter 12 as well as in the POV Interview with Michael Phillips, Avid's principal product designer.

Among these three applications, my recommendation is personal; I happen to use Final Cut Pro and am happy with it. That said, I think Premiere Pro and Media Composer are both worthy editors, and it's worth your time to test drive each before making your choice. The cross-platform packages have time-limited demos that you can download and install on your own system. Final Cut Pro isn't available as a downloadable demo, but you can walk into an Apple Store and try it there. Whichever application you go with, make sure it works well with the particular RED workflow you plan to use, whether it's offline or online, RAW or baked in, or native/proxy/transcode.

Storage Options

Almost as important as choosing a platform and an editing application is storage (hard drives). The storage used for your postproduction system is generally separate from the storage you use with your camera in the field (see Chapter 14 to learn more about that). You want as much fast hard drive space as possible, because RED projects will take up all you can spare.

JBOD

"Just a bunch of disks" (JBOD) is a cute phrase for single-disk drives that are not configured into RAIDs (described in detail in the next section). You can get powerful and vast storage with FireWire 400/800, USB 2.0, and eSATA connections. Some solid brands include G-Tech, CalDigit, and Dulce Systems. These sorts of single-drive units are great for storage but not so good for editing directly from. You can use them to transfer assets from one place to another, or even onto and off your set, but I think you'll find much better performance editing from RAID solutions.

RAIDS

A Redundant Array of Independent Disks (RAID) is essentially multiple hard drives electronically linked together to provide extra speed and/or redundancy. I'm a big fan of RAIDs. See **Table 8.1** for some of the more common RAID configurations.

TABLE 8.1 COMMON RAID CONFIGURATIONS

	RAID 0	RAID 1	RAID 5	RAID 0/1 (RAID 10)
Description	Data striping (no data protection)	Disk mirroring	Data striping with distributed parity	RAID 0 and RAID 1 combined
Minimum number of drives	Two	Two	Three	Four
Benefit	Highest performance	Data protection through redundancy	Best balance of cost/performance/data protection	Highest performance with data protection

You can get a simple RAID housed in a portable enclosure. You can also create a RAID in software by linking several drives either mounted inside a desktop machine or connected via FireWire or eSATA. From there you can move up to a more robust solution that comes with a special RAID controller card. Finally, there are storage area networks (SANs) that use a very powerful array of RAIDs to service several users across a network to centralized storage.

For software RAIDs, you can begin with the built-in tools that come with your OS. On the Mac, use the Disk Utility in the Applications > Utilities folder (**Figure 8.5**). First click the RAID tab, and then drag the drives you want to associate as RAIDs into the window. The drives must be identical in size and type to function as a RAID. This method is very easy to set up, but it's not the most powerful RAID you can have.

The next step up is a drive in a single enclosure that is actually two drives running together. This can be a nice starter system because the costs are low and the performance is noticeably better than a single-drive system. Some examples are the G-Tech (www.g-technology.com) G-RAID2 and G-RAID3, which are mostly RAID 0. These are great little units, with USB, FireWire 400/800, and eSATA connections at up to 3 TB (terabytes—a terabyte is 1,000 GB), and they range in price from $300 to $650 depending on capacity. G-Tech also offers bus-powered portable versions, though these are a little less speedy, and more powerful G-SAFEs and G-SPEEDs, which move you up to RAID 1 for mirrored/redundant storage. You can't go wrong with any of these units—as with anything else important, don't pinch pennies on good hard drives. Remember, that's your hard work in there.

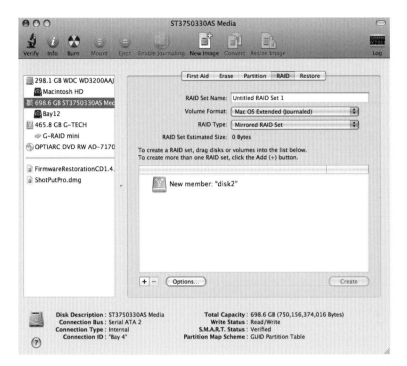

Figure 8.5 Creating a software RAID using Disk Utility. Add another drive of the same size and capacity, and you're all set.

TIP RAID 0 is considered in some circles to not be a true RAID because it offers no redundancy. But you can use a RAID for performance, protection, or both.

Another step up is a RAID that connects to your system via a RAID controller card. This card boosts performance another notch and may be more suitable for intensive color correction and effects work or when you're working with a multilayered sequence in your editing application. I like the CalDigit HDElement (www.caldigit.com), which comes complete with a RAID card and can be set up in a number of different RAID level configurations (**Figure 8.6**). For less than $3,000, this is a bargain that can give you up to 370MB/second of playback speed. As with the rest of the components surveyed here, when it comes to RED, there's no such thing as too much power.

For the really high end, when you want to support several editing stations across a network with really fast performance, you'll need to create a SAN. A SAN is one very powerful set of hard drives that other computers connect to via Ethernet or Fibre Channel rather than FireWire or eSATA. This arrangement affords centralized administration as well as sharing of assets across many artists and postproduction personnel. For this setup, I recommend

Figure 8.6 CalDigit's HDElement RAID unit and controller card.

something like the Active Storage XRAID (www.getactivestorage.com), which starts at $11,999 for 8 TB. (See Chapter 14's "Post-production Archiving" section for an image of the XRAID.) That may sound pricey, but it's still less than the camera body you have, and it can play uncompressed 2K footage; try doing that with FireWire!

As with the all of the items covered so far, scale your system to your needs. If you're doing moderate amounts of editing as a single-person operation, a nice external RAID connected via RAID card or FireWire 800/eSATA will get the job done. If you're working with a group of editors in a production house or TV network, move up to the higher-performance RAID drives or consider a full-blown SAN.

Monitor Options

The last of the most critical purchases is the monitor. You'll likely be spending a lot more of your time staring into your computer monitor than the camera's electronic viewfinder. Thus, it makes a lot of sense to get the highest-quality monitor you can afford—for your own eye comfort, for the accuracy it will help you achieve, and for your own image and reputation working in front of a client.

When working with RED footage, or footage from any camera for that matter, you really need to understand the difference between a computer monitor and a display or broadcast monitor. A computer monitor uses RGB color space and is optimized for displaying the output of a computer's graphic display card. A broadcast monitor uses YUV color (like a TV) and is typically fed a composite or component video signal. Therefore, you should consider two different monitors: First, you need an RGB monitor for your computer's desktop and your editing application's timeline. Second, you need a YUV monitor, which is important for color correction and more accurate evaluation of your footage.

NOTE YUV refers to a color television display, where Y indicates the luma (brightness) value and U and V refer to the chroma (color) components.

COMPUTER MONITORS

Before considering *which* computer monitor you need, you should consider *how many* you need. There are two schools of thought on this: that you should get either one big monitor or two (or more) medium-sized ones. If you're cramped for desk space or you don't edit constantly, a single large monitor may be more than enough. If you edit all the time, you might find having two monitors much more user-friendly. You can put all of your source clips on one monitor and have your Timeline and program window on the other.

TIP Although it's possible to color correct footage using an RGB monitor alone, it's inaccurate compared to a true broadcast monitor. So if you're doing work for broadcast or theatrical release, don't even think about color correction on anything other than a broadcast monitor.

Liquid-crystal display (LCD) flat-panel monitors have largely replaced the cathode ray tube (CRT) displays of a decade ago. This is great because LCDs have gotten very accurate, they take up less space, and they are more mobile than CRT monitors. If you're working with a Mac, the Apple Cinema Displays are very popular. They are nice and sharp, perfectly matched to the Mac Pro's output resolutions, and look very high-end sitting on your desk. Apple recently switched over from LCD to light-emitting diode (LED), which is supposed to offer an even brighter picture. Apple's 30-inch LCD runs about $1,799 (**Figure 8.7**) while the 24-inch LED Cinema Display goes for $899. Some other solid LCD monitor brands to consider are Dell, Asus, Samsung, ViewSonic, and HP.

TIP Make sure you get a display that matches your computer's output. DVI and DisplayPort are the most popular display interfaces.

Figure 8.7 An Apple 30-inch LCD Cinema Display. (Courtesy of Apple Inc.)

BROADCAST MONITORS

As with computer monitors, you can work with one or multiple broadcast monitors. The principal purpose of a broadcast monitor is accuracy for color correction and compositing. You also need a converter card to display HD video properly on a broadcast monitor (more on converter cards in the next section).

If you're working mostly on your own, a decent-sized (15- to 21-inch) HD display should do the trick. However, if you're often working in front of a client, you might want to consider a larger display, such as a large LCD or plasma screen (you can find surprisingly high quality and affordable ones at the big chain stores such as Best Buy and Costco) for clients to sit and watch the work. Then you can have your smaller and more accurate HD broadcast monitor for the critical decisions. It's up to you and, of course, your budget.

For smaller HD displays, I'm a big fan of the Sony and Panasonic HD production monitors. Sony offers the LUMA, PVM, and BVM (some of which are still CRTs) series for a variety of budget and quality levels. Sony's Trimaster BVML170 LCD (about $13,000) is a particularly impressive and accurate LCD monitor to check out.

On the Panasonic side there's the BT-LH series LCD monitors; the BT-LH2550 is a nice value at $5,995. For the big plasma client display, I'm also partial to Panasonic's offerings, such as the TH-42PF11UK for about $2,400. Panasonic has been making and perfecting plasmas for a long time, and when you walk down the aisles at electronic trade shows such as NAB, you see Panasonic plasmas in *lots* of booths. Image is important both literally and figuratively, so don't skimp on monitors if you can afford not to.

CONVERTER CARDS

If you choose to work with a broadcast monitor, you need a special conversion or capture card to output a proper high-definition component video signal from your computer to the monitor. Typically, these are PCI cards that go into a desktop machine, which is another advantage over a laptop. There are two brands I recommend for this task: AJA (www.aja. com) and Blackmagic Design (www.blackmagic-design.com). To work at some of the higher resolutions, you'll also want a powerful RAID system to support the increased bandwidth. Consult the companies' respective Web sites to determine specific hardware requirements.

AJA offers several different cards for displaying footage on an HD monitor. My favorite is the Kona 3 (about $2,700), which enables SD, HD, and even 2K output via SDI and HD-SDI connections. The Kona 3 also supports integrated real-time ProRes encoding, so if you're working in a transcoded files workflow, you can play ProRes footage directly out to your monitor in high quality without rendering. The Kona 3 is very well integrated with Final Cut Pro.

> TIP AJA also makes the io HD, which allows you to connect a laptop to HD monitors, should a high-end desktop machine be out of the budget. It's a portable solution for displaying high-definition video on a monitor and getting native ProRes support directly from a laptop.

Figure 8.8 Blackmagic Design's DeckLink HD Extreme capture card.

Blackmagic Design's cards are a little more affordable while offering many of the same features as the AJA cards. The DeckLink HD Extreme ($995) offers SD, HD, and up to 2K monitoring with real-time down-conversion (**Figure 8.8**). For example, if you want to view a 2K edit on a standard-definition monitor to get a sense of how it might look on a DVD, you can do that. DeckLink is also well integrated with Final Cut Pro and Premiere Pro.

> TIP Both the AJA and Blackmagic cards also offer HD and SD input capabilities, ideal if you need to mix RED footage with other sources.

RED ROCKET

RED has entered the display card market with its sub-$5,000 RED Rocket. It offers an accelerated transcode of 4K R3D files in real time to any system codec. RED Rocket also plays full-quality 4K from its DVI output and 2K and 1080p scaled from 4K to any application that uses the RED SDK, which includes the editing applications mentioned in this chapter. The RED Rocket promises to shake up and greatly accelerate postproduction workflows for RED.

The bottom line is that a nice Mac Pro, armed with a reasonably powerful RAID, along with desktop and broadcast monitors and a capture card, will give you everything you need to edit and finish RED-originated projects. You can scale everything up or down to suit your budget and needs. With what you've learned in this chapter, you'll be well positioned to make informed decisions about the system that will form the heart of your postproduction workflow.

Michael Cioni has some fun with a vintage instant photo booth.

Michael Cioni
FOUNDER AND CEO, LIGHTIRON DIGITAL

Michael Cioni has more than a decade of progressive postproduction filmmaking experience. He cofounded and built one of Hollywood's first desktop-toolset postproduction facilities, PlasterCITY Digital Post in 2003. While at PCDP, Michael ran day-to-day operations, assembled what quickly became an industry-respected team of artists and technologists, and led the organization's business development efforts.

In 2009, Michael launched his new postproduction facility, LIGHT-IRON Digital, LLC. LIGHTIRON is the first Hollywood-based facility focusing entirely on end-to-end, file-based workflow sequencing. Coupling state-of-the-art technology with cost-conscious business acumen, LIGHTIRON has a multi-faceted approach toward serving the post-production community.

In addition to scores of RED commercials and music videos, Michael has been involved with several high-profile features during the initial few years of the camera's existence. These have included Steven Soderbergh's *The Informant*, starring Matt Damon; *Manure*, starring Billy Bob Thornton, directed by the Polish Brothers, and shot by M. David Mullen, ASC; *S. Darko, A Donnie Darko Tale*, photographed by Marvin Rush, ASC; and *Hybrid*, shot by John R. Leonetti, ASC.

"My team is made up of data-centric enthusiasts working almost entirely with digital cameras," says Cioni. "Fifty percent of our recent projects are RED-based, and the other half come from cameras such as the Vision Research Phantom, Sony F23, Panavision Genesis, ARRI D-20/D21, and the Thomson Viper. Some of those are tape-based cameras, but we encourage filmmakers to transfer their project into a tapeless workflow as early as possible. Then we can start to cut out all the time-consuming and limiting issues tape entails, such as cross-conversion, frame rate concerns, resolution, and aspect ratio incompatibilities, and help our customer start saving money.

"We have many RED ONE workflow guides we use that ask the client which camera build, aspect ratio, frame rate, resolution, and so on," adds Cioni. "Then they specify whether they want to edit with Avid, Final Cut Pro, or Premiere and have footage delivered on tape or hard drive. It's like buying and configuring a car online, for example: Do you want four-wheel drive, an eight-cylinder engine, etc.? And with our checklists we can tell them, 'That car doesn't exist.' In other words, 'That workflow won't work, but here's one that will.'"

Along with educational outreach, Cioni tries to make sure LIGHTIRON's workload is balanced between larger projects and more independent fare. "I have worked on well over 100 indie projects," he says. "It really helps when producers on a tight budget do their homework and determine how much work they can do on their side of the fence and how much they need us to do. They might, for example, do all their editing offline, and then we come in and conform and color correct their material."

Regarding RED's proliferation across the Internet and the heated online discussions it often stimulates, Cioni takes a hands-off approach. "I typically stay away from the boards," he says. "We come by our post information through firsthand experience. My team has executed around two hundred RED jobs and counting, and we've worked hands-on with the camera for the last few years. We've had our share of mistakes and successes, and all of that feeds into our ongoing development."

With a dozen Final Cut Studio workstations, LIGHTIRON has extensive capabilities with Final Cut Pro and QuickTime in the high-end arena of 2K and 4K digital intermediates. "Because LIGHTIRON is tapeless, it's very easy for us to move up and down the ladder between different resolutions up to 4K uncompressed DI mastering," Cioni notes.

"We're building 500 TBs of storage with a four-lane and eight-lane Fibre Channel infrastructure," he continues. "That encompasses a 175 TB Apple Xsan along with a couple of smaller ones and Promise Technology RAIDs, which enable users to achieve over 2 GB per second of throughput. With a series of LTO-3A and DLT-S4 drives for archiving, we can back-up every project asset and then vault that for long-term storage. When completed, an entire feature can easily fit into a shoebox.

"The RED shoots compressed REDCODE to a relatively small file of around 36 MB per second or approximately 100 GB per hour," Cioni says. "When you process to uncompressed for the DI, it can get up to 50 MB a frame. At this point we're not doing uncompressed dailies, so instead we do real-time transfers to compressed media files or out to HD videotape. It's easy to create real-time DNxHD files for Avid and ProRes for Final Cut Pro since some productions want tape, and others want hard drives."

When it comes time to finish a project, LIGHTIRON brings heavy-duty hardware to bear. "Our color-correction suite features Quantel's 4K Pablo, which is one of the premiere DI tools in the world right now," emphasizes Cioni. "The system allows us to produce 4K DPX files, suitable for film or tape output. We can edit, color correct, and composite in 4K all in real time. Almost no other system can do that. It's a great way to color-correct high-resolution footage like RED and the work looks beautiful on the big screen. Our team is used to doing two to three features a month along with music videos, commercials, and other short-form work. It's all pretty challenging for a DI lab, but we work hard to be fast and efficient."

Asked about his own expectations for digital cinema's future, Cioni is highly optimistic. "I'm looking forward to the next generation of RED cameras with even higher image quality and lower compression," he says. "This is really just the beginning. Imagine how much time it took for Ford to build the first Model-T and then how long for cars to evolve into how we know them today; with this camera, that's all happening overnight. Other manufacturers are now building their versions of the RED, which means more competition and cameras to choose from. It will also inspire everyone to switch to tapeless, and we see that as the most exciting thing for this industry."

Michael Cioni's Web site is www.lightirondigital.com. ∎

9 USING HELPER APPLICATIONS

As noted throughout this book, the ends determine the means when working with RED footage. In other words, the type of final output you need determines your workflow. Depending on the path you take, some of the utility applications covered in this chapter will be useful to you, and others won't apply.

This chapter notes the main uses for each of these applications and details some of the most common working methods. We begin by looking at the applications RED offers directly and then explore some third-party applications. This list is by no means exhaustive, because many third-party applications have emerged and continue to evolve.

RED Applications

All the RED applications discussed in this section are available free from the company's Web site at www.red.com/support. Their primary use is viewing and transcoding native R3D files. This function used to be of greater importance because no other applications were available that could play back RED's file formats. However, with the QuickTime Player plugin and broad editing software support, plenty of alternatives are available now. Some of the RED applications are Mac-only, so factor that in when choosing a RED editing/finishing system (and refer to Chapter 8 for further Mac versus PC discussion). With that in mind, let's look at how you can use each RED application in your workflow.

> NOTE As this book went to press, RED announced a new generation of helper applications including ROCKETCine-X and REDCINE-X. They are designed to be easier to use while offering all of the functionality of the original applications. For more details, visit this book's Web site at www.peachpit.com/red.

RED ALERT!

RED Alert! was one of the first applications released by RED. It's designed primarily as a quick shot development/one-light grading station. RED Alert! can work on only a single clip at a time, which limits its usefulness for processing vast amounts of footage. You can work in one of two modes: re-grading *proxies* (lower-resolution QuickTime versions of R3D files created by the camera) or transcoding from R3D to another format such as DPX or TIF.

> NOTE Film labs refer to the initial prints made from processed negatives as *one-light* because they give all shots the same settings and don't manually correct for variations in color and exposure. It's just a quick way to see what's been photographed.

Working with proxies is useful because they allow you to tap into the RED RAW workflow without doing a lot of transcoding up front. For example, say you have a shot that was taken with the wrong color temperature or you just want to warm up the look a bit. Load up an R3D into RED Alert! and adjust the Kelvin (color temperature) slider until you get the color balance you want. Then choose File > Make QuickTimes. You'll instantly have a full set of all the different QuickTime proxy sizes with those new settings "baked in." **Figure 9.1** and **Figure 9.2** show Red Alert! creating different looks by adjusting the color temperature.

TIP Watch out for noise when you correct directly to the QuickTimes, especially in the blue channel.

Figure 9.1 RED clip corrected for a "day for night" and a cool color temperature look in RED Alert!

Figure 9.2 The same image, corrected for a warm, saturated, overexposed look.

To go back to the way the files looked straight out of the camera, reload the R3D, and click the Metadata button. You might do this if you don't like the way your corrections turned out or if you want to compare to the original look. Choose File > Make QuickTimes, and your proxies will return to their original settings (**Figure 9.3**). Altering the proxies is instant and allows you to quickly experiment with different looks. Another benefit is that if you are editing with proxies, your changes in RED Alert! immediately update in your NLE software.

Figure 9.3 Reset to the original camera settings.

Two other useful features of RED Alert! are the Histogram and the Zebra. The Histogram (**Figure 9.4**) is essentially a graphical analysis of the brightness values of red, green, and blue in your clip. The more the peaks hit the top part of the graph, the more your shot is exposed in that color. Peaks toward the left indicate underexposure, while peaks toward the right mean overexposure.

Figure 9.4 Using the Histogram to measure the relative brightness values of red, green, and blue in an image.

The Zebra superimposes a zebra-striped pattern over areas of your image that are overexposed by a certain percentage. In **Figure 9.5**, I've set it for 95 percent. That means the areas on the cars' hoods that are covered with the zebra pattern are more than 95 percent exposed. I could turn my exposure slider down just a bit so these areas won't read as pure white in my QuickTime movies.

TIP Remember, the original R3D file contains more information and detail than the QuickTime proxies, so this is where you want to squeeze out the best exposure and color you can.

Figure 9.5 Zebra set at 95 percent reveals portions of the image that are 95 percent or more exposed.

Each time you make adjustments in RED Alert!, a new RSX settings file is automatically created in the folder of the clip you are adjusting. The next time you open the R3D in this folder, that RSX file will be loaded as well, showing all the image adjustments you've made.

Remember the RSX file, because some of the other tools covered in this chapter can also use it.

REDCINE

REDCINE is intended as a color correction suite and is available for both Mac and PC (**Figure 9.6**). Its purpose is to take the place of a telecine transfer session in a traditional film workflow. You can perform color corrections and export to a variety of movie and still image formats with plenty of down-conversion and image-cropping options along the way.

Figure 9.6 The REDCINE main application window.

The color controls are configured differently from RED Alert!'s, but REDCINE can load groups of clips simultaneously and apply settings globally. Also, REDCINE can process and output shots in batches. So you could, for example, load an entire magazine's footage and correct it all at once. Be aware that REDCINE has a limit as to the amount of footage you can load, which comes out to approximately 10 minutes for 4K.

NOTE   REDCINE runs as a maximized application in Mac OS X at all times. It will not minimize or play in a window and doesn't hide with the Command-H key. This can be a little disconcerting at first compared to most other OS X applications. To switch to another program without quitting REDCINE, press the F11 key.

You need to learn two main sets of controls to start working with this program. In the main window on the top-left side, you'll find four radio buttons. These allow you to toggle through most of the other controls, organized into four groups: Project, Shot, Color, and Output (**Figure 9.7**).

Figure 9.7 The Project, Shot, Color, and Output buttons in REDCINE.

- Project is where you choose the global settings for your project, such as the format type, frame rate, aspect ratio, output resolution, and whether you want to apply frame guides to your exported footage.
- Shot lets you adjust the in and out points of your shot, such as if you have a particularly long take and you want to process only part of it, for example. You can also reframe and scale shots if you are going from 4K to HD and you want to crop out a part of the frame, for example. You can't key frame cropping (or anything else), so if you want to make changes over time, you need to do that in another application.
- The Color section gives you access to most of the same color correction options in RED Alert! They are organized a bit differently but are mostly the same concepts.
- Finally, the Output section is where you make format adjustments when you export a shot or group of shots. You can export to QuickTime in a variety of codecs as well as to image sequence formats such as DPX and Cineon (a format originally created by Kodak for the digital storage of film material). You can also choose to superimpose timecode on your shots, which can be useful if you're working offline and want everyone who sees your footage to have visual verification of timecode.

REDCINE TO SCRATCH

REDCINE was developed by ASSIMILATE, makers of the sophisticated SCRATCH, a real-time color correction conform and online application. REDCINE is a good deal since you get free access to some of the functionality of SCRATCH, which is quite expensive. If you really like what REDCINE can do and want a much more powerful solution, consider investing in SCRATCH. (Learn more about SCRATCH in Chapter 13.)

Another key feature of REDCINE is the Library/Player button (**Figure 9.8**). This button toggles back and forth between the main window, where the image-adjustment controls are, and the Library view (**Figure 9.9**), where you can see all the clips associated with a project. You can also stack different versions of your grades so you can easily toggle between them and decide which one you like best.

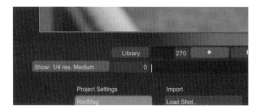

Figure 9.8 The REDCINE Library/Player toggle button.

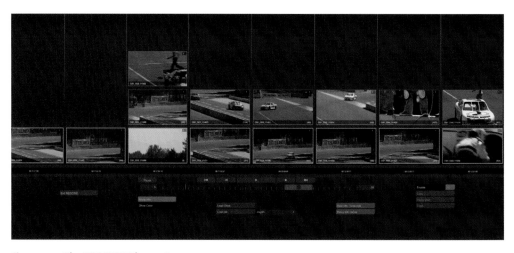

Figure 9.9 The REDCINE Library view.

REDRUSHES

REDrushes (**Figure 9.10**) is an application from RED designed to batch process single clips or large groups of R3D files all at once. You can use it for tasks such as creating offline copies of your RED footage for viewing or editing or for making online HD down-conversions of your footage for use as a finishing format. You can also use REDrushes to create new QuickTime proxy versions of footage with different color space settings.

NOTE   REDrushes gets its name from the term *rushes*, which some film crews (especially in the United Kingdom) use to describe the first set of lab prints or dailies from a day's work.

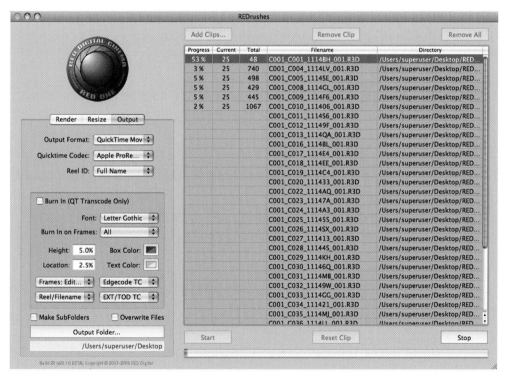

Figure 9.10   REDrushes, main application window.

REDrushes doesn't have the viewing or image-grading capabilities of RED Alert! or RED-CINE, but it makes up for that with speed and simplicity. The application features a single window with controls for render quality, resizing/cropping, and file type output on the left and a list of currently loaded clips on the right.

The workflow for REDrushes is straightforward if you follow these steps:

1. Open your R3D file in REDrushes and click the Add Clips button.

2. Navigate to the first folder of RED shots you want to process. Then choose your clip settings.

3. On the Render tab (**Figure 9.11**), you'll find the options Debayer Quality, Timecode, Look Source, Color Space, and Gamma Space. Pick your settings according to your project needs.

   • Debayer Quality determines how good the footage will look by how the raw sensor image data is being reprocessed. Full is the highest quality but requires the most time to process; the others are Half Res (resolution), Quarter Res, and Eighth Res. It's worth experimenting with each Debayer Quality setting to see which speed/quality combination you like best.

   • Next you can choose whether the timecode source will be from the time-of-day counter on the camera or the edge code, which starts from zero on each shot. The Look Source setting will match either the LOOK settings originally set in the camera or an RSX file you may have generated using RED Alert!

   • Color Space determines which color space to work in: Look Source, REDspace, CameraRGB, or REC 709.

   • Gamma Space lets you choose between gamma settings such as Linear Light, REC 709, REDspace, REDlog, and PDlog 685. (For more details about these options, see the "Color and Gamma Space" section later in this chapter.)

4. The Resize tab (**Figure 9.12**) has options for cropping and scaling footage. You might want to extract a 4:3-sized frame for standard-definition TV viewing, for example. You'll also find some presets for 1080 and 720 HD resolutions as well as 2K film resolution. Finally, there's a Resample Filter option that determines the quality and look of the scaling; some algorithms are faster than others. The filters each have a different degree of sharpening as well, so it's worth a little experimentation to determine which results you prefer.

5. The last tab, Output (**Figure 9.13**), contains the export options. You can choose to output to a QuickTime movie or a TIFF or DPX image sequence. A QuickTime movie is best used for both offline- and online-quality editorial, and the still images are best used for visual effects work, high-end color correction, or output to film. You can choose from a variety of codecs and can determine whether you want to use the full name of the clip's reel or one shortened to eight characters.

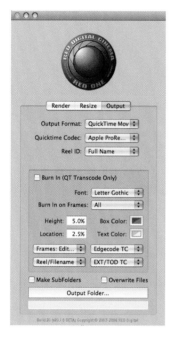

Figure 9.11
REDrushes Render tab.

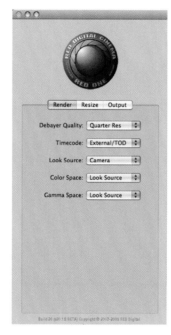

Figure 9.12
REDrushes Resize tab.

Figure 9.13
REDrushes Output tab.

6. A couple of other REDrushes controls can be helpful. Choose Settings > Render and you can choose to render multiple clips simultaneously; if you have a powerful desktop machine, try cranking these up to the maximum for faster processing. The QT Wrappers menu gives you options for creating new proxies with the current settings built-in. The File menu offers a couple of edit decision list (EDL) formats that can assist in importing footage for editing.

7. When you have all the settings the way you want them, select your output folder by clicking the Output Folder button, and click Start.

REDLINE

REDLine (**Figure 9.14**) is a Mac-only, command-line application that gives you access to all of the same transcoding and rendering operations that RED Alert! uses via the Terminal window (Terminal is available in your Applications/Utilities folder). It's not nearly as user-friendly as some of the other applications, but if you're familiar with the Terminal in Mac OS X, RED-Line gives you powerful automation capabilities. It's especially useful if you're processing lots of clips and projects. To see all the options REDLine has, open a Terminal window, and type **redline**.

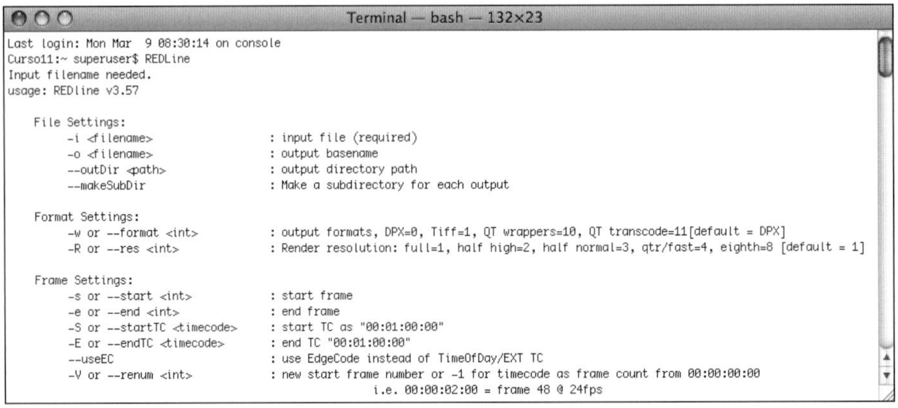

```
 ● ● ○                         Terminal — bash — 132×23
Last login: Mon Mar  9 08:30:14 on console
Curso11:~ superuser$ REDLine
Input filename needed.
usage: REDline v3.57

    File Settings:
        -i <filename>           : input file (required)
        -o <filename>           : output basename
        --outDir <path>         : output directory path
        --makeSubDir            : Make a subdirectory for each output

    Format Settings:
        -w or --format <int>    : output formats, DPX=0, Tiff=1, QT wrappers=10, QT transcode=11[default = DPX]
        -R or --res <int>       : Render resolution: full=1, half high=2, half normal=3, qtr/fast=4, eighth=8 [default = 1]

    Frame Settings:
        -s or --start <int>     : start frame
        -e or --end <int>       : end frame
        -S or --startTC <timecode>  : start TC as "00:01:00:00"
        -E or --endTC <timecode>    : end TC "00:01:00:00"
        --useEC                 : use EdgeCode instead of TimeOfDay/EXT TC
        -V or --renum <int>     : new start frame number or -1 for timecode as frame count from 00:00:00:00
                                     i.e. 00:00:02:00 = frame 48 @ 24fps
```

Figure 9.14 Some of the command-line options available in REDLine.

Third-Party Applications

As with RED's applications, more third-party applications are available for Mac than PC at the moment, so that's something to consider when choosing your RED postproduction platform. Applications such as Crimson Workflow, Monkey Extract, and Clipfinder help you view footage and transcode to HD, 2K, and even 4K versions. In this section, you'll learn how each utility operates on a typical project.

CRIMSON WORKFLOW

Crimson Workflow (www.crimsonworkflow.com) is a powerful program. Its main focus is importing a Final Cut Pro XML file and using it to extract full-resolution footage from original

R3D camera files in a wide variety of user-selectable formats. (XML stands for *Extensible Markup Language*, a universal data exchange format that can be used to export edit decision lists.) Once the footage is rendered at the desired settings, Crimson Workflow creates an updated XML file for Final Cut Pro with pointers to the new media.

Alternatively, if you want to do an extensive color correction session with REDCINE, Crimson Workflow can generate a special XML file that REDCINE can use to import only the parts of the R3D media you used in your edit. You then render your corrected clips out of REDCINE, generate a new round-trip XML file in Crimson Workflow, and re-import with the updated media into Final Cut Pro.

Let's take a look at how to extract footage to 1080/24p HD from RED files:

1. Starting in Final Cut Pro with a completed edit, select your sequence, and then choose File > Export > XML (**Figure 9.15**). Choose version 4 in the Format list of options, and then save the XML with the default options (as shown in the figure).

Figure 9.15 Exporting an XML from Final Cut Pro.

2. Import the XML into Crimson Workflow by clicking the Choose button (**Figure 9.16**). Drag the folders where your camera originals are into the Search Folders window, and click Match. Crimson Workflow should match the XML edits to the R3D files.

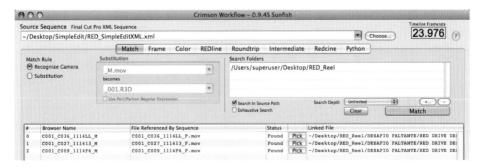

Figure 9.16 Importing XML into Crimson with matched R3D files.

Now you can use the REDLine tab to render your footage out directly, or you can export a REDCINE XML and do additional color correction there. Let's start with the REDLine method.

3. Click the Frame tab, and choose High Definition 1080p as the Preset option (**Figure 9.17**).

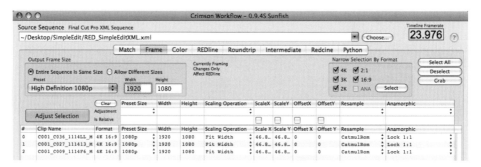

Figure 9.17 Frame tab in Crimson Workflow.

4. Click the REDLine tab, and choose the Output Format and QT Codec. I've chosen QT Movie and Apple ProRes 42 in **Figure 9.18**. Click the Render with REDline button to begin rendering.

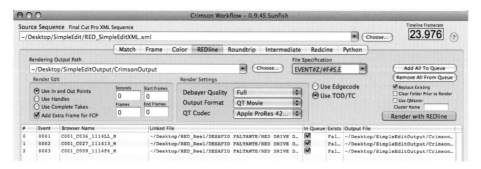

Figure 9.18 REDLine tab in Crimson Workflow.

5. When rendering is complete, switch to the Roundtrip tab (**Figure 9.19**). Make sure the locations of your original Final Cut Pro XML file and your rendered files are correct. Then click Generate Roundtrip XML.

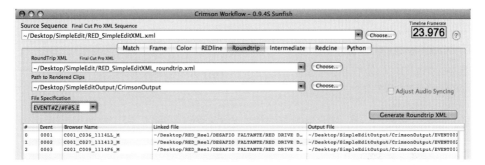

Figure 9.19 Generating round-trip XML.

6. Open Final Cut Pro, and import that XML. It should now point to the newly rendered footage you created in Crimson Workflow.

The alternate method for working with Crimson Workflow is to send the footage to REDCINE for color correction:

1. Click the REDCINE tab in Crimson Workflow, and click the Export Redcine XML button (**Figure 9.20**).

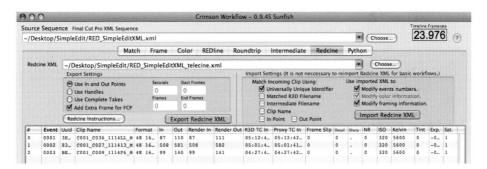

Figure 9.20 The REDCINE tab in Crimson Workflow.

2. Import the clips you made with Crimson (they're stored in Documents/crimson by default) with the Load All command.

3. In REDCINE, open the telecine file you exported from Crimson. Do your one-light color correction work, and save a new XML in REDCINE when you're done.

4. Return to Crimson Workflow and reload that newly-saved XML for rendering.

MONKEY EXTRACT

Monkey Extract (www.rubbermonkeysoftware.com) is a Mac-only tool designed to import an edit decision list (EDL) from your editing program (or an XML from Final Cut Pro) and export the footage used in your edit to another format. Its chief advantage over Crimson is ease of use, with most of the power hidden under the hood of a simplified interface (**Figure 9.21**). Make sure you have the latest version of RED Alert! installed before running Monkey Extract, because it uses RED Alert!'s rendering engine.

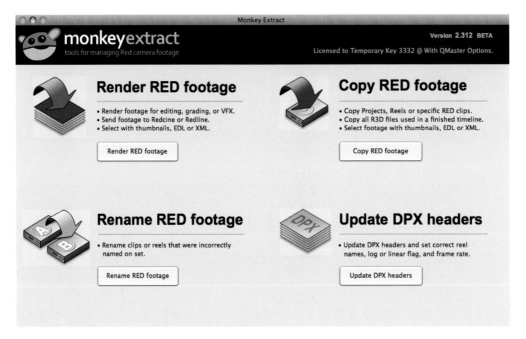

Figure 9.21 Monkey Extract's main application window.

In addition to rendering footage from an EDL, Monkey Extract can also copy RED footage in batches, rename footage, and update DPX metadata. Sometimes it's necessary to change DPX metadata because settings such as the timecode, frame rate, and reel names of your edit don't match the DPX files you want to work with. Also, by exporting an updated EDL, you can go directly into an application such as Color, which supports DPX, while skipping Final Cut Pro, which does not (at least not without a plugin). Another feature of Monkey Extract is its upgradeable capability to use multiple computers in parallel and speed up rendering of a project via Apple's Qmaster network management utility.

Let's take a look at how to extract footage for a 1080/24p HD down-convert from RED files using the same project we used for Crimson Workflow:

1. Starting in Final Cut Pro with a completed edit, select that edit, and then choose File > Export > EDL (**Figure 9.22**). Choose CMX 3600 for the Format option and save the EDL with the default options (as shown in the figure).

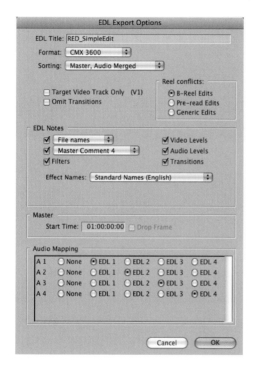

Figure 9.22 Exporting an EDL from Final Cut Pro for Monkey Extract.

2. Switch to Monkey Extract, and click the Render RED footage button. Load the EDL you just exported, and then select the folder containing original camera files (**Figure 9.23**).

3. Finally, select an output folder for the converted files—make sure this is not the same folder as the one that holds your camera files. Then click the Start Render button (**Figure 9.24**).

When rendering is complete, you'll have the footage in the desired output format; you'll get a new EDL to import into a color correction program and an XML to reload into Final Cut Pro when you choose File > Import in Final Cut Pro. Monkey Extract is easy to use, and it offers a powerful way to render only the portions of RED footage you actually use in an edit.

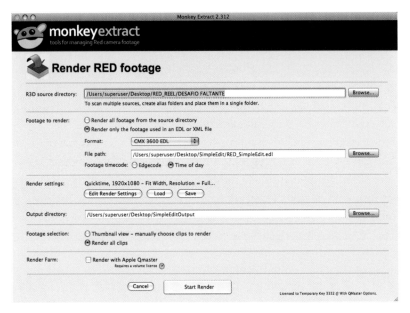

Figure 9.23 Ready to render from a Final Cut Pro EDL using Monkey Extract.

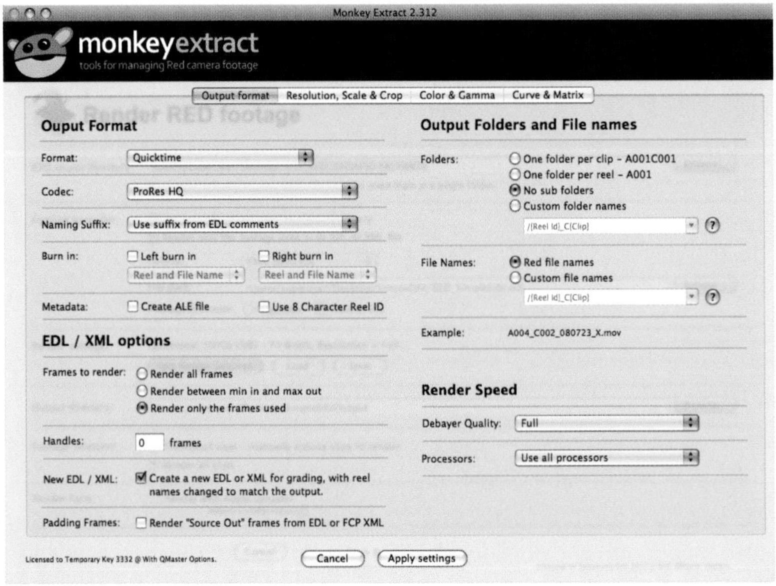

Figure 9.24 Choosing ouput settings.

CLIPFINDER

Clipfinder (www.daun.ch/software) is a Mac-only RED R3D clip-browsing tool with some additional useful features. Think of it as iPhoto on steroids for your RED clips. You can drag and drop entire magazines or folders of RED footage directly into Clipfinder and quickly see thumbnails of each shot. Clipfinder can also easily swap proxies in a Final Cut Pro Timeline. For example, you could edit with M proxies and switch to H whenever you want.

Some other nice features are Lift & Stamp, which applies look settings from one clip to all selected clips. You can also "Data Exchange" clips directly into Final Cut Pro with names and custom field data. Do this by pressing Alt-Command-F. Clipfinder can also output Web pages and PDF contact sheets of your clips, along with metadata and thumbnails. Clipfinder has two basic viewing modes: a standard list layout (**Figure 9.25**) and a thumbnail layout (**Figure 9.26**). You can toggle back and forth between these modes by pressing Command-T.

Figure 9.25 Clipfinder list mode.

Figure 9.26 Clipfinder thumbnail mode.

Figure 9.27 Clipfinder Loupe.

Clipfinder also has a Loupe viewer (**Figure 9.27**) that zooms into a portion of a clip at a 1:1, 100 percent resolution, which can be helpful for checking the sharpness of a clip or the amount of grain/noise present.

In addition to viewing clips, Clipfinder can also speed up and automate your workflow. You can use it to process footage into other formats and make outputs, similar to the way REDrushes works. You can also set up a watch folder for Clipfinder to monitor. Then, whenever new clips are moved or copied into this folder, Clipfinder will automatically process them according to the current output settings.

Color and Gamma Space

Color space and gamma were briefly mentioned earlier in this chapter and elsewhere in the book, and now we'll get into greater technical detail. Color and gamma space are especially important to understand because they determine the appearance of your footage. Learning about color and gamma will help you get a final image that looks the way you intended when you shot it.

Color space is a mathematical way to describe how color will be represented on a given medium—in our case, a computer screen. If you've ever worked with Adobe Photoshop, you've probably heard of the RGB and CMYK color spaces, which are typically used for computer and print output, respectively. (RGB stands for *red, green, blue*, and CMYK stands for *cyan, magenta, yellow, key*—or *cyan, magenta, yellow, black*.)

Gamma refers to how the tonal range from light to dark is expressed on your computer monitor. The RED ONE is capable of capturing a greater range of gamma than can be accurately displayed on your computer or a TV screen. So, you must apply some sort of gamma correction to try to squeeze what's really in the RAW footage from the camera onto your screen. The different gamma and color space settings available to many RED applications determine how the conversion is handled.

COLOR SPACE SETTINGS

In the RED camera and RED applications, three color spaces are currently available: CameraRGB, REC 709, and REDspace (**Figure 9.28**).

Figure 9.28 RED color space settings.

CameraRGB is the original, uncorrected sensor data without any sort of profiling applied (called RAW on the camera controls). To the eye it can look a bit washed out and devoid of color, but this is more because of monitor limitations than reality. REC 709 is the standard color space specification for high-definition video and is the format you should use if you're planning to finish your project for HD. Finally, REDspace gives you an expanded color space over REC 709 and is intended for film output and digital cinema mastering.

NOTE   REC 709 is short for *Recommendation BT.709* from the International Telecommunication Union (ITU) and comprises the agreed-upon technical standards that make up high-definition TV.

GAMMA SPACE SETTINGS

For gamma, you have more settings than Color Space (**Figure 9.29**).

Figure 9.29   RED Gamma space settings.

The available options are REDspace, REDlog, REC 709, PDlog 685 and 985, and Linear Light (**Figure 9.30**). Linear Light is the baseline, with no gamma adjustment made at all to the original sensor data. As with the CameraRGB color space setting, Linear Light can look a bit flat to your eye, which is accustomed to seeing gamma-corrected images on monitors. REC 709 is the standard gamma for viewing footage on an HD monitor. REDspace is reasonably similar to REC 709 but has been adjusted by the engineers at RED to look more appealing via increased contrast and brighter midtones. REDlog converts the 12-bit native RED gamma curve into a 10-bit curve that is more suitable for display on a monitor while keeping as much of the data as possible intact for later color correction. PDlog 685 is another kind of logarithmic display setting that is useful for film transfer. PDlog 985 is similar to 685 but with an increase in brightness sensitivity. PDlog 985 also uses more of the R3D's available data; your post house should inform you which it prefers.

So, what settings do you use and when? REDspace is especially useful for reviewing footage on set and at the start of editing because it gives the closest approximation of what your eyes see when looking at the image in front of the camera. REC 709 should be used primarily when working toward a video finish in HD. REC 709 will give you the must accurate representation of your footage as it will look on an HDTV monitor.

Figure 9.30 Clockwise, starting from the top-left image, RED Gamma space settings include REDspace, REDlog, REC 709, PDlog 685, PDlog 985, and Linear Light.

REDlog attempts to preserve more detail in the image, especially when going to DPX and eventually onto film. REDlog may look flat on your screen, but more information is being preserved for later usage in color correction. The PDlog modes are designed specifically for film output and working with Cineon files. You probably won't get into those settings unless your post house or film lab specifically requests them.

BITS AND LOGS

Terms such as *12-bit* and *10-bit*, refer to the amount of data used to record color information. Computer displays are typically 8-bits per color channel. That means you have 256 possible values for each of the red, green, and blue channels in an image. Moving up to 10-bit gives you 1,024 values per channel, and 12-bit yields 4,096.

You can also describe images as *log* (logarithmic) or *linear*. Linear Light expresses all values equally across the entire range of latitude, which can sometimes mean redundant data in parts of the spectrum that are very similar. Logarithmic works on a curve that more accurately mimics the way film (and the eye) captures light, where there is greater detail in the darkest and brightest values.

In general, log is considered more suitable for intensive color grading because you can push it a lot further while retaining detail in the brightest and darkest zones of the image. With linear, what you see is generally all that's there. The higher up the latitude you go toward white, the more precision you have. That's why log images look washed out—the image is biased toward brightness where there's more accuracy.

This chapter has thrown a lot of technical data at you, and it's not necessary to understand every last bit to work with RED. It's important to know which mode to use for what occasion to keep your work accurate and your final outputs as expected. Most of the applications surveyed in this chapter can switch between these modes as you transcode and move from RAW 12-bit R3D to 8-bit and 10-bit finishing formats. As with everything else in this book, experiment to find the applications and settings that work best for the type of project you're creating.

Brook Willard (left) makes a point on the set of the NBC cop show *Southland*.

Brook Willard
DIGITAL IMAGING TECHNICIAN, *ER*

ER cinematographer Arthur Albert (whose POV interview you can also find in this book) initially expected that the changeover of his show to digital would mean a reduction in the size of his crew. He quickly realized it would actually need to grow. "You'd think the film loader position would no longer be necessary, but the loader does a lot of other tasks, like moving gear around, prepping, and slating shots," says Albert. "We needed the help as well because the RED camera has more parts and accessories to keep track of than our previous Panavision cameras. Then we also added a digital imaging technician (DIT) to be responsible for footage downloads, backing data up, and everything technical to do with the camera."

The DIT position went to Brook Willard, who has lots of experience with RED and a wide variety of other high-definition and film cameras. His credits include dozens of commercials and other TV series. Willard also spends some of his available spare time as a forum moderator on Reduser.net. He first got the call for *ER* via his work with the same producers on another show.

"I had recently worked with RED on the NBC pilot for *Southland* as a DIT, and we were also just finishing up with a live-action shoot for the videogame *Need for Speed: Undercover*," Willard recalls. "Robert Keslow, of Keslow Camera in Santa Monica, brought me in. Keslow is the biggest RED rental house in Hollywood right now; they have 27 RED bodies. Robert reserved five the day camera reservations were first opened at NAB [in April 2007]."

Willard gives some insight into his daily routine as a DIT on *ER*. "I split my time between running data and transfers at my cart and working alongside the camera," he reveals. "In the beginning I was spending more time at the camera, helping the crew get accustomed to the RED and how it operates. I've built and rebuilt this camera 1,000 times, and they were coming from a Panavision package, so we spent a lot of time adapting their techniques. I'm also on top of exposure; Arthur [Albert] and I will sit together at the monitor and work out the appropriate stop for a shot. Most of the stages are prelit, so 98 percent of the time, we set the stop for a scene and forget about it."

Even though the show is broadcast in high definition and standard definition, it's being shot at RED's highest-quality settings. "We shoot 4K HD at 23.98 with REDCODE 36," says Willard. "The HD frame is easier on post than 2:1 or 16:9, and it transcodes much more quickly. For optics, we use the ARRI primes and all four of the major Angenieux Optimo zooms, including the 17–80mm and the 24–290mm. We also shoot with Cooke S4i's, but the Optimos are really the primary workhouse with all of our Steadicam and handheld work."

The *ER* crew recorded to CompactFlash cards instead of hard drives. "We managed to obtain about 30 16 GB cards for the show," says Willard. "This allows us to hold onto cards for 36 hours from when they're shot until they go back into a camera again. So if there are any issues, I can go right back to the original and re-transfer. Every card is labeled with the current reel number. When the crew rolls out on a shot, they eject the card and put tape over the pins. From there it goes into a special Pelican case on the DIT cart, and I provide them with a fresh one from another marked case. I also reformat the cards in a special way so that the camera thinks they're empty but the footage can still be accessed. If the ACs load a card I haven't cleared like that, they get an in-camera formatting error, and they know something is wrong. That way it's always clear which cards are ready for reuse."

Willard's cart features a Mac Pro in a shock-mounted hard case connected to an HD monitor via a Blackmagic HD-SDI output card. The system has 14 TB of RAID 6 storage capable of read/write speeds up to 800 MB per second. "I back up every shot onto various different drives and RAIDs," he notes. "Then I create initial grades before sending footage off to post-production. For CF card readers, I've built a few eSATA units of my own based on Addonics parts connected to a Sonnet eSATA card in the Mac Pro. I also have Hama USB and FireWire 800 readers and a SanDisk FireWire 800 reader as backups."

To do the actual copying from CF card to hard drive, Willard uses a modified version of the OS X Finder. "I've got it configured to do a checksum, so I know every copy is perfect," he explains. "I've tried some of the dedicated data transfer applications, but I found them to be a bit more unstable than I'd like, so I've stuck with the Finder.

For audio, the show recorded double-system sound, and the sound department had its own recording device. "We have a Denecke SB-T Time Code Generator on top of every RED," says Willard. "We considered recording RED audio as well, briefly, but there was ultimately no reason to have it. The assistant editor syncs up the takes in postproduction."

ER partially leveraged RED's RAW workflow before finishing in a more conventional tape-based color correction session. "We send R3D and RSX files with each hard drive after doing some initial grading on the set," Willard notes. "The R3D files are then transcoded by R!OT Post directly to Avid's DNxHD format. They make a DNx36 transcode for editorial on the

Avid. Then they do a higher-quality DPX encode for the high-definition tape-to-tape the color correction on a da Vinci at Level 3."

Taking note of the impact of a show like *ER* switching to RED, Willard observed a lot of interest during his time on the set. "We had directors of photography and producers from every show you can imagine stop by," he says. "They all wanted to know how well it was working and what the footage looked like. *ER* was the big show that opened the floodgates and made it a whole lot easier to accept the idea of using this camera."

Brook Willard's Web sites are www.brookwillard.com and www.4kninjas.net. ∎

10 APPLE FINAL CUT PRO WORKFLOW

You can edit a RED project with Apple Final Cut Pro in a number of ways, and each has its own strengths. The amount of options can be overwhelming, so in this chapter we'll focus on the transcode to Apple ProRes workflow via the Log and Transfer window , which is currently favored by Apple. You'll learn how to ingest your footage properly, send it to Apple Color, work with Cinema Tools, and export using the Share feature in Final Cut Pro. After you have the recommended workflow down pat, we'll look at some alternative methods that you might find useful for certain types of projects.

System Requirements

Final Cut Pro is optimized for the ProRes compression format. Using this format gives you real-time performance and access to all effects, assuming you meet the minimum system requirements according to Apple.

You need to be aware of a couple of issues when you're using the recommended workflow. First, there is a waiting period between shooting and editing because transcoding from R3D to ProRes takes time. The amount of time depends mainly on the speed of your system processor and the amount of RAM. I recommend an eight-core 2.26 GHz or faster Mac Pro with at least 4 GB of RAM.

The other issue with transcoding from R3D to ProRes is that once you begin color correction, you're locked into the color space and gamma, set in the Log and Transfer window. For many productions, this is not that big of a deal, and if you think about working with footage from any other non-RAW camera, that's the usual way. You can get around this limitation with an easy side trip to Cinema Tools, which you'll explore later in this chapter in the "Using Cinema Tools" section.

I recommend using Final Cut Pro 7 or later for the best performance. You'll also need RED's software, which enables support for Final Cut Pro, Color, and QuickTime. You'll find the latest version at www.red.com/support.

Ingesting Footage

This workflow will be familiar if you're used to working with other tapeless formats in Final Cut Pro such as P2 or XDCAM EX. For the best results, keep all of your original RDM folders intact and organized. The general rule of thumb is to copy all files and directories the camera makes and not to remove files, rename files, or rearrange folders. This is especially important if you're planning to do RAW color correction using Cinema Tools.

1. Begin the ingest process in Final Cut Pro by choosing File > Log and Transfer, or by pressing Command-Shift-8. The Log and Transfer window appears.

2. Specify which ProRes format you want to transcode to. Click the small gear icon in the Log and Transfer window, and choose Preferences from the Action menu.

3. In the Import Preferences dialog, choose the desired transcode format in the Target Format column (next to RED Digital Cinema REDCODE) (**Figure 10.1**).

   As of Final Cut Pro 7, you have a number of ProRes formats to choose from, each with a different level of quality and corresponding bitrate. The quality levels start at ProRes

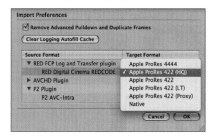

Figure 10.1 Selecting a ProRes format.

422 (Proxy) and go up to ProRes 4444 (check with Apple for the exact data rates). If the footage you're ingesting is intended to be your online or final version, pick one of the higher bitrate flavors such as ProRes 422 (HQ) or 4444. Keep in mind that each level as you go up requires more storage and a faster hard drive for optimum editing performance.

If you're treating the initial edit as offline and you plan to either re-ingest the footage to a higher-quality format or reconnect to the R3D files via Cinema Tools, choose one of the lower bitrate ProRes formats such as LT or Proxy. Keep in mind that those lower-quality ProRes formats can still look pretty good, especially when going out to standard-definition DVD or the Internet. We'll use ProRes 422 (HQ) for this example.

4. Once you've selected a ProRes format, drag and drop your RDM folders from the Finder into the Log and Transfer window. After the scanning is complete, all the shots from each folder should appear in the Log and Transfer window (**Figure 10.2**).

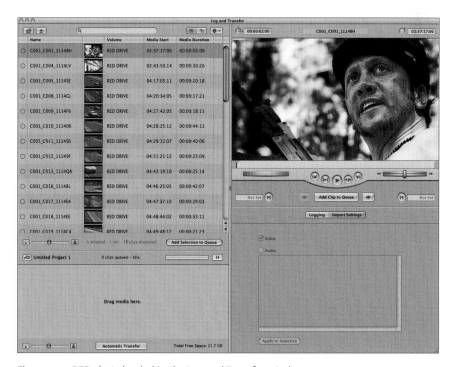

Figure 10.2 RED shots loaded in the Log and Transfer window.

NOTE   You have the option to ingest with or without audio by clicking the Import Settings button under the Log and Transfer preview area. I suggest simply bringing everything in as it was shot.

5. Select the clips you want to ingest, or press Command-A to select them all.
6. Click the Add Selection to Queue button.

    Final Cut Pro will begin to ingest the clips one at a time. This is likely to take a while, depending on how many clips you plan to import and how long they are. Ingested clips will appear in your Project window (**Figure 10.3**).

7. Repeat as needed for each reel. When the process is complete, close the Log and Transfer window. All clips are transcoded to ProRes at 2K in Final Cut Pro.

Figure 10.3 RED ProRes clips viewed in the Project window.

Editing

Once you've ingested your footage, editing RED footage in Final Cut Pro isn't too different from editing other types of footage.

1. To start editing, create a new sequence by choosing File > New > Sequence, or press Command-N.
2. Drag a single clip into the new sequence.

3. When prompted to change the sequence settings to match the clip settings, click Yes. Your resulting sequence settings should look something like **Figure 10.4**.

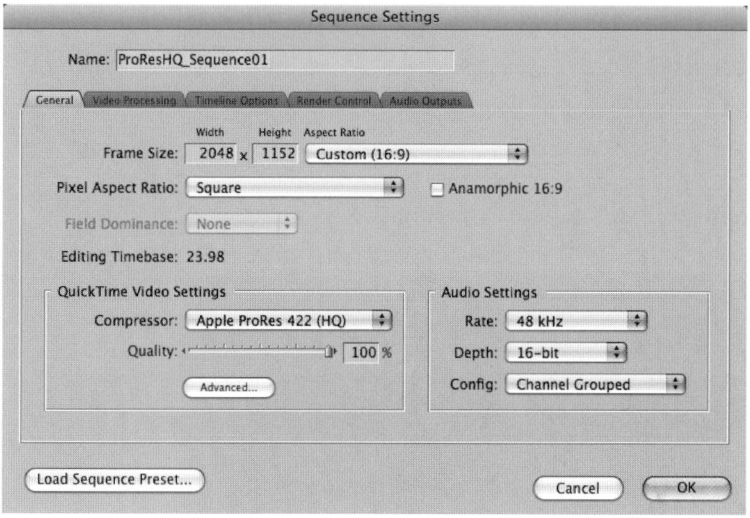

Figure 10.4 Sequence settings for 2K ProRes 16:9 footage.

The nice aspect of transcoding is you get excellent performance with all your real-time filters and effects via the extensive ProRes support in Final Cut Pro. If you can live without the RAW workflow for color correction, you can use 2K ProRes transcoded files as your master for high-definition and standard-definition projects. If you do need to go RAW, say for extensive visual effects or a 4K film finish, refer to the "Using Cinema Tools" section of this chapter.

Color Correcting

Once you've completed an edit with Final Cut Pro, you can send it to Apple Color for color grading. Technically, a locked edit is not essential for color correction, but it's much simpler and avoids redoing work. (For other color-correction applications, refer to Chapter 13.) The color space and gamma latitude of ProRes files are sufficient to finish for high-definition, and this process is easier and quicker than accessing the native RAW metadata.

For a majority of RED projects, especially those destined for DVD, HD, or the Web, you'll be all set with this method and can begin working in Color right away. For more critical projects, however, you'll want to access the power of the RED RAW workflow with Cinema Tools.

SENDING TO COLOR

To go from a transcoded 2K edit in Final Cut Pro into a ProRes color-correction session in Color, the simplest method is the following:

1. In Final Cut Pro, select the sequence you want to correct in Color by clicking it in the Project window.

2. Choose File > Send to Color.

    Color should start up, and your Timeline should load automatically. If you've set up everything properly, your Color project settings should look like **Figure 10.5** (your own project settings will vary).

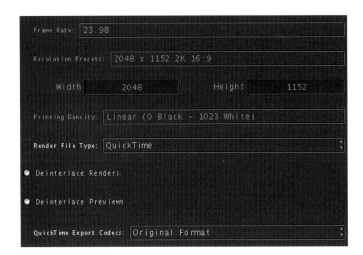

Figure 10.5 Project settings for a ProRes 2K project in Color.

3. Confirm that your resolution and frame rate match your Final Cut Pro sequence settings. If not, you can manually reenter them. This might, however, indicate an incorrect setting in the original sequence, so go back and re-check your settings.

TIP   For projects destined for DPX and film output, Color works best with simplified Timelines from Final Cut Pro. Stick with standard dissolves, and remove speed and motion effects. You should create those after a Color session, because many of these effects will be discarded when you export directly from Color to the image sequence formats.

USING CINEMA TOOLS

If you're working toward a film finish or 4K output, you'll want the higher latitude of the original R3D media when you color correct. This gives you access to all original RAW color and exposure data out of the camera. You'll use Cinema Tools (included as part of Final Cut Studio) to enable Color's RED metadata control tab using an EDL from Final Cut Pro. (This method requires Final Cut Pro 7 or later.)

1. Start in Final Cut Pro, and select the sequence you want to color correct.

2. Choose File > Export > EDL.

   The EDL Export Options dialog opens.

3. Choose the CMX 3600 format, and select None for each channel in the Audio Mapping list. (The EDL will automatically be titled according to the current sequence name.)

   Color doesn't import audio, and omitting it will make for a more trouble-free EDL export; just be prepared to realign your audio tracks with the completed color-corrected footage when you send them to Final Cut Pro from Color.

4. Match what you see in **Figure 10.6** for the rest of the settings. Click OK, and save the EDL.

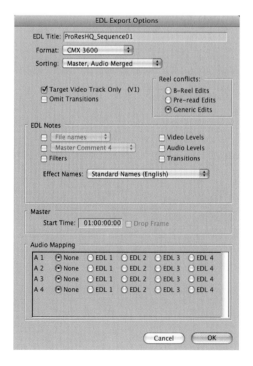

Figure 10.6 Follow these export options for your EDL from Final Cut Pro.

5. Launch Cinema Tools, and create a new database by choosing Database > New Database. Accept the default settings, because these settings don't affect RED projects.

6. Load all the reels you've used in your RED project into Cinema Tools by dragging them from the Finder. This is when keeping things organized and not changing filenames or reel names will make your life a lot easier.

7. Switch from the default Keycode view to the Video view to see more details about your database (**Figure 10.7**).

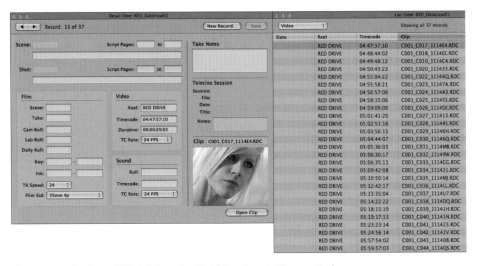

Figure 10.7 Viewing a RED database in the Video view in Cinema Tools.

TIP If you need to move footage around or change reel names, make sure to do this before you ingest into Final Cut Pro or create a Cinema Tools database; otherwise, you may have problems reconnecting the original media to your EDL.

GOING TO COLOR

Once you've created a Cinema Tools database, the next step is linking it to the EDL you exported from Final Cut Pro. This creates a Color project with your edited sequence that references the original R3D files instead of the transcoded ProRes material.

1. Launch Color, and open the EDL you saved in Final Cut Pro.

   The EDL Import Settings window appears. Confirm that your frame rate and resolutions match your original shooting settings. I've chosen the 4K 16:9 preset and set my frame rates to 23.98.

2. To select your source directory (**Figure 10.8**), click the Browse button, and search for the Cinema Tools database you saved (it should have a .ctdb file extension).

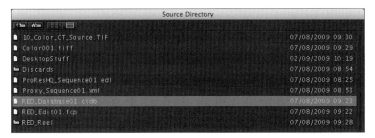

Figure 10.8 Choosing the Cinema Tools database as the source directory for the EDL import.

Figure 10.9 Accessing the RED tab in the Primary In room.

3. Click the tab for the Primary In room.

   You should now have access to the RED control tab (**Figure 10.9**). This gives you the ability to alter the RAW metadata, including exposure, color temperature, gamma and color spaces, and more.

   TIP For more training on Color, check out *Apple Pro Training Series: Color* (Peachpit Press) or my Digital Color Correction DVD from Call Box (www.callboxlive.com).

4. When you're done grading in Color, click the tab for the Setup room. Choose an export format on the Project Settings tab. You can export at 4K or down-convert to 2K. I recommend exporting to at least 2K because you can use that to derive most other formats you'll need.

5. Choose one of the ProRes formats such as ProRes 4444 (**Figure 10.10**).

   Each level up provides more image quality, but also larger files and increased drive speed requirements. A ProRes 4444 file at 4K is not likely to play reliably on most systems because of its very high data rate, but it's fine as a source master for transcodes to other formats. Run some tests to determine the best combination of quality versus file size on your system. 2K ProRes HQ is usually a solid bet, for example.

Figure 10.10 Choosing an output format for rendering in Color.

6. Click the User Preferences tab to choose your render proxy setting. Choose Full to render to 4K or Half for 2K.

7. When you are finished with settings, click the tab for the Render Queue room. Click the Add All button to load your sequence clips into the queue. Then click the Start Render button.

NOTE   Because you're actually correcting directly from the R3D files, you can switch between 2K or 4K at any time without having to redo any of your work. Everything automatically scales, including Secondary In room masks.

For a film output, check in with your film recording service. You'll likely export to ProRes or to DPX files ready for direct recording to film, depending on their requirements. If you want to bring footage back into Final Cut Pro from Color for additional editing, choose File > Send to Final Cut Pro.

Final Cut Pro will automatically reload the new sequence, and you'll find it in 4K if you've corrected in Color with 4K. Otherwise, it will likely be 2K. You can now do additional sound work or export from Final Cut Pro to a variety of formats such as high definition and DVD.

Sharing with Other Formats

Final Cut Pro 7 offers new export options such as Blu-ray and YouTube. Instead of exporting footage to Compressor or DVD Studio Pro only, you can now use the Share menu in Final Cut Pro following these simple steps:

1. Select the current sequence in your Project window.

2. Choose File > Share, and then select your output format (**Figure 10.11**).

3. You can quickly and easily make a Blu-ray disc with the default settings.

    Remember, you'll also need a Blu-ray burner to make Blu-ray discs. (Alternately, you can use the AVCHD setting and burn footage to standard DVD-Rs that will play on most Macs and PlayStation 3 in high definition.)

NOTE　For more information on exporting your project and Blu-ray, refer to Chapter 13.

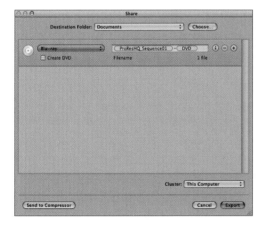

Figure 10.11 Making a Blu-ray disc in Final Cut Pro from the Share menu.

Alternate Workflows

Now that you have the basic Final Cut Pro workflow down, you should be aware of a couple alternative methods for working with RED footage in Final Cut Pro. Because Final Cut Pro was the first editing application to support RED, it has a variety of options that have been developed and used since RED cameras hit the market. We'll focus on two of the most well-known workflows: native-wrapped and proxies.

THE NATIVE-WRAPPED METHOD

For the native-wrapped method, you create a special kind of QuickTime file that points directly to the R3D file, essentially coming the closest to a native workflow. In theory, this workflow gives you the best of both worlds: you have the ability to edit clips in Final Cut Pro while maintaining a connection to the R3D files for RAW color correction. It does require very high-end system specifications to perform reliably, which is its chief drawback. You also have to wait while footage is converted from R3D to native-wrapped QuickTime in the Log and Transfer window, but not nearly as long as you do with transcoding. I find it works best with a top-of-the-line Mac Pro with 16 GB or more of RAM and a RAID hard drive.

> NOTE This method is referred to as "native-wrapped" because Final Cut Pro makes a special copy of the R3D file with a set of translation instructions (also known as a *wrapper*) for QuickTime to directly access the original RED video, audio, and metadata.

INGESTING

The native-wrapped QuickTime workflow is similar in operation to the transcoding workflow:

1. In Final Cut Pro, open the Log and Transfer window. Click the gear icon to open the Import Preferences dialog. This time, instead of a ProRes codec, select the Native option (**Figure 10.12**).

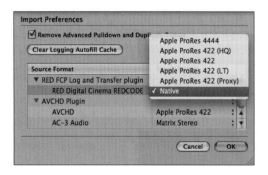

Figure 10.12 Selecting Native in the RED Import Preferences dialog.

2. You also have some image preprocessing options, which include As Shot, Tungsten, Daylight, and others (**Figure 10.13**). I recommend keeping this set to As Shot, which preserves your original camera metadata settings. Color space is something you'll want a lot more control over than a blanket preset, and you'll get that control later when you go into Color for finishing.

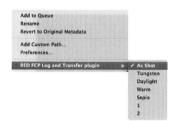

Figure 10.13 Image preprocessing options in the Log and Transfer window.

TIP   Transcoded and native-wrapped footage will be stored wherever you've set your Video Capture location in System Settings. Confirm you have plenty of disk space at the chosen location before you start ingesting.

3. Once you've chosen your options, select the clips you want to ingest, and then click the Add Selection to Queue button.

    Clips will begin processing and appearing in your Project window. This process is much faster than transcoding to ProRes because the clip is basically receiving some translation data and then being copied.

4. When all the clips have been ingested, create a new sequence by choosing File > New > Sequence.

5. Drag a single native-wrapped clip into the new sequence. When prompted to change the sequence settings to match the clip settings, click Yes.

    Your native-wrapped sequence settings should look like **Figure 10.14**. Even though you're working with REDCODE native files, your sequence codec is ProRes because you cannot directly encode to REDCODE at this time in Final Cut Pro.

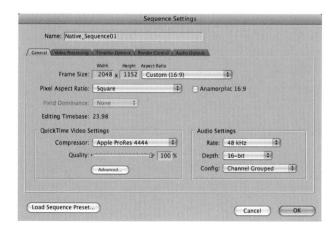

Figure 10.14 Native-wrapped Final Cut Pro sequence settings for 16:9 footage.

TIP   Make sure your Sequence RT tab is set to Unlimited RT. Otherwise, your sequences will require rendering for playback. Try Low or Medium Playback Video Quality and Full Playback Frame Rate.

COLOR CORRECTION

The native-wrapped workflow offers the easiest path from an edit in Final Cut Pro to a native-enabled color-correction session in Color. All you need to do is the following:

1. In Final Cut Pro, choose File > Send to Color.

   Your sequence will then appear in Color, ready to take advantage of the RED metadata controls. Because Final Cut Pro's working resolution is 2K, you'll need to reset the Color project to 4K if you want to work at the higher resolution.

2. In Color, click the tab for the Setup room, and then click the Project Settings tab.

3. Choose the 4K-resolution preset that matches your project's original settings, such as 4096 x 2304 4K 16:9.

Now you might be asking, "If this is so simple, why don't I always use the native-wrapped method as my workflow?" As mentioned earlier, there's a delay while the files are ingested via Log and Transfer, and you need very powerful hardware to get reliable performance in Final Cut Pro. But if you test this workflow and it works well on your system, go for it. It's the most straightforward of method for getting to a RAW finish.

THE PROXY METHOD

Because the RED ONE creates QuickTime-compatible proxy files that you can play back in Final Cut Pro, you can actually drop a proxy file into a Final Cut Pro sequence and immediately start to cut. (A *proxy* is a special translator file that gives all QuickTime-compatible applications, such as Final Cut Pro, access to the original R3D data.)

The drawbacks to using proxies include increased system requirements and instability. You'll find that a number of Final Cut Pro's real-time effects and transitions require rendering, and you need to maintain very specific sequence settings, typically starting from 4K 16:9, 2:1, or HD footage. You also need to keep careful track of your RDM folders, because they must remain in the same place for the proxies to keep functioning as you edit.

I'm covering the proxy workflow here because folks are already using it in the field, even though I do not recommend it without extensive testing. Proxies can be useful in certain situations when you need to do a quick edit—as in, immediately. When you get into color correction in Color, the proxy files can point back to the R3D originals, and you'll be able to access the RAW metadata for color correction.

> NOTE Proxy is an unsupported workflow because it ignores all kinds of other things under the hood that help maintain stability. So if you go with this workflow, proceed at your own risk.

INGESTING

Unlike the transcode and native-wrapped workflows, you don't use the Log and Transfer window; however, you'll need to have Final Cut Pro open. To begin a proxy edit, you'll use your Finder window.

1. At the Finder, navigate to the top-level directory of one of your RED reels. Find all the files with _M.mov as the filename within the directory (**Figure 10.15**). This will give you a window with all the medium-sized proxies in the reel.

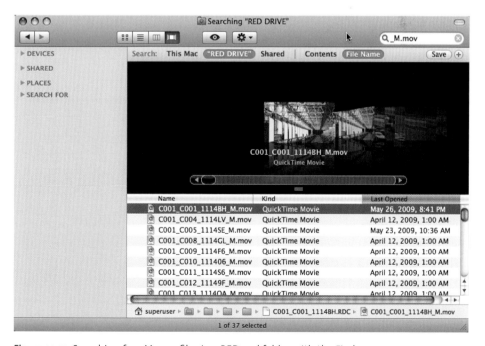

Figure 10.15 Searching for _M.mov files in a RED reel folder with the Finder.

2. Select all these files by pressing Command-A. Then drag the files into a bin (the folders you sort footage with) or your Project window in Final Cut Pro. It's better to use a bin so you can easily keep reels separated and organized (**Figure 10.16**).

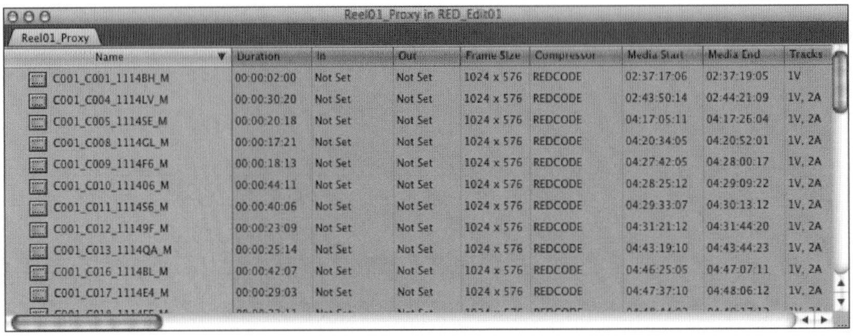

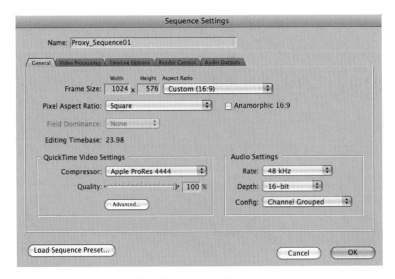

Figure 10.16 Medium-sized proxy files loaded into a bin in Final Cut Pro.

3. To begin a proxy edit, use the same technique as used in the transcode workflow. Create a new sequence by choosing File > New > Sequence or by pressing Command-N. Drag a single clip into the new sequence. When prompted to change the sequence settings to match the clip settings, click Yes.

Your resulting sequence settings for a medium proxy edit of 16:9 4K-originated footage should look like **Figure 10.17**.

Figure 10.17 Sequence settings for a proxy edit.

TIP Control-click or right-click in the Project window, and choose View as Large Icons. You'll see an icon preview for each proxy clip.

Note that you're working at approximately 1K resolution, comparable to standard-definition (1024 x 576 versus 720 x 480 pixels). I don't recommend making final output at this resolution, but it's high enough quality for an offline edit. The sequence codec defaults to ProRes 4444, but I suggest throttling this down to ProRes HQ or even ProRes Proxy for better performance.

COLOR CORRECTION

Once you've completed your editorial work with proxy footage, you need to relink that footage with the original R3D files in order to utilize the RAW workflow with Color. This is where things get a little tricky. Again, I emphasize this is an unsupported workflow that isn't recommended for long-form projects because of its potential instability. Save it for brief projects for which you need to turn something around very quickly.

1. Start in Final Cut Pro by selecting the sequence you want to color correct in the Project window, and choose File > Export > XML. Keep the default XML format version 5, and make sure "Save project with latest clip metadata" is selected. Save the XML file (**Figure 10.18**) by clicking OK.

Figure 10.18 Saving an XML file out of Final Cut Pro.

NOTE It's also possible to use the Send to Color command for proxy sequences, but I find the XML method more reliable.

2. Launch Color, and navigate to the XML file you just saved in Final Cut Pro. Click the file to open it.

    Assuming your footage hasn't moved since you brought it into Final Cut Pro as a proxy, it should automatically link to the original R3D media. Confirm this by checking to see whether you have access to the RED control tab in the Primary In room.

NOTE   You can also use the Clipfinder application mentioned in Chapter 9 to process a proxy XML file out of Final Cut Pro for use with Color, often with more stable results. Check out Clipfinder's Web site to see how this can be done (*www.daun.ch/software*).

3.   Click the Setup room tab. Check the Project Settings tab, and you'll notice there's one problem: The sequence is still at the medium proxy resolution size. In this example, the resolution is 1,024 x 576 for 16:9. Fix that by choosing the 4K 16:9 preset from the Resolution Presets menu (**Figure 10.19**).

Figure 10.19 Resetting the project resolution in the Setup room.

That's the workflow for migrating a proxy edit into Color and maintaining the connection to the original RED metadata. It's not the most stable approach, but it can get the job accomplished quickly if you need to do a fast color grade on the set. For more complex projects, stick with the transcode method or native-wrapped method. They require more time for ingesting footage, but you'll be rewarded with a more stable workflow and quicker editing performance.

As you've learned in this chapter, Final Cut Pro offers several methods of working with RED footage. It's crucial that you test each workflow with your system before selecting one. The transcode to ProRes workflow gives you the best performance within Final Cut Pro, but it requires you to do some careful work to get to a native color correction. The native-wrapped workflow gives you the easiest path to RAW color correction in Color, but it requires higher system specifications for optimal performance in Final Cut Pro. The proxy workflow allows you to start cutting immediately, but it requires a fair amount of diligence to get the maximum benefits in Color and is not recommended because of potential instability. For more guidance, download the latest RED workflow guide for Final Cut Studio from www.red.com/support.

Evin Grant

DIRECTOR OF PHOTOGRAPHY, 4K NINJAS

Evin Grant shooting with RED in the New Mexico desert. (Photo by Kiana Grant.)

I met director of photography and stills photographer Evin Grant several years ago when we were both testing the new Panasonic DVX100 camera. As the first prosumer 24p DV camera, we realized this was the turning point in what we as indie filmmaker-types could achieve. We'd no longer need to rent high-end HD or film cameras to get that elusive cinematic look. When the RED came along, Grant procured camera serial number 199. He later cofounded the 4K Ninjas, a Los Angeles–based group of RED owner/operators and workflow specialists (including Brook Willard, whose POV interview you'll also find in this book). In addition to rentals and technician services, 4K Ninjas offers the Road Grader, a Scratch Cine and Final Cut Studio suite rolled into a minivan, for intensive on-location color-correction work. The group has supported hundreds of projects ranging from music videos to commercials to short films and features. Their clients have included Jaguar, Toyota, Nike, Microsoft, and Leonard Cohen.

Grant explains the idea behind 4K Ninjas. "We're all 'Ronin' as it were [hired samurai in feudal Japan]—each independent but functioning as a group to spread the workload and projects around," he says. "This gives us a brand identity in the community as next-generation camera support. Our service is partially rentals and is partially technicians. We don't assume that any job has any more or less need. We have six camera ninjas (four of us own cameras) and one for post. We kind of come in and handle the jobs that best suit our talent on a per-job basis."

Grant offers his current workflow (as of this writing), noting with a grin, "As of two days ago, I shoot at 4K HD in REDCODE 36. After production, I offline edit in Final Cut Pro with the H QuickTime proxies (of course, you have to have a fast enough computer for that). I get high-quality 1080p playback using a BlackMagic Design DeckLink Extreme. When I'm done cutting, I'll duplicate the sequence and pull out all of the time changes and other sorts of effects to simplify the timeline. I export to Crimson Workflow and then go through REDCINE, where I can do a pretty good basic primary color correction. If it's something that needs a true secondaries grade, I'll export to DPX and go to Color. But most projects don't have the time or energy to do that."

While on set, Grant keeps one eye on the camera operations and another on constantly downloading footage. "You have to know your timing well," he observes. "I never let RED-DRIVEs go below 80 percent free because the transfer will start to slow down shooting. I'll always do a double-simultaneous backup to G-Tech drives and LaCies. The work is equal parts IT, data wrangler, and camera technician."

When asked what his greatest challenge has been with RED, Grant is quick to respond. "It's postproduction," he says. "Post isn't so much a technical problem as it is an informational one. When I talk to producers, I talk in simple terms: round holes and square pegs, with the pegs being RED footage. The director of photography wants to shoot high end, but the production can't afford to shoot with a Viper or Sony F23 and a more accepted workflow. Then there's an editor who is very comfortable on his Avid machine and a post house that doesn't understand that it's not uncompressed 4K, but they want to charge for 4K uncompressed storage anyway. You can see how it can become an ugly, gnarled hole. So, I come in and help sort all of that out."

Another area of concern for Grant is potential infrared (IR) contamination (which you can read more about in the "Filters" section of Chapter 4). "You have to think of regular neutral-density (ND) filters as IR pass filters," Grant advises. "Most normal ND filters block visible light instead of IR. Once you get to a .9 ND, light rays shift into a visible cyan color as you get IR contamination. At a 1.5 or 1.8 ND, it can be a visible difference as fabrics and polyesters will take on a magenta hue. This isn't specific to the RED, as all CMOS-based cameras are susceptible. To counter this, I use Formatts, which are ND filters combined with a hot mirror filter. They reflect the visible and IR light in the same amount. You can also try hot mirror filters combined with ND filters and then a polarizer, but in some lighting situations, that can produce triple and double reflections. So, you have to experiment as there really isn't one solution."

Grant expresses satisfaction with the 4K Ninjas' technical achievements while noting that knowledge is still the most important part of the job. "The hardest part for producers is getting past the preconceived notion that RED is an upstart kid," he says. "Surprisingly, some people are really into the camera for its size. It's not like a little EX1 or HVX200 that they wouldn't want on a big-budget commercial spot, but it's also not a behemoth like the Panavision Genesis or the Sony F23. Once you've mounted the body with a lens, follow-focus, batteries, and RED-DRIVE, you're back up to the size of a Panavision Panaflex Gold 35mm camera from the mid-'80s. Many of the individual qualities can be argued plus or minus, but RED knocked it out of the park with the EVF and the LCD for weight and build quality. For a professional director of photography, the operating experience is at least as important as the final quality of the image."

Evin Grant's Web sites are www.evingrant.com and www.4kninjas.net. ∎

11 ADOBE PREMIERE PRO WORKFLOW

As mentioned in Chapter 8, Adobe Premiere Pro is the only one of the three editing applications covered in this book to support a truly native RED workflow. What that means is that you can drag and drop R3D files from your hard drive directly onto a sequence in Premiere Pro without having to transcode to another format first or work with proxies. This has distinct advantages both in the reduced amount of time you have to wait to start editing and in the flexibility you have with outputting a completed edit. Let's get started with Premiere Pro.

Setting Up Your System

Because you'll be decoding R3D files on the fly as you edit, the Premier Pro workflow demands a bit more out of your system than Avid or Apple Final Cut Pro do. The more RAM, processor speed, and fast hard drives you can throw at Premiere Pro, the better performance you'll achieve. That said, you can also change the working resolution to suit a more modest system's power (more on that later in this chapter).

Adobe recommends Mac OS X or Windows Vista 64 for the best performance, along with a minimum of 4 GB of RAM (with a maximum of 32 GB for effects-intensive work). A fast laptop is capable of running the RED native workflow, but I recommend a high-end desktop machine for the ultimate performance. You need to have at least Adobe Premiere Pro CS4 and the latest REDCODE CS4 installer from www.red.com/support.

The Premiere Pro workflow is equivalent on Mac and Windows. In the following examples, I'm working with a Mac version of Premiere Pro, but the workflow is identical on Windows. The primary difference is the operating system's appearance and that you use the Control key in Windows instead of the Command (aka, Apple) key.

Figure 11.1 Selecting the 1080p/16:9, 23.98 RED sequence preset from the New Sequence dialog box.

When working natively, how you set your initial project sequence settings is not that critical. You can, for example, start with a 4K project timeline and start cutting away. Later, if you decide to work at HD resolution, all you need to do is make a new sequence in HD and drop the R3D files onto it. No matter which resolution you work in, the R3D files are automatically scaled to fit. You never need to reimport footage once you have it loaded into your project.

For a demonstration in the sections that follow, I'll start a new project and work in a 1080p sequence. But everything I'm doing would be the same in a 2K, 3K, or 4K sequence. The most important part is making sure your sequence's frame rate and aspect ratio match what you shot so you can avoid having to render shots to fit. In this case, my original footage was shot in 4K/16:9 at 23.98. To begin working with RED footage in Premiere Pro, choose File > New > New Sequence and choose a RED preset of 1080p in 16:9 and 23.98 (**Figure 11.1**).

Ingesting Footage

You can ingest R3D clips directly into Premiere Pro in one of two ways. In the first method, open the Media Browser and then point to your RED RDM directory (**Figure 11.2**). Select all of your R3D files, Control-click (right-click), and choose Import. Alternatively, you can search for R3D files on your hard drive and drag them directly into your Project window.

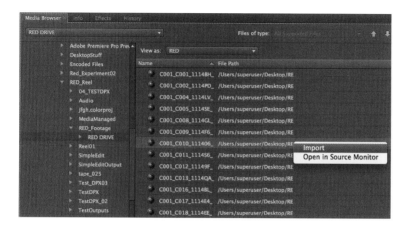

Figure 11.2 Using the Adobe Premiere Pro Media Browser to load RED R3D files.

Figure 11.3 R3D files imported into a bin in the Project window.

Dragging the files directly into your Project window works better if you have a lot of clips in different folders that aren't in the same directories the camera put them in. You can control exactly what goes into the project, and when dragging it doesn't matter as much if there is a complete RDM structure. To simplify this method, navigate to your footage folder and do a search for R3D files. Drag the search results into a bin of the Project window, and you'll be all set (**Figure 11.3**).

Editing in Premiere Pro

To work with RED files in a sequence, you do exactly what you're used to doing with other media formats in Premiere Pro. You can either double-click a clip in your Project window to load it into the Source window or drag an R3D file directly onto your Timeline.

You will, however, need to do a little bit of specific system tuning for optimal performance:

1. Click Play in the Source window. You will probably see things moving very slowly because the default R3D playback resolution is Full.

2. Control-click (right-click) anywhere in the Source window, and select Resolution from the pop-up menu.

   You can now choose the playback resolution (**Figure 11.4**). I get pretty good performance with the Quarter Resolution setting on my eight-core 3 GHz machine with internal SATA drives and 4 GB of RAM, which I consider a moderate system.

Figure 11.4 Selecting RED playback resolution for the sequence.

TIP   When you set the resolution, it's only for playback. The actual project and source footage resolution retains its original quality. Experiment with different playback resolutions and project resolutions to determine the best mix of performance and viewing quality on your system. Remember, even Quarter Resolution is still higher than standard definition and should be more than enough quality for editing.

Once the working resolution is properly tuned, you can edit normally (**Figure 11.5**). The goal of the Premiere Pro workflow is to make editing R3D as simple as editing DV. You can also drop other footage formats and resolutions into the same sequence with RED footage, and they will be converted to match the sequence settings in real time. The playback performance of mixed edits will depend on your system specifications.

Figure 11.5 Working with RED footage in an Adobe Premiere Pro sequence.

NOTE   The Resolution settings for the Source and Program windows are independent of each other. So if you find a setting you like in one window, be sure to match it in the other for consistency.

Regarding the visual quality of R3D shots, with Premiere Pro CS 4.1 and newer, you have direct access to most of the RED native format controls in your Project window. To make changes to a clip, select it in the Project window, Control-click (right-click), and choose Source Settings from the clip's pop-up menu. You'll now have access to many of the RED R3D meta-data settings, such as the color temperature, exposure, ISO, color space, gamma space, and decoding quality (**Figure 11.6**).

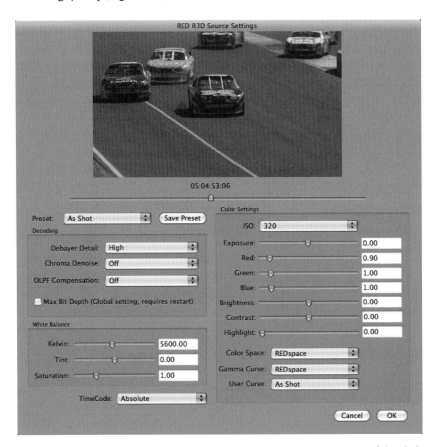

Figure 11.6 The RED R3D Source Settings window gives you access to many of the clip's native metadata controls.

Within the Source Settings window, you can also apply a preset look. This can be a look you save using the Save Preset button, the default settings, or the original settings used on the camera when the clip was shot. Having full access to the source settings within Premiere Pro means you can do a significant level of color correction as you edit.

TIP To access the source settings from a clip in your edit sequence, Control-click (right-click) the clip, and select Reveal in Project from the pop-up window. The original clip is then highlighted in the Project menu, and you can access its source settings there.

Exporting Your Project

When you've completed your edit, you can export your project to a variety of different file sizes and formats. To start the process follow these steps:

1. Highlight the sequence you want to export.

2. Choose File > Export > Media. This opens the Export Settings window.

   In this example, I'm exporting to an HD QuickTime file at 1920 x 1080, 23.98 (**Figure 11.7**). Since the edit uses the 4K R3D files as its source, you can just as easily export a DPX image sequence at 2K or 4K or a QuickTime file at standard definition, 2K, or 4K.

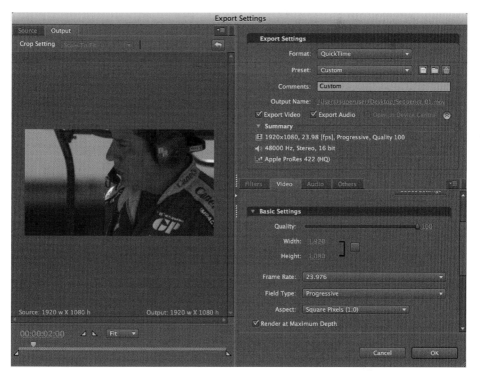

Figure 11.7 The Export Settings window set for a 1920 x 1080 23.98 ProRes HQ QuickTime format export.

3. Click OK; the Adobe Media Encoder application automatically launches (**Figure 11.8**).

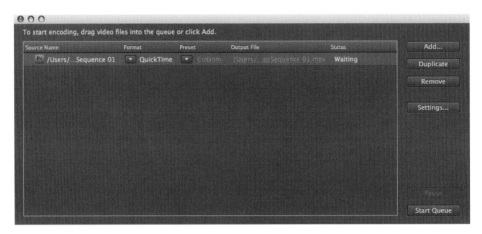

Figure 11.8   Adobe Media Encoder handles the output of your RED project to any desired format.

4. Confirm the filename and destination settings and then click the Start Queue button. Your sequence starts rendering and appears wherever you set the destination as soon as it's complete. You may find that the encoding times vary quite a bit, depending on how large you make the export and how long the original sequence is.

TIP   Adobe Media Encoder can take a little while to load up the first time you invoke it from Premiere Pro. So, I recommend leaving it running after your first export to speed up subsequent sequence outputs.

ADOBE AFTER EFFECTS

If you want to do additional effects or compositing work while in the native RED workflow, you can open your Premiere Pro project in Adobe After Effects. Start After Effects, and choose File > Adobe Dynamic Link > Import Premiere Pro Sequence. Navigate to your Premiere Pro project and choose the sequence you want to import. Place the imported sequence into a composition (**Figure 11.9**). It will match the sequence in Premiere Pro, including all transitions and effects.

Figure 11.9 Premiere Pro Sequence loaded into After Effects.

BLU-RAY

In After Effects, you can also export to a Blu-ray high-definition disc. Follow these steps to do this:

1. Start with a composition open in After Effects, and then choose Composition > Add to Render Queue.

2. Once the Render Queue appears, click the Output Module button for the settings.

3. Click the Format button and choose MPEG2 Blu-ray from the Format list of options.

4. In the MPEG2 Blu-ray dialog that appears (**Figure 11.10**), you can choose 720p or 1080p resolution as well as pick the compression quality and frame rate settings. Click OK to finish the export.

   Once you export the MPEG2, you can use the Adobe Encore application, available as part of Adobe Creative Suite Production Premium and Adobe Creative Suite Master Collection (which also includes After Effects).

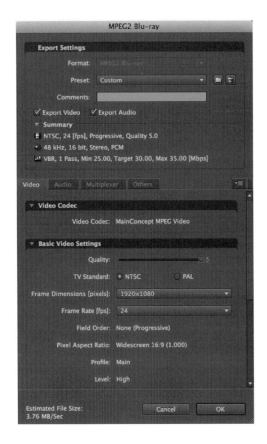

Figure 11.10 Exporting an MPEG2 for a Blu-ray high-definition disc in After Effects.

You can also export to an H.264 Blu-ray format from Premiere Pro, which gives you higher image quality. To do this, follow these steps:

1. In Premiere Pro, Choose File > Export > Media to send your project to the Export Settings window.

2. Click the Format button, and choose the H.264 Blu-ray preset from the Format list of options. Then you have the option to make 720p or 1080p Blu-ray files.

3. Once the media has been encoded, bring it into Encore for the Blu-ray authoring.

That completes this look at the Premiere Pro native workflow. Adobe has worked closely with RED to make its software as user-friendly with the camera's footage as possible. To learn of new changes to the Premiere Pro workflow, visit the RED support area at www.red.com/support and Adobe's support area at www.adobe.com/products/premiere.

12 AVID WORKFLOW

Using an Avid system for your RED projects involves a two-step process that combines transcoding and native workflows. You begin by editing a project in Avid Media Composer, using footage transcoded by Avid's MetaFuze utility from R3D to DNxHD-formatted MXF files. (DNxHD is Avid's native video codec, optimized for all of its applications, and Material Exchange Format [MXF] is Media Composer's native editing file format.) You then complete final color correction natively with R3D files using Avid DS. It may sound a little complex at first, but if you have some familiarity with the Avid system, this is a similar workflow to film or HD online finishing. Avid has worked hard to adapt the RED workflow to its software, rather than the other way around.

Setting Up Your System

The Apple Final Cut Pro and Adobe Premiere Pro workflows function well on the Mac platform, but for Avid I recommend going with a Windows machine. Media Composer is cross-platform, but MetaFuze and DS, which are central to the process, are Windows-only. You can run them in Windows virtualization on a Mac via Boot Camp or VMware's Fusion (www.vmware.com), but you'll face potential performance and disk-formatting issues. If you've ever exchanged media projects between Mac and Windows, you know this can be a real pain.

> NOTE   Although this book focuses on Avid Media Composer for editing, the Avid Symphony editing suite is also capable of utilizing RED DNxHD transcoded footage from MetaFuze.

> TIP   One way around the MetaFuze requirement, if you're on a Mac, is to use RED's REDCINE application to derive your transcoded files for editing. This steps outside of Avid's product line a bit, but it can make all the difference in successfully completing a Mac-only RED project. For demonstration purposes, this chapter uses MetaFuze, but the methodology is essentially the same once you complete the conversion of R3D to DNxHD. It's just a different application doing the actual transcoding.

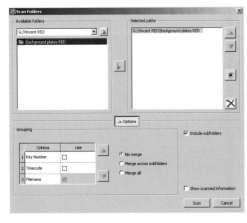

Figure 12.1 MetaFuze set up to scan a directory for R3D files.

Ingesting Footage

To begin a project, first organize your RED media files under a single main project folder. This is not essential—and may not even be practical if you have a huge project or if you're ingesting footage on a daily basis—but it will make your work go faster. You can rerun the MetaFuze transcoding process as needed while you continue to edit. For each directory, simply point Meta-Fuze to the top level containing your RDM folders, and it will scan for all available R3D files (**Figure 12.1**).

(Make sure to include subfolders in the scan.) You can also choose the destination media folder for completed transcodes.

Once the R3D files are all loaded, you can set the transcoding format options and which level of DNxHD compression you want to use (**Figure 12.2**). The higher the number after DNx, the better the image quality. DNx 36 is suitable for offline editing with minimum hard drive space requirements. DNx 175 is of sufficient visual quality to potentially be usable as a finishing format. You'll want to evaluate for yourself whether the image quality is truly acceptable for online at 175 or whether you want to continue into an R3D native finish in DS. For example, the postproduction team on *ER* determined that DNx 175 wasn't working for certain shots, so they re-exported to DPX files for their final color correction outputs (though at the time they were using a version of DNx 175 that had not been fully optimized for the RED).

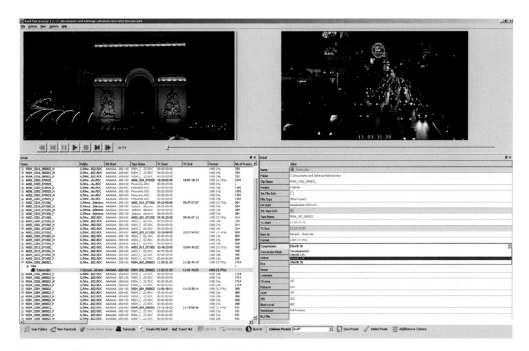

Figure 12.2 Choosing transcoding options in MetaFuze.

In addition to standard formatting options, RED-specific transcoding options in MetaFuze can help determine the visual quality of your transcoded files (**Figure 12.3**). You can adjust the debayer quality, ISO, optical low-pass filter (OLPF) compensation (which helps determine the transcoded image's sharpness), and decoding resolution (full, half, quarter, or eighth).

Each of these selections determines how the resulting transcodes look, but the higher the quality, the longer the transcodes will take. Experiment to determine the best trade-off of time versus quality for your own process. If you've done any preliminary color correction in RED Alert!, you can also import the resulting RLX file and apply it to the transcode.

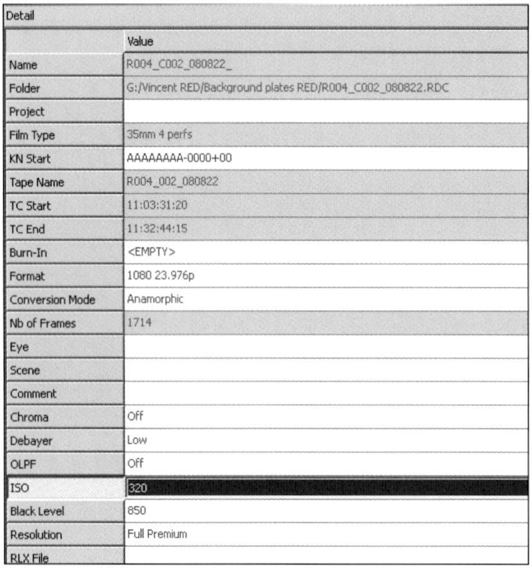

Detail	
	Value
Name	R004_C002_080822_
Folder	G:/Vincent RED/Background plates RED/R004_C002_080822.RDC
Project	
Film Type	35mm 4 perfs
KN Start	AAAAAAAA-0000+00
Tape Name	R004_002_080822
TC Start	11:03:31:20
TC End	11:32:44:15
Burn-In	<EMPTY>
Format	1080 23.976p
Conversion Mode	Anamorphic
Nb of Frames	1714
Eye	
Scene	
Comment	
Chroma	Off
Debayer	Low
OLPF	Off
ISO	320
Black Level	850
Resolution	Full Premium
RLX File	

Figure 12.3 Choosing RED-specific image quality options in MetaFuze.

TIP   Once you've found a favorite combination of settings for a project, you can save a preset by clicking the Save Preset button on the lower-right side of the MetaFuze application window.

An option that will be familiar to Avid veterans is the ability to set a timecode burn-in, which appears as visible metadata directly overlaid onto the transcoded footage (**Figure 12.4** and **Figure 12.5**). Burn-ins can be very helpful to verify timecode across departments, help assure audio sync, and give precise frame counts to visual effects and animation crews. In addition to standard edge code and time-of-day timecode, you can also burn in a wide variety of other metadata from the original R3D files, such as ISO, debayer mode, camera clip name, and so on.

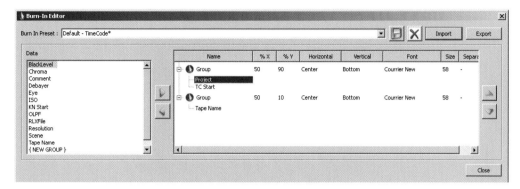

Figure 12.4   Setting the burn-in options in MetaFuze.

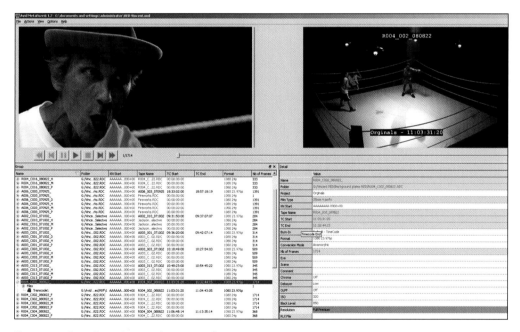

Figure 12.5   Burn-in option results on RED footage in MetaFuze.

NOTE   Because MetaFuze outputs R3D files to HD-resolution files, the gamma space is always REC 709. Keep this in mind if you've been monitoring your camera footage with a different gamma profile, such as REDspace, so you're not surprised if your footage looks different in editing.

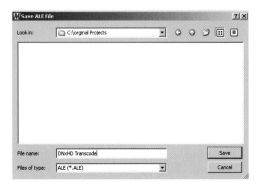

Figure 12.6 Saving an ALE file out of MetaFuze.

Once you've set everything the way you want, click the Transcode button at the bottom of the MetaFuze window and wait. The files will be transcoded and will begin appearing in the destination media folder. When the process is complete, the final step in MetaFuze is to create an Avid Log Exchange (ALE) file. This file is a record of all the files you transcoded in this session, along with their settings, and will assist the import process in Media Composer. To create the ALE file, click the Export ALE button at the bottom of the application window, and save the file with the name of your project (**Figure 12.6**).

Editing in Avid Media Composer

The next phase is editing with Media Composer. As I mentioned at the start of this chapter, Avid's approach calls for doing creative editing work in Media Composer, with final color correction and high-quality format output in Avid DS. The image quality in Media Composer can be very high, depending on the DNxHD compression settings you chose in MetaFuze. But keep in mind that footage will look even better once you get to the last steps in DS, working directly from the R3D files. (Finishing from the R3D files should be considered essential for film outputs and 2K or higher, while HD and SD work can be finished in Media Composer from DNx 175 files.)

To begin editing your RED footage in Avid Media Composer, create a new project in Media Composer using the same frame rate of the R3D files (such as 23.98 or 25) and the resolution of the MetaFuze DNxHD transcodes (typically 720p or 1080p). Then follow these steps:

1. Start Media Composer. The Select Project dialog opens.
2. Click New Project and enter the name of your project.
3. Click the Format menu, and then pick your footage frame rate and DNxHD footage resolution. Then click OK. Your new project opens.

4. Next, import the ALE file you created in MetaFuze by choosing File > Import (**Figure 12.7**). Then choose your ALE file and click OK, which should bring in all of the associated transcoded media (**Figure 12.8**).

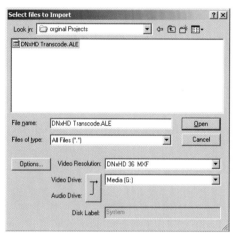

Figure 12.7 Launching the Import dialog in Media Composer.

Figure 12.8 Importing the MetaFuze-created ALE file into Media Composer.

5. If any media doesn't come across, launch the Avid Media tool by choosing Tools > Media Tool, and manually drag the transcodes into a bin.

Once you have all of your DNxHD transcoded footage loaded properly into Media Composer, you can edit as you would any high-definition project (**Figure 12.9**). One consideration is where you intend to finish. The nice aspect of finishing in Avid DS is that it's a very simple process to get from a Media Composer edit; additionally, all the filters and effects you apply in Media Composer are automatically translated into your DS project. I will assume that's your intended workflow as this chapter continues.

When you have completed your editing work in Media Composer and are ready to move onto finishing in DS, you need to export an Avid File Exchange (AFE) file. AFE is a special format designed to facilitate project sharing between Avid applications. To create the AFE file, simply select the current sequence, and choose File > Export (**Figure 12.10**). Select AFE as the Export setting, and click the Save button.

Figure 12.9 Working with RED-originated DNxHD files in a Media Composer project.

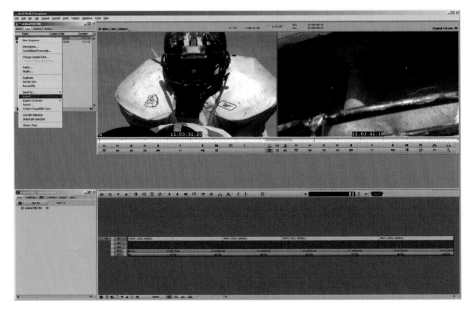

Figure 12.10 Exporting an AFE file from Media Composer.

Conforming in Avid DS

Conforming is the process of taking the offline edit you made in Media Composer and cor-relating it to the original R3D files using Avid DS. This gives you the maximum possible image quality and resolution to derive your final outputs such as HD and film. To begin the conform process in Avid DS, follow these steps:

1. Create a new project. Make sure to match the resolution, aspect ratio, and frame rate of your original R3D files (not your Media Composer edit). You'll find presets for all the available RED formats under the Film settings in DS. In **Figure 12.11**, I'm setting up to conform a project shot at 2K 16:9 and 24p (23.98) using the Video Settings section of the New Project dialog.

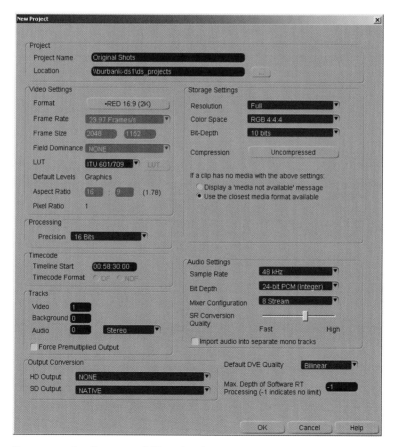

Figure 12.11 Creating a new RED project in DS.

TIP   DS will only import R3D footage when using an AFE file to conform a Media Composer RED project, so make sure no other formats (such as DPX) are part of your sequence edit. DS will ignore those formats.

2.   Next, choose File > Open and load the AFE file. You'll notice it contains not just your sequence but all the media used in the Media Composer project (**Figure 12.12**).

Figure 12.12   Opening an AFE file in DS.

3.   Select the sequence you want to conform (**Figure 12.13**). Select the Create Associated Clips, Create Linked Clips for Files Sources, and Use Alternate Video Sources check boxes. Then click the Configure button.

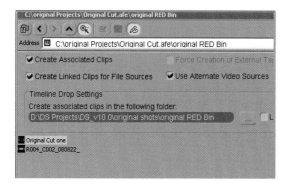

Figure 12.13 Selecting the Media Composer sequence to conform in DS.

4. In the Choose Alternate Video Sources dialog that launches, select the top-level folder containing your R3D camera originals (**Figure 12.14**). Make sure no other formats (such as DPX) are in here.

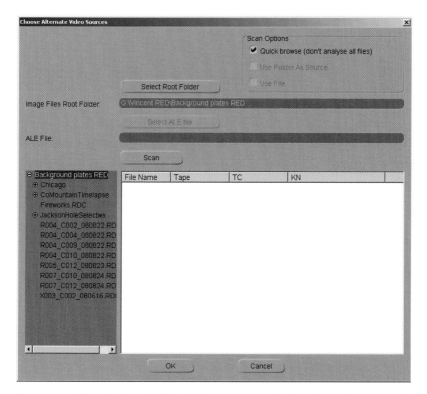

Figure 12.14 Choosing the R3D files to bring into DS with the Choose Alternate Video Sources window.

5. Confirm that all the directories and clips you expect appear in the window, and click OK.

   The Color Management window launches (**Figure 12.15**). You'll find these controls familiar if you've worked with RED applications such as RED Alert! Since DS uses the SDK from RED, many of the options here are identical.

6. Within the Color Management window, you can access the R3D files directly and choose important options such as your gamma and color space, extensive color and exposure controls, and debayer method. You can also load RLX files from RED Alert! if you want to reuse color corrections you made before starting postproduction. (You can always return to this window on a shot-by-shot basis from within DS by right-clicking a clip in the Timeline and selecting the Properties option.)

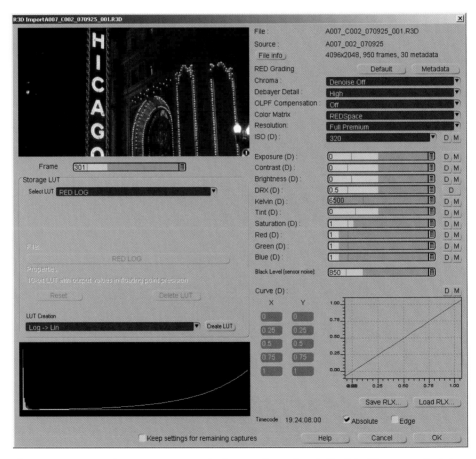

Figure 12.15 You can select gamma space and color correction options in the Color Management window.

7. Once you set the Color Management options, drag the sequence directly into the Timeline. It should now be a complete conform of your Media Composer offline edit pointing to the full-resolution, native R3D files (**Figure 12.16**).

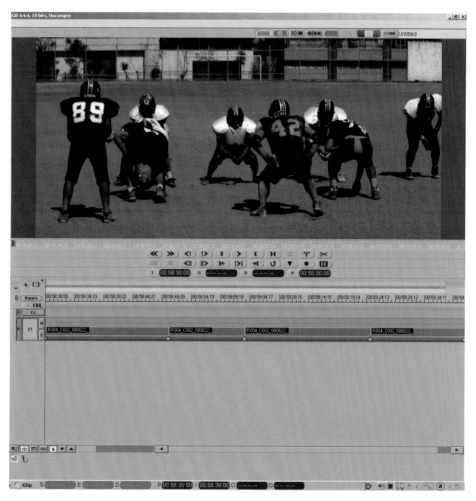

Figure 12.16   A conformed Timeline in Avid DS.

Now that you have a conformed project in Avid DS referencing the native R3D files, your options are wide open. You can easily create an HD or SD down-conversion to a variety of formats, either compressed with the codec of your choice or uncompressed. You can also export to DPX image sequence files if, for example, your final destination is a film print.

To create a DPX output, follow these steps:

1. Select the sequence and then choose View > Single Instance View > Output Tool. The Output Tool opens (**Figure 12.17**).

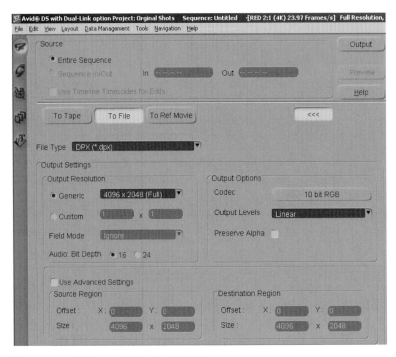

Figure 12.17 Setting up DPX output in DS.

2. Click the To File button.

3. Next choose your output format options. In this example I've chosen to output Entire Sequence as my Source to DPX. I've also chosen 4096 x 2048 for a full 4K output resolution.

You can also create a custom color lookup table (LUT) to go with your DPX files (**Figure 12.18**). This is a key step because you can load LUTs in most color correction suites (such as a da Vinci), and it will go a long way in assuring that the look of footage you're seeing in DS is the same as in the color correction suite.

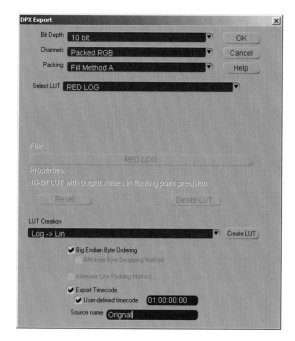

Figure 12.18 Creating a custom LUT for DPX files in DS.

TIP The export process is the same for outputting your project to HD or SD—just choose the desired resolution and file format in place of DPX and 2K.

Avid's approach has evolved significantly since the RED camera first came out and may have changed even more by the time you read this chapter. For the latest techniques and updates, visit the book's companion Web site at www.peachpit.com/red or Avid's RED support page at www.avid.com/RED.

Michael Phillips

PRINCIPAL PRODUCT DESIGNER, AVID TECHNOLOGY

Michael Phillips working with RED on a project he produced and edited. (Photo by Howard A. Phillips.)

As principal product designer for nonlinear editing pioneer Avid, Michael Phillips has observed multiple digital revolutions in the movie business. One revolution happened in 1992 when Avid (www.avid.com) introduced Film Composer, the first native 24 fps digital nonlinear editing platform, enabling moviemakers to edit projects on a computer rather than directly slicing pieces of film. Over the years, Avid's software has evolved to support many different cameras and resolutions from standard-definition videotape all the way up to 2K/4K file-based finishing and beyond. With the RED ONE, Phillips is watching another digital revolution change the movie world.

Avid's interest in RED began as soon as the camera was unveiled in April 2006. "We saw the camera at NAB when it first came out," recalls Phillips. "Within three months we visited RED at their offices at Oakley and said, 'Whenever you have something available to test, please let us know.' They went through many development phases, which took about a year. Then it became a real workflow solution project for us, learning what the camera could do."

While analyzing the camera and its file-based methodology, Phillips took note of how working methods were evolving over time. "It's interesting to see how much postproduction is moving onto the set," he notes. "As a camera operator, assistant, or DIT, you need to be aware of post more than ever. It's not as easy as the good old days when you handed over a roll of film or a tape and said good-bye. There's a real convergence of post and camera coming to a head right now. RED is leading the charge on that because of its immediate accessibility.

"Anything that's a disruptive technology is very interesting to watch," Phillips adds. "When Film Composer came out in 1992 as a true 24-frame digital editing system, you saw a very quick adoption rate. Panasonic's DVX100 was another disruptive technology. As the first 24p DV camera, it was outselling every other DV camera at the time 10 to 1 in the filmmaking market. RED has a fantastic marketing strategy that keeps interest at an all-time high. They also maintain good customer interactions, with Jim Jannard directly engaging customers on REDuser (www.reduser.net). You couldn't do all of that as a public company, but a private company has that ability."

Avid uses RED's software development kit (SDK) to be able to read RED's native R3D files and access their metadata in order to facilitate ingest into its products like Avid DS and Avid Media Composer. A special Avid-designed utility called Avid MetaFuze handles the conversion from R3D to Avid's MXF-wrapped DNxHD codec.

"I don't think it's necessary to be able to transcode back to R3D right now," Phillips says. "At some point they will need some sort of encoder, especially when they release the RED-RAY [RED's proposed player device for R3D files encoded on disc]. It will also help in other places to do native R3D encoding. If you look at Adobe doing native, unless you're doing a bunch of straight cuts, you're going to have to render at some point, whether it's color correction or effects. That's going to be some other format that isn't R3D. You can't stay fully native throughout the production process."

Phillips continues, "The workflow doesn't lend itself to native all the time either. The bonding company wants to know where those R3D files are going and who really owns them. The turnaround deliverables on a production also remain the same, regardless of the acquisition format. On TV and features, the next morning after a shoot, they want to start editing and need viewing DVDs and H.264s for producers to review on a Web site. People are looking for pipelines that allow them to maintain all those expectations."

Turning to the world of independent production, Phillips observes that time is often more available than money. "There's still going to be a performance benefit to transcoding to DNxHD or ProRes, and if it takes you an extra day, that's what you'll do," he says. "Editors have a certain expectation as to what they can do in real time, like eight streams of DNx36 on multicam shows, and so on. I don't think you'll get that with native RAW files for a while because the decoding is a computationally expensive process."

For Phillips, the question is whether the transcoding will be done by the editors themselves or farmed out to post-production facilities. "The issue is scaling for many different deliverables versus one tape," he observes. "If you have one system that can churn out dailies at something less than real time and you have just one project, you can turn it around within 24 hours. But if you have 20 projects, that's a different story. Solutions like ASSIMILATE's SCRATCH CINE or Baselight Transfer (BLT) become interesting because they can play RED footage in real time with color correction. Then one post room can handle multiple projects in a more streamlined manner. That's where you have to decide whether you're going to do a tape-based workflow or a transcode/file workflow. In the end you're still getting the same edit from the same media—it's just how fast you get it that's driving decisions."

Asked about Avid's long-term goals for working with cameras like RED, Phillips envisions a further expansion of support. "There are lots of cameras out there, and RED is certainly a priority right now," he says. "But what's even more important is the infrastructure we're putting in place to allow camera manufacturers to come into the Avid world themselves. We want to place an open, native wrapper around incoming camera formats that goes directly into the editorial environment without Avid adding support directly for every model. AMA (Avid Media Access) was released with version 3.5 of Media Composer. That initiative's acceptance is based on priorities and engineering resources at each company."

As someone who's seen many new technologies alter the movie industry, Phillips expects a continued evolution for the foreseeable future. "It's just human nature that bigger and better formats mean bigger and better quality," he says. "Now all the tent-pole directors like Spielberg want to shoot IMAX for certain scenes because *The Dark Knight* did it. IMAX looks better, and it's a creative challenge for them. You'll see that in file-based cameras that will go to 2K, 4K, 6K, 8K, and just on and on. You'll probably always be editing with a proxy while the CPUs catch up to the playback speed of newer formats. We're all just chasing the technology."

Avid's Web site is www.avid.com.   ∎

13 FINISHING YOUR PROJECT

With luck you've made it through the rigors of RED production and editing. All your creative work is complete except for two last tasks: *color correction* (also called *grading* or *finishing*) and *outputting* your project. At this stage, you'll balance the colors and gamma of footage you shot on the RED ONE, set a creative look, and then export the footage to a distribution format. This could take the form of a standard-definition DVD, film print, Blu-ray disc, HD tape, or Internet file. (You'll likely export to several different formats.)

Because you started with 4K resolution footage, you can derive just about any common distribution format in very high quality. In this chapter, we'll look at methods for finishing RED projects on 35mm film, survey desktop color-correction tools—including Apple Color, ASSIMILATE SCRATCH, and IRIDAS SpeedGrade XR—and cover mastering to DVD, Blu-ray, and Web formats.

Film Workflow

If you're planning to finish a RED project onto 35mm film, you're probably working with a significant budget. I wouldn't advise printing a project to film unless you've already got theatrical distribution lined up. Without distribution, it's not too likely that you'll get a movie into wide release in cinemas, with all the big studio content crowding theaters these days. Also, film festivals are happy to project projects from tape. Digital projection from a high-definition tape format such as HDCAM or even a standard-definition format like DigiBeta is more than acceptable to festival judges and audiences. You won't need a film print unless someone who's willing to pay for it asks for one.

Figure 13.1 An ARRILASER 2 film recorder outputs digital files to film one frame at a time.

If you need to make a film print from your RED project, the bulk of the work will be handled by a lab, because to date there are no viable options for affordable desktop film printing. You'll work with a postproduction facility that has the ability to record digital files onto film (**Figure 13.1**). To get a project ready for a film output, you need to go one of two routes: (1) turn over your edit and source media to a full-service postproduction facility and have them derive all of the necessary digital files to make a film print, or (2) deliver camera-ready digital files of your project, usually as DPX or Cineon files, to a facility with a film recorder.

For the first workflow, the most important consideration is careful coordination with your chosen post facility. Find one that has experience finishing RED projects on film, such as Plaster-CITY in Los Angeles or Technicolor in New York. They will need all of your original R3D files and an XML or EDL output of your final edit, which you'll deliver on one or more hard drives. (This is when all that organizational work discussed throughout this book is going to pay off.)

If you want to do a bit more of the creative work yourself, save a little money, and deliver files ready to be recorded to film, you'll use a desktop color-correction application that supports RED footage. We'll look at three such applications in this chapter. You may also want to be able to work with corrected image sequences formats such as DPX files in your editing application. Some editors support these formats directly, such as Adobe Premiere Pro and Avid DS; others require the use of a plugin. To load DPX and Cineon files into Apple Final Cut Pro, for example, you need the Glue Tools plugin (www.gluetools.com).

DIGITAL INTERMEDIATES

In film parlance, scanning 35mm film negative into a computer for color correction is known as a *digital intermediate*. This is compared to the old way of photochemically *timing* a negative. Because RED is already digital at the moment of acquisition, it's not technically a digital intermediate. But you can use the same color-correction tools intended for digital intermediates with RED footage. This includes the really top-end hardware systems such as da Vinci (www.davsys.com) and Pogle (www.pogle.pandora-int.com).

Desktop Color Correction

Desktop color-correction software has brought high-quality grading out of the realm of $500-per-hour finishing suites. In this section, we'll take a look at Apple Color, ASSIMILATE SCRATCH, and IRIDAS SpeedGrade XR.

APPLE COLOR

Apple Color (www.apple.com/finalcutstudio/color) is one of the better bargains in desktop color correction (**Figure 13.2**). Once a $25,000 editing application called Final Touch, Apple acquired it in 2006 and bundled it as part of Final Cut Studio (now only $999). Color is not the easiest program to learn, but what you invest in learning, you gain tenfold in power. We're going to spend a lot more time going over the specific workflow with Color and Final Cut Pro in Chapter 10. Let's take a brief look at what's involved in working with the RED camera and Color.

Figure 13.2 You can run Color on one monitor but it is more effective across two.

If you're grading in Color, I recommend Final Cut Pro as your editing application. This is not a requirement, but the two applications are well integrated. You can move projects between them via Send To commands in their respective File menus. Otherwise, from most applications, you can use XML or EDL exports, but the import into Color can be a little more complex.

Color is capable of accessing RED metadata directly via the RED tab (**Figure 13.3**)—if it receives access to the original R3D files. To do this, you need to send an XML file or edit from Final Cut Pro referencing either proxy files or QuickTime-wrapped R3D files. If you work with transcoded ProRes QuickTime files in Final Cut Pro, you won't have access to the RED tab without relinking back to the original R3D files in Cinema Tools. We'll look at this in more detail in Chapter 10.

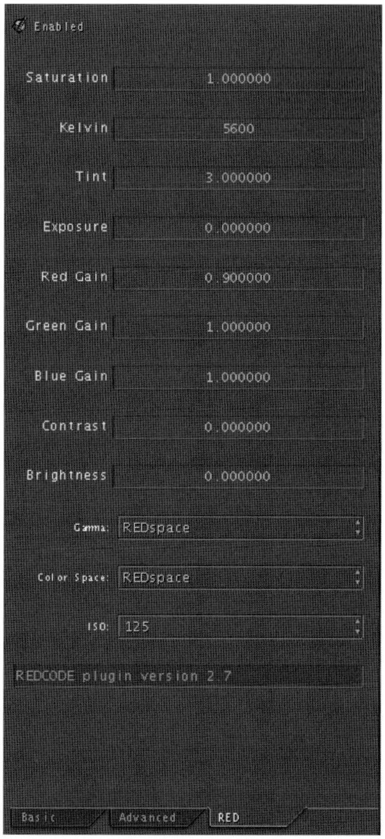

Figure 13.3 The RED tab in the Primary room of Color can access clip gamma and color space, exposure, ISO, color temperature, and other native R3D metadata.

WORKING WITH LUTS

Most color grading applications (such as those in this chapter) have the ability to import and output custom lookup tables (LUTs) for your project. A *LUT* is a special calibration file that profiles your display monitor to give you an accurate preview of your project as it will look when output to another medium, such as film. High-end film post houses can typically provide you with a LUT calibrated to their film recorder and the specific 35mm film stock you're using for the final output. This gives you a much higher degree of accuracy, and the resulting film print will be closer to your creative intentions.

ASSIMILATE SCRATCH

ASSIMILATE SCRATCH (www.assimilateinc.com) is a powerful, real-time color-grading application that has offered native support for R3D files since the early days of RED. The makers of
SCRATCH also developed REDCINE, so you may notice some shared DNA and user interface
components (**Figure 13.4**). While I recommend SCRATCH, it's important to understand that it
is an expensive solution, with a base price of $65,000. If you're grading projects every day or
planning to work as a color-correction service bureau, the expense is worthwhile.

Figure 13.4 Working with native RED R3D files in SCRATCH.

TIP ASSIMILATE also offers SCRATCH CINE, which restricts you to only RED-originated
footage, but includes much of SCRATCH'S grading power for a relatively more affordable $17,500.

SCRATCH is a Windows-only solution, so take that into consideration if you're working with an editing program on the Mac. The good news is that most SCRATCH setups come with integrated hardware, so you can treat a SCRATCH system as a dedicated workstation and send completed projects over Ethernet connections or hard drives. Just be aware of OS-specific requirements such as using a disc format that is compatible on both Mac and Windows, such as Window NT File System (NTFS).

> TIP To read and write to NTFS-formatted hard drives on the Mac OS, get the Paragon NTFS for Mac plugin (www.paragon-software.com/home/ntfs-mac).

The key to SCRATCH's power is scalability, meaning you gear the program up or down to best suit the power of your hardware. Because the application is capable of working with R3D files natively, there's never any reason to transcode to other codecs. You simply load in R3D files linked to an EDL of your final edit and then work in the resolution that offers you the best performance on your system. Once you've completed all of your color grading work, you export the final edit as DPX frames or whatever format is required for the final outputs. That output then becomes the final version of your project, and essentially you're done.

The lack of transcoding makes workflows with SCRATCH very simple. In fact, you don't even need to worry as much about keeping all of the original files and folders from the camera intact. The application doesn't require the RDM or RDC folders, nor the QuickTime proxies to function; only the R3Ds are necessary (although I recommend the habit of keeping everything organized).

Here are the basic steps:

1. In SCRATCH, load an EDL into a new CONstruct (timeline).

   You will be prompted for the location of R3D files. If any files conflict (for example, have the same name), an alert requests a resolution.

2. Once you have a project's footage loaded, SCRATCH gives you the option to select your working resolution. No matter what the viewing resolution is, you are always working from the full 4K RAW files as your source.

   The application is intelligent enough to automatically scale any work you do—such as color keying and SCAFFOLDs (masks)—within the frame as you change resolution (**Figure 13.5**).

Figure 13.5 Frame-specific effects such as SCAFFOLDs are automatically scaled as you switch resolutions in SCRATCH.

3. You'll also have access to all of the built-in color and gamma spaces that the camera is capable of shooting. That means you can quickly toggle back and forth between the settings you shot at (for example, REDSpace) and the finishing space (such as REC709 for high-definition output). Define your desired resolution, gamma, and color settings before outputting your project.

4. To output the project, open the PLAYER and play your footage out (for example, directly to HDCAM SR tape, as shown in **Figure 13.6**). Or you can use the PROCESS command from within PLAYER to output your shots to formats such as QuickTime and DPX.

Edit #	Reel	Shot Name	Effects	Source In	Source Out	Record In	Record Out	Match
1	A004	A004_C329_0902SU[3]	C	17:30:35:10	17:30:36:17	00:00:00:00	00:00:01:07	TRN 1
2	A004	A004_C244_0902J8[3]	C	09:02:20:00	09:02:21:02	00:00:01:07	00:00:02:09	TRN 2
3	A004	A004_C220_09017S[2]	C	16:32:54:02	16:32:55:04	00:00:02:09	00:00:03:11	TRN 1
4	A004	A004_C316_0902Q9[3]	C	16:01:39:06	16:01:42:17	00:00:03:11	00:00:06:22	TRN 1
5	A004	A004_C332_0902NR[4]	C	17:44:06:08	17:44:08:13	00:00:06:22	00:00:09:03	TRN 1
6	A004	A004_C266_0902AD[3]	C	10:07:43:14	10:07:47:19	00:00:09:03	00:00:13:08	TRN 1
7	A004	A004_C216_09013M[3]	C	15:08:23:20	15:08:28:02	00:00:13:08	00:00:17:14	TRN 1
8	A004	A004_C236_0901DT[4]	C	18:01:31:03	18:01:48:13	00:00:17:14	00:00:35:00	TRN 1

Figure 13.6 Assembling a project for output in SCRATCH.

Because all work is resolution independent, you'll find the SCRATCH workflow is simple and straightforward.

IRIDAS SPEEDGRADE XR

IRIDAS SpeedGrade XR (www.speedgrade.com/xr) offers real-time color correction of RED R3D files. The application also supports a number of other digital motion-picture camera RAW formats, such as ARRI D20, DALSA Origin, and Phantom HD. This can be advantageous if you need to support projects shot on a variety of cameras. IRIDAS's secret weapon is tapping into the graphics processing unit (GPU) of powerful computer graphics adapters to provide the real-time decoding of RAW formats for instant playback (**Figure 13.7**).

Figure 13.7 SpeedGrade XR can play and color-correct R3D files natively in real time.

NOTE   IRIDAS recommends working with high-powered Nehalem processors or better for ideal performance.

You can customize SpeedGrade XR to play back R3D files at the ideal combination of quality and performance, to tailor the software for your system. You do this through the Dynamic Quality panel, which gives you the option to set separate playback and paused resolution settings. This is great because most of the intensive detail work in color correction is done on single frames while moving frames are used to show how adjustments play out over the course of a shot. For example you could set the resolution to 1:2 quality for playback to get

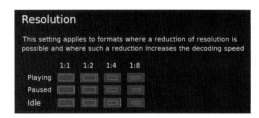

Figure 13.8 Choosing Play, Pause, and Idle resolutions in the Dynamic Quality panel.

responsive performance, then leave it at 1:1 quality when paused to see the best quality preview of the corrections you've made.

To adjust the Dynamic Quality settings in SpeedGrade XR, you can either press the S key or open the Dynamic Quality settings panel (**Figure 13.8**). You'll see choices for three different modes in this window: Playing, Paused, and Idle. Playing and Paused function as you'd expect while Idle is intended for the desired resolution when you have SpeedGrade running in the background. Idle mode can be useful if you're doing edits or effects work in another application and want to view your color-correction work as a reference.

The other important aspect of working with RED in SpeedGrade XR is the global R3D settings control (**Figure 13.9**). You have the option to either use each incoming clip with its original metadata or set a standard interpretation for all clips. This can be useful, for example, if you've shot everything at daylight color temperature and you want to view everything tungsten balanced, or if you want to apply a global change to the ISO settings. You can also select specific gamma and color space settings to override the camera metadata.

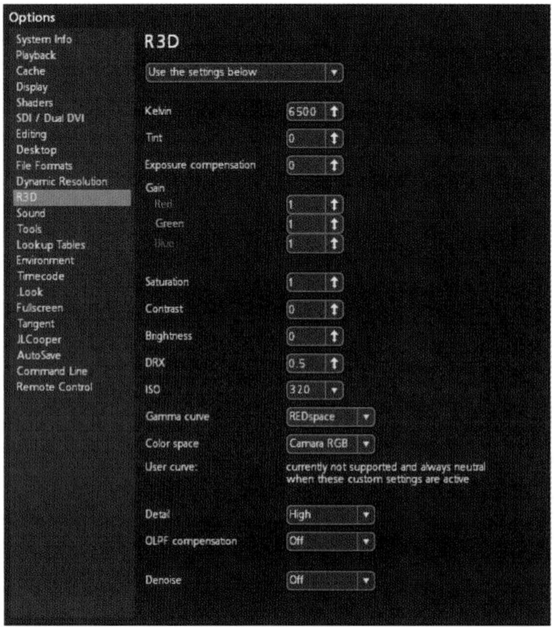

Figure 13.9 Choosing global metadata options with the R3D settings controls.

SpeedGrade XR is expensive ($19,999 for the software version, $45,399 for an integrated hardware solution), but the results and real-time feedback are worth the expense. SpeedGrade XR is available for Mac and Windows, giving you a bit more of a cross-platform option compared to other grading applications. Of course, when compared to million-dollar dedicated color-correction suites, all these desktop solutions are bargains.

REDCINE-X AND ROCKETCINE-X

As this book went to press, RED introduced two new applications designed to assist with desktop grading. ROCKETcine-X is a viewing/output tool designed specifically for the REDROCKET accelerator card (mentioned at the end of Chapter 8) for footage playback and transcodes; its predecessors are RED Alert! and REDrushes. REDCINE-X is a look development and grading tool optimized for REDROCKET (but not requiring it); its predecessor is REDCINE. With an intuitive, iPhoto-like browsing interface, each application offers a quick selection of R3D clips along with intensive color-correction and export options. By the time you read this, they should be available from RED and will make a powerful addition to your desktop color-correction toolset. Check this book's companion Web site at www.peachpit.com/red for updated information.

Outputting for Other Formats

Although the color-grading applications mentioned above are mostly geared to outputting in high definition and on film, they can also derive a RED master version for output to other possible destinations, such as standard-definition DVD and the Internet. The best way to get a good final output is to know from the start of a project which formats you want to deliver.

DVD

To make a nice 24p 16:9 DVD, I suggest you shoot in 4K HD or 4K 16:9 and then edit in HD (or higher) resolution. When you're finally done, you'll down-convert your entire work to standard-definition 24p, 16:9 (or 25p for PAL). Typically, it's a good idea to do the final down-conversion after color grading is complete. This way, you have a high-resolution master ready for other format outputs, and all your color grading is in higher precision than standard definition.

DVD STUDIO PRO

Companies such as Sonic and Roxio offer standalone applications for making DVDs, but most editing application bundles include integrated DVD authoring software. Apple Final Cut Studio comes with DVD Studio Pro, which can make standard-definition DVDs—but not Blu-ray discs (**Figure 13.10**). (You can, however, make simple Blu-ray discs directly from Final Cut Pro as of version 7—more on that in the "Sharing with other formats" section of Chapter 10.) DVD Studio Pro can also make HD-DVDs and record them onto regular DVD-R discs that play on HD-DVD players and Macs. But because HD-DVD is an abandoned format, you're essentially limited to standard-definition PAL and NTSC discs within DVD Studio Pro as of this writing.

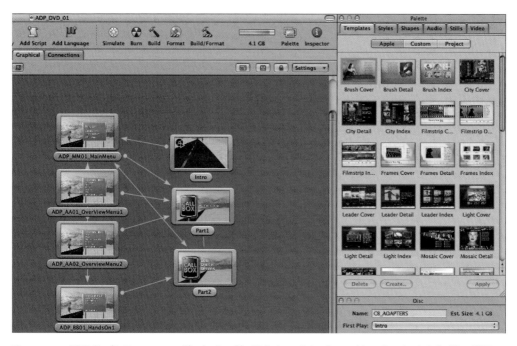

Figure 13.10 DVD Studio Pro comes with plenty of built-in templates for making standard-definition DVDs.

ADOBE ENCORE

Adobe Premiere Pro's companion authoring application is Adobe Encore, available individually for $799 or as part of Adobe Creative Suite Production Premium and Adobe Create Suite Master Collection. Encore (**Figure 13.11**) is capable of authoring standard-definition discs as well as Blu-rays. You need a Blu-ray burner to create Blu-ray discs (more on that in the

"Blu-ray" section). Encore can also convert a DVD project to Flash video for export to the Internet, meaning you need to author a project only once for multiple delivery options.

Figure 13.11 Adobe Encore runs on Mac or Windows and can make DVDs and Blu-rays.

AVID DVD

Avid's DVD authoring software is Avid DVD by Sonic. Avid DVD ($1,300 or $2,400 with Media Composer) is capable of making standard-definition discs as well as Blu-ray. It's Windows only, so take that into consideration as part of your authoring system setup. Avid DVD is well integrated with Media Composer, enabling the creation of chapter points and thumbnails while editing. Media Composer also provides a one-step Send to DVD command.

CREATING A DVD FROM RED FOOTAGE

Here are some quick tips for making a standard definition DVD. I'm using Final Cut Pro and DVD Studio Pro in this example, but the basic workflow is the same for any authoring program.

1. Start with a finished edit (use the final graded version if available) and export a self-contained file as uncompressed or with high-quality compression in standard definition. This will accomplish the down-conversion that's required and leave only MPEG-2 encoding for the next step. I'm going out to ProRes 422 (HQ) at 720 x 480 23.98 16:9 in

this example (**Figure 13.12**), which is the maximum resolution you can put on an NTSC DVD. In Final Cut Pro, choose File > Export > Using QuickTime Conversion.

Figure 13.12 Exporting a QuickTime file as standard definition from Final Cut Pro.

2. The next step is to import the resulting file into your MPEG-2 encoder. Most authoring applications have built-in encoders, but I prefer to do the encoding in Compressor where I have more control. If you use Compressor, you'll see a Batch window when you launch the program (**Figure 13.13**).

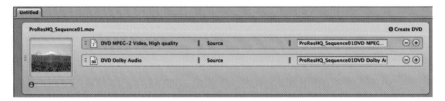

Figure 13.13 Standard definition DVD presets automatically loaded into Compressor's Batch window.

3. Click on and drag the preset for standard-definition DVD at High quality from the Settings window into the Batch window.

4. Drag the QuickTime file you created in Final Cut Pro from the Finder into this new batch setting. Then press the Submit button to automatically create an M2V file for the video and an AC3 file for the audio.

5. Double-click the DVD video preset to check the format settings in the Inspector. Verify your settings as NTSC Video Format, 23.98 Frame Rate, 16:9 Aspect Ratio, and Progressive Field Dominance (**Figure 13.14**). Click the Submit button to start encoding.

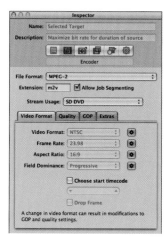

Figure 13.14 Verifying video format settings in Compressor's Inspector.

6. When encoding is complete, launch DVD Studio Pro to create a basic project.

7. Drag the M2V and AC3 files you made in Compressor directly onto the Track 1 container in the Graphical view (**Figure 13.15**). This automatically imports the footage and sets the track up for 23.98, 16:9 display.

Figure 13.15 16:9 footage loaded into a video track container in DVDSP.

8. Control-click on the video track and choose First Play from the pop-up menu.

9. Press the Simulate button and you should have a DVD playing video (**Figure 13.16**).

Coming from RED footage, your DVD should look awesome but if it doesn't go back and re-check your export settings in Final Cut Pro and Compressor. One common mistake is encoding footage first to a web format such as H.264 before going to MPEG-2, which adds re-compression and quality loss.

Figure 13.16 Viewing a completed DVD in 16:9 using the Simulator.

That's a simplified look at making a DVD. You can create more complex and fancy projects on disc if you spend time learning authoring. For more help, check out *Apple Pro Training Series: DVD Studio Pro* (Peachpit Press) or my own training disc, *DVD Studio Pro: Special Edition*, www.callboxlive.com.

BLU-RAY

To make a Blu-ray disc, you'll need a Blu-ray–capable authoring application, such as the ones mentioned in the previous section, and a disc burner. Some good options include Pioneer's

Figure 13.17 Pioneer's BDR-203 burner mounts internally in a desktop computer.

BDR-203 burner (**Figure 13.17**), which you can find for less than $300 as of this writing, and LG's GGW-H20, which sells for about $200. These are internal burners meant for desktop machines; for external burners, try the OWC Mercury Pro (around $350) or the LaCie D2 ($450).

Blu-ray discs can be encoded in standard definition as well as high definition at 720p, 1080p, and 1080i resolution. Because you're coming from a 4K master, I recommend always encoding at 1080p for the best quality. On a 720p display, 1080p footage is automatically down-converted and looks just that much sharper than 720p-encoded footage. Footage that originated in 16:9 or HD aspect ratios on the camera will fit onto a Blu-ray disc perfectly. Footage originated at 2:1 will need to be either cropped or letterboxed to fit into the 16:9 frame of Blu-ray.

The compression bitrate for Blu-ray is lower than REDCODE (approximately 5 MB per second for Blu-ray versus 36 MB per second for REDCODE36). So, do your final compression only once and from as uncompressed a source as possible. Don't output an edit to H.264 for the Web and then use that file as a source for high definition, for example. If you follow these guidelines, your Blu-ray footage will look as clean and free from compression artifacts as possible.

> NOTE   Direct Blu-ray playback is not currently supported on the Mac OS. To view a disc authored in Encore, you'll have the best luck viewing it on an external Blu-ray player.

HD

Part of the appeal of a camera such as the RED ONE is going tapeless, but many distribution outlets still require projects to be delivered on tape. These include video distributors, film festivals, and broadcasters. You'll need to interface with a tape deck using a video card capable of outputting to HD-SDI, such as a Blackmagic DeckLink or an AJA Kona 3. (Learn more about video cards in Chapter 8 in the "Converter cards" section.)

One of the most universal HD tape formats is Sony's HDCAM. HDCAM decks can run into the high five figures, so I recommend a rental if you're doing only occasional *laybacks* to tape. Also, most postproduction houses equipped with HDCAM offer a transfer service that involves bringing in a digital movie file on hard drive for output to tape. Check with the facility you intend to use for format specifics.

> NOTE   When you export to HD tape or to Blu-ray, you're going from a RAW color and gamma space to a high-definition color and gamma space. So, be sure to check your color correction with the REC709 settings of your grading application to get a better sense of how your project will look in high definition.

INTERNET

I spoke about some of the specific compression settings and sites for Internet video in the "Delivering for the Internet" section of Chapter 3. As it relates to color grading, you may want to switch the gamma and color spaces of your grading application to RGB so that you have a better sense of what footage looks like on a computer monitor. You'll probably be making a QuickTime MOV, Windows Media Video WMV, or Flash FLV file and hosting it directly on your own site or sending it to a third-party video-sharing site. Unfortunately, the proprietary compression technologies of these Web sites can compress your gamma and color space in unpredictable ways.

I recommend plenty of testing with your project and the intended Web video codec or site. People who work with Web video often have their secret recipes for getting the best online results. Some tools that can help you make better Web video are Sorenson Squeeze (www.sorensonmedia.com) and On2 Technologies (www.on2.com).

There's a reason the position of postproduction supervisor has existed for so long in the movie business. Tracking all the creative assets of a movie project and following through on all the technical details needed for the final output formats is a lot of work. So, more than anything else, knowing the specifics about your final destination as you begin a project is very important. Now that you've seen where projects can end up, take some time to review Chapter 3 again. Stay organized, and you'll save a lot of time and money in post by avoiding extra conversions and work you don't really need to do.

Simon Duggan, ACS
DIRECTOR OF PHOTOGRAPHY, *KNOWING*

Simon Duggan, ACS, on the set of *Knowing* in Australia. (Photo courtesy of www. vincethephotographer.com.)

Australian cinematographer Simon Duggan, ACS, made a name for himself shooting commercials beginning in the early 1980s. He went on to win numerous advertising and cinematographers' guild awards over the years before transitioning to features starting with the 1998 film, *The Interview*. Rising quickly in profile, Duggan's resume grew with big-budget features such as *I, Robot* with Will Smith, *Die Hard IV* with Bruce Willis, and *The Mummy: Tomb of the Dragon Emperor* with Brendan Fraser. Duggan also has the distinction of shooting one of the first major Hollywood productions on the RED ONE, the science-fiction/action-adventure *Knowing*, starring Nicholas Cage and directed by Alex Proyas (*The Crow, Dark City*).

Duggan and Proyas first started discussing the potential of shooting with the RED in 2007. "Alex mentioned he had seen the results of a RED test shot in Sydney with the Australian Cinematographers Society," Duggan recalls. "He liked the look of the images, and we both liked the look of the CMOS sensors in our digital still cameras. So, we decided to do some testing of our own with the RED.

"We took the camera out and tested some really unforgiving high-contrast interior/exterior scenes, along with some available-light night exteriors," Duggan continues. "In general, we both agreed the colors and skin tones felt natural. The RED had its very own look that was closer to film than high-definition video. The dynamic range in the highlights was less than film and more typical of all other digital/video formats, however. I found the workaround in extreme contrast conditions was to expose for the highlights, knowing that I could lift the shadows back up [in postproduction] without creating excess noise."

The cinematographer and director then sat down to plan the visual aesthetic of *Knowing*. "Alex wanted a very realistic and yet immediate feel," remembers Duggan. "Both the 4K quality and lack of grain helped give the look we were after. Our visual effects supervisor, Andrew Jackson from Animal Logic, was also very positive about using the RED. The R3D files could be taken straight into the FX pipeline without having to make selections and negative scans outside of their facility."

As production moved forward, Duggan was able to adapt his standard film crew to working digitally. "We had a normal complement in the camera department supplemented with two digital imaging technicians (DITs)," he says. "Our on-set DIT was always close to the camera setting looks, carrying out initial logging, and checking R3D files. Our second DIT was nearby in a truck with Mac Pros and LCD monitors. He created color-timed QuickTime proxies based on the on-set grade references we made and then made two backups of every file. One copy would go to editorial, and an additional two backups would be copied to LTO tape—one for Animal Logic and one for [Peter Jackson's] Park Road Post, which was doing the digital intermediate (DI). Park Road also supplied final quality-control checks before we recycled any hard drives or CompactFlash cards." (*Knowing* utilized 150 8 GB CF cards and 26 RED-DRIVEs throughout production.)

Duggan's optical and lighting equipment package was very similar to his preferred film setup. "The camera was identical to my usual requirement except that the film camera body was replaced with the RED camera body," Duggan explains. "I lit and exposed with a light meter. I did experiment with the histogram but found it like using any in-camera meter: You end up with exposures based on contrast differences within each shot rather than an exposure that works for the continuity of a whole scene. I used the onboard exposure tools for highlight control and REC 709 gamma and color space for monitoring. I would adjust the color-temperature settings to create a look for each scene. The look for our dailies was being set as we shot, keeping in mind that none of these metadata settings were affecting the RAW capture of the camera's sensor."

In general, Duggan had very few issues working with the RED on *Knowing*. "On one occasion we were caught out when jumping between shooting speeds at 24 fps to over 30 fps," he recalls. "This changes the image capture size from 4K to 3K, which requires a wider-angle lens to match the field of view from 4K. Most other issues were resolved by restarting the camera. We also found that it is always best to use RED-RAM drives or CF cards, as the RED-DRIVEs are susceptible to vibration. The in-camera fault-detection warnings are very good, and there weren't any surprises. One added bonus was the in-camera playback, so we would always do a quick focus check after each take."

Though Duggan was working with an earlier version of the camera (Build 15), he found the greatest technical challenge was locating a postproduction house that could handle the R3D files. "Park Road Post in New Zealand had been doing a lot work with the RED camera the previous year for Peter Jackson's short film *Crossing the Line*," Duggan notes. "I flew down a few times while we were shooting to check how the material was looking on the big screen through their pipeline using a Quantel Pablo system. The results were amazing, and there were no problems with compression patterns or noise, even in the moodiest of scenes.

"The images looked like 70mm film, with a real three-dimensional quality," Duggan adds. "Grading the final files was very easy with the Pablo, and we had no noise problems pulling up shadow detail or blacks. During the DI, we changed most of the green foliage to an autumnal mix of oranges and pinks with no problems. We were slightly shocked seeing film grain again with the release print, but it looked great, and most people wouldn't pick it for a digital origination."

With *Knowing* successfully released, Duggan is intrigued by the next generation of cameras. "The RED has gone through many improvements since our production," he observes. "Postproduction workflows have also come a long way. I'm looking forward to testing the new cameras and sensors as they come out."

Simon Duggan's Web site is www.simonduggan.com. ∎

14 ARCHIVING YOUR MEDIA

Many first-time RED users come from the worlds of video-tape or film, where you shoot media once, and it immediately becomes your archive. After film negative is exposed, it goes into a lab vault for long-term storage or for later use in negative cutting for a theatrical release print. Videotape can be reused, but most producers choose to keep their original tapes as back-ups, since buying more tape is much cheaper than the average cost of a day of production.

With RED, archiving requires more thoughtful preparation and work. The CF media, RED-DRIVEs, and RED-RAM storage systems are (as of this writing) too expensive to employ as archival media. So, they must be recycled once footage is offloaded to other media, such as another hard drive, for editing. Choosing a reliable, long-term archiving solution is therefore critical to preserving footage and preventing the possibility of data loss. The costs of reshooting lost footage far exceed the prices of readily available and proven data-archiving systems. With that in mind, in this chapter you'll find recommended equipment and workflows for saving footage.

An old film school buddy of mine used to always say, "Pain is temporary—film is forever." With the RED, you just have to work a little harder to make that a reality. Initially, you transfer footage to external hard drives for editorial usage. Hard drives are excellent for quickly accessing media during postproduction but are not durable enough to reliably sit on the shelf for many years because of technical issues like *stiction*, which causes hard drive failure (see Note below). You never know when you might need to revisit a project, right? Production footage can easily run into the hundreds of gigabytes, so optical disc-based formats such as DVD-R and Blu-ray don't offer enough practical capacity.

NOTE *Stiction* is short for static friction, a condition in which a hard drive's read/write heads become stuck to the disk's platters with enough strength to keep them from spinning, resulting in hard drive failure. This can happen when a hard drive sits unused for an extended period of time. It's less likely to happen with tape-based storage, which is why that format is preferred over magnetic hard drives for long-term storage.

Optical disc formats are also physically vulnerable to damage, though arguably less so than magnetic hard drives. Solid-state drives are slowly becoming another option, though they're currently pretty expensive on a per-gigabyte basis. Digital tape-based systems such as LTO drives (**Figure 14.1**) offer the best combination of speed, capacity, affordability, and long-term endurance.

Figure 14.1 A Quantum LTO-3 internal tape drive with cartridges, software, and cleaning kit.

NOTE LTO stands for Linear Tape-Open and was developed in the late 1990s; capacities range from 100 GB for LTO-1 to 800 GB for LTO-4.

Archiving in the Field

Tape drive transfer speeds are slower than magnetic hard drives, so tape-based archiving is typically run overnight, or after production has completed shooting. The RED-DRIVE and RED-RAM have FireWire and USB 2.0 connectors that you can attach to a laptop and start using to transfer footage immediately. In the field, where you typically need to turn around RED-DRIVEs and CF cards quickly, use fast external FireWire 800 or eSATA drives for initial backups (**Figure 14.2**).

Figure 14.2 An external hard drive with FireWire 400/800, USB 2.0, and eSATA connectors.

NOTE eSATA stands for External Serial Advanced Technology Attachment. All you really need to know is that it's a very fast connection for external hard drives.

RECOMMENDED EQUIPMENT

RED CF cards require a card reader. I recommend getting as fast a unit as possible, such as the SanDisk Extreme FireWire Reader (**Figure 14.3**). The SanDisk costs a bit more than a standard-issue card reader, but if you have FireWire 800 as a connection on your laptop, it's blazingly fast and can

Figure 14.3 SanDisk Extreme FireWire Reader is fast.

help eliminate bottlenecks when shooting with the RED to CF. If you're working with a USB 2.0 connection, try the Lexar Pro CF Reader.

For production storage, get the fastest, highest-quality hard drives you can afford. Remember, once you transfer your footage onto a hard drive and put the CF cards or RED-DRIVEs back into circulation, that's your entire production on a little spinning platter. You

may be tempted to build your own drive system with off-the-shelf components, but it's worth splurging a bit on a complete, integrated solution with a full warranty.

My current favorite hard drive manufacturer is G-Technology. G-Technology offers compact, portable FireWire 400/800, USB 2.0, and eSATA drives in standard and Redundant Array of Independent Disks (RAID) configurations (**Figure 14.4**). With a couple of G-RAIDs or G-SAFEs attached to your laptop, you'll be all set. Some other hard drive brands I like are CalDigit and Dulce Systems.

Figure 14.4 G-Technology G-SAFE external hard drive.

NOTE   RED's Leader of the Rebellion, Ted Schilowitz, previously worked full-time for G-Tech, and there's reportedly a lot of affection for the hard drive brand internally at RED.

LAPTOP VS. DESKTOP FOR FIELDWORK

Laptops are limited in their expansion capabilities to external interfaces, such as USB 2.0, FireWire, and ExpressCard. That means your transfer speeds can be only as fast as those bus connections. You might not think so, but a desktop machine sitting on a cart can be more versatile and powerful as your transfer machine, though of course you'll need AC power. With a desktop, you can add a RAID expansion card internally and create a much faster drive system than a laptop could accommodate. If you're shooting on stage or in a studio, this is a good alternative to consider for superior performance.

TRANSFERRING FOOTAGE

It's completely feasible to manage RED file transfers by drag-and-drop copying as you would copy to any other media drive on your computer. The only drawback is that you usually don't get copy verification (at least not by default). If you're copying footage from a CF card onto a backup hard drive and something goes wrong, you might get an error message, or you might not. An error is pretty rare, but that's a lot to risk when you have critical footage on the line.

USING YOUR TIME WISELY

Take advantage of any available downtime to offload footage; don't wait until hard drives are completely full. A full RED-DRIVE can take a long time to copy over. You might suddenly need to start shooting again, but be forced to wait for the copying to complete. Also, if you download footage several times during the day, you can quickly spot any problems and fix them, rather than finding out at the end of a shoot day, when it may be too late.

OFFLOADING UTILITIES

If you want to have a little more security and peace of mind, try one of the following footage-offloading utilities and use copy verification. (Keep in mind that copy verification does slow down the transfer process, so build a little extra time into your workflow.)

Imagine Products' (www.imagineproducts.com) Shotput Pro, which goes for $89, is a highly versatile media offloader available for Mac and Windows. In addition to copying RED material, Shotput Pro also supports a variety of other HD and still-camera file formats. This can be very useful if you're working on a variety of different productions and you want to standardize your archive workflow across every format. Shotput is very easy to use: You simply mount a RED CF card or RED-DRIVE onto your desktop (**Figure 14.5**), and it automatically makes several backups organized into folders (*reels*) while copying with verification. It also generates reports and activity logs (**Figure 14.6**) that outline every copy operation and even makes automatic backups to Blu-ray if you have a burner.

When used properly, Shotput can make field downloading much simpler and more reliable. (Imagine also makes ProxyMill, which automatically derives self-contained QuickTime movies directly from RED proxies.)

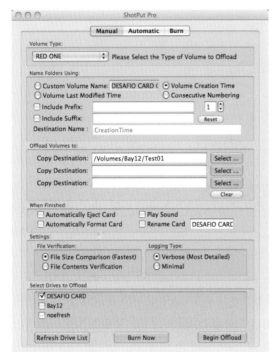

Figure 14.5 Shotput Pro's main interface.

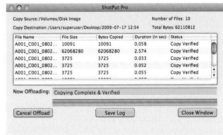

Figure 14.6 Shotput Pro offloading log.

R3D Data Manager ($79 at www.r3ddata.com) is another application designed for RED offloading with versions for Mac and Windows. Like Shotput Pro, Data Manager offers automated copying with verification (**Figure 14.7**) and activity logging. It's focused specifically on R3D files and doesn't support other still or HD formats. So if you only work with RED material, R3D Data Manager may be the right move. Some nice features include the capability to directly format RED CF cards for faster turnarounds, cell phone notification of completed transfers, and direct render to DPX. It's also a little less expensive than Shotput, so if you don't need those additional features, you can save a little money.

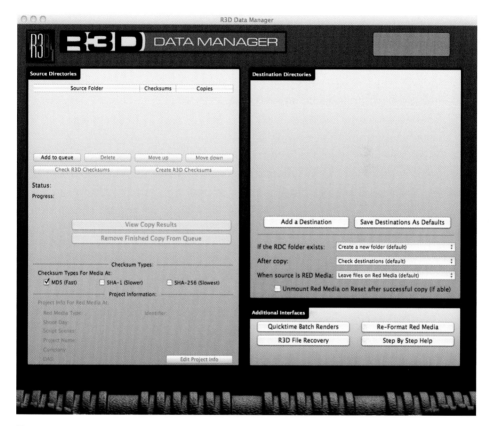

Figure 14.7 R3D Data Manager main transfer window.

OFFLOADING VIA THE FINDER

Many RED owners simply transfer their footage by dragging and dropping and have no issues. If that's the workflow you'd like to go with, I have an important recommendation: to copy absolutely everything recorded onto the CF card or RED-DRIVE by the camera from the top-level directory on down and keep that directory structure intact (**Figure 14.8**). Copy every proxy file; every RDC, RSX, and R3D; and any other files or folders on the CF card or RED-DRIVE to your transfer hard drive. Many postproduction applications that are RED-aware require that the full directory structure be intact in order to operate properly.

Figure 14.8 Copying RED footage from a CF card to a hard drive in the Finder.

DIRECTORY NAMING CONVENTIONS

Make sure each card goes into its own discrete directory as you transfer. The directory naming convention is up to you, but be consistent and pick a logical method that anyone who receives the directory on a hard drive (such as another editor or a post house) will easily understand. You could name each directory according to project name, date, time of day, camera, and card number.

Here's an example: **Commercial_110409_1330_A01**.

In this naming convention, that directory is for my "commercial" project, shot on November 4, 2009, and transferred at 1:30 p.m., from A camera, reel 01. Another method is simply to take the first clip name created by the camera on each reel and make that the directory name. So, each directory would look something like **REEL_A001_C001_1114BH**. This can look a little confusing, but it's a quick and easy way to be consistent.

> TIP Computers sort numbered files according to two digits, so always enter single-digit numbers as double digits. For example, use 01 instead of 1. Otherwise, the computer won't sort the directories the way you'd expect, and it can be a little confusing when you're searching for a specific folder.

You can also pick a very short and simple name and go by reels, like **Commercial_Project01_Reel01**. Since you'll already have the time and date stamp created by the camera in the Finder, this is a pretty easy way to go. Use whatever method makes the most sense to you. And remember, you'll also need to set up a separate set of folders for sound files if you've recorded double-system audio. Just be sure to have a method and use it consistently. Don't let a pile of untitled folders happen to you.

> TIP Get into the habit of using underscores (_) instead of blank spaces in directory names. Some operating systems and web interfaces choke on filenames with blank spaces, so do yourself the favor of omitting them throughout your workflow. (This is especially true with LTO tapes, where blank spaces can make directories unreadable.)

Postproduction Archiving

It might seem premature to discuss archiving before you've even had a chance to start edit-ing, but you can do a lot of prep work that will serve you well down the road. You shouldn't edit directly from the copies you made in the field. If anything goes wrong—such as an acci-dental file deletion—that clip will be gone forever. If you used one of the offloader applica-tions, you'll already have a working copy and a backup. If not, you need to work on creating an archiving setup.

INITIAL SETUP

In general, you want to edit using the fastest hard drives you can afford. A nice RAID setup (**Figure 14.9**), depending on the amount of footage you have and what editing workflow you decide to use, is a good call (you can find more details on RAIDs in Chapter 8). In contrast, the drives you might use for initial archives during postproduction need not be that fast. You can easily get away with relatively inexpensive FireWire or USB 2.0 drives that you'll put on the shelf for the moment. Those drives can later form the basis of your archive should you choose to back up everything from a production.

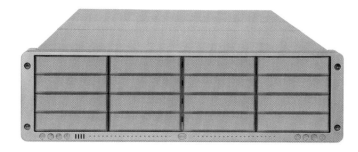

Figure 14.9 An Active Storage XRAID unit.

SELECTIVE VS. COMPLETE ARCHIVES

At this point in postproduction you should start thinking about whether to back up every frame of footage you've shot or just preserve the parts of your media you used in the final edit. This depends on the kind of project you're working on, the likelihood of ever coming back to reedit, and your budget for additional storage.

Are you shooting daily sports or news events that require only a single edit, giving you tons of footage you'll never need again? Would any of your footage be usable in complete takes to sell as stock footage? Is the footage once-in-a-lifetime/irreplaceable footage? Will you be creating a director's cut, extended version, or DVD "extras" someday? You need to decide for yourself how important it is to keep every shot. If you can afford a tape drive, you'll have vast amounts of relatively inexpensive storage. Tape makes the prospect of preserving everything in a project much easier.

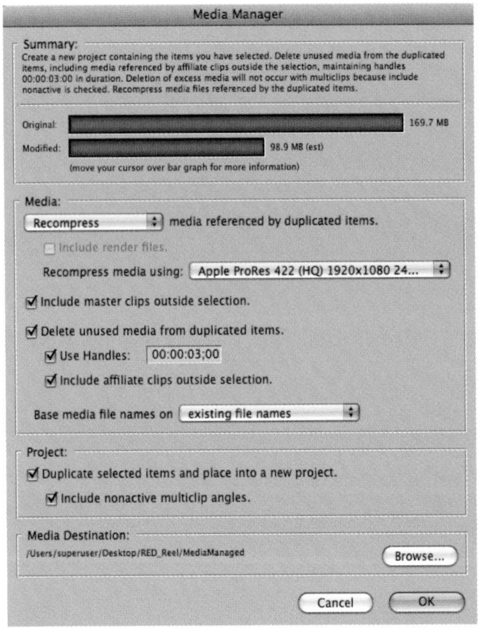

If you ultimately conclude that it's not possible or necessary to save everything, you'll be well served by at least archiving the final edit itself as discrete media clips. Most editing applications, such as Final Cut Pro, offer a method of media management (**Figure 14.10**) in which you can export only the media used in the final edit, plus a little extra in the form of *handles* (extra frames before and after edit points). I recommend at least three seconds worth of handles before and after each clip. That gives you enough to finesse edits a little bit should you need to, while still not taking up a lot of space.

Figure 14.10 Using Media Manager in Final Cut Pro.

The process becomes a bit more complex in the world of the RED, though, because you might not be editing R3D files natively, so you'll need to transcode RED footage to another format in order to create a selective archive. For this reason—along with the low cost of storage compared to the cost of going back and completely reshooting something deleted—I recommend archiving both a selective version with just the media used in the edit as well as a complete archive of everything you shoot. You can quickly restore the selective archive if you just need to do a quick touch-up or output to another format. And if you need to do a more complex reedit using a lot of extra footage, you'll then have the option to take the time and do a complete restore from the full archive.

WORKING WITH TAPE

Over the years, many different digital tape-based storage formats have been introduced. These include Advanced Intelligent Tape (AIT), Digital Linear Tape, (DLT), Digital Audio Tape (DAT), and Linear Tape-Open (LTO).

LTO has emerged as the most popular of the formats for digital footage archiving and is the one I recommend for the RED. LTO is fast, reliable, durable, and relatively affordable.

The two types of LTO most prominently in use today are LTO-3 and LTO-4. The differences in the two iterations include speed, capacity, and cost. **Table 14.1** outlines the major differences, including the older LTO and LTO-2 for comparison.

TABLE 14.1   LTO TAPE FORMATS COMPARED

	LTO	LTO-2	LTO-3	LTO-4
Release date	2000	2003	2005	2007
Native data capacity	100 GB	200 GB	400 GB	800 GB
Max speed (MB/s)	15	40	80	120
WORM capable	No	No	Yes	Yes
Average drive cost	$500	$750	$2,000	$3,000
Average tape cost	$15	$25	$50	$75

CATCH THE WORM

LTO-3 and LTO-4 include support for Write Once, Read Many—or WORM. WORM tapes can be physically written to one time only. They cannot be erased or overwritten without physically destroying the media. This seeming limitation can be a desirable feature because it builds in an additional layer of foolproof protection to your footage by preventing it from accidental erasure. Of course, it also means WORM tapes cannot be reused, so keep that in mind budget-wise before committing to the technology.

Recommended Hardware and Software

This section spells out some specific LTO drive recommendations. Note that most LTO-3 and LTO-4 drives rely on Small Computer System Interface (SCSI) and Serial Attached SCSI (SAS) connectors, rather than FireWire or USB.

SCSI (**Figure 14.11**) has been around since the mid-1980s, if you can believe it. It used to be a common interface on desktop computers, but now you usually need to purchase a special interface card in order to use it.

SAS was initially designed as an update to the SCSI format. It offers faster transfer speeds and more devices per bus (although certain flavors of SCSI are now as fast or faster). ATTO Technology and LSI make some of the more reliable SCSI- and SAS-to-PCI adapter cards. Check carefully which kind of SCSI your drive uses, because the connector

Figure 14.11 A SCSI cable and connector.

comes in several iterations. Shop around to determine which drive type offers the best possible compatibility and performance within your budget.

> TIP SAS cables can lose signal quality quickly over long distances, so use the shortest possible cable between your desktop system and tape drive for maximum throughput and data reliability.

Figure 14.12 Quantum ProVideo A-Series series LTO-3 drive.

RECOMMENDED LTO DRIVES

I've always liked the Quantum ProVideo A-Series (**Figure 14.12**). These affordable, LTO-3 drives are optimized for video with direct MXF awareness that provides automatic proxy clips and timecode search capabilities. Unfortunately, this search feature doesn't extend to R3Ds at the moment, but it's still a great drive for RED. What's nice about the Quantum is that it's a network attached storage (NAS) device that connects to your computer via Gigabit Ethernet. You can access it directly across a network without a SCSI or SAS card. This feature makes the drive more expensive, at about $7,500, but the convenience of Ethernet access deserves a serious look. Quantum also makes LTO-4 drives, though at the time of this writing, none are configured for NAS. The drives are firmware upgradeable just like the RED, and Quantum provides good tech support.

Dell offers its PowerVault series of LTO drives (**Figure 14.13**), with prices ranging from just less than $2,000 for an LTO-3 entry-level drive to about $3,000 for a high-performance LTO-4 drive. HP also has a selection of LTO-3 and LTO-4 drives that work well for archiving footage. HP's StorageWorks LTO Ultrium Tape Drives (**Figure 14.14**) are available in a variety of LTO-3/LTO-4 internal/external and SCSI/SAS configurations at prices similar to Dell's.

Figure 14.13
Dell PowerVault
124T LTO drive.

Figure 14.14
HP StorageWorks LTO
Ultrium Tape Drive.

TAPES

In addition to your drive, you'll also need LTO tape stock. The 400 GB LTO-3 tapes start at about $50 each, and 800 GB LTO-4 tapes cost about $75 and up, as of this writing. Your major cost is the tape drive itself; once you've gotten past that initial investment, the media is relatively inexpensive.

Figure 14.15 Dell PowerVault ML6020 LTO tape library.

TAPE LIBRARIES

Most tape drive manufacturers sell single drive units as well as tape libraries and autoloaders (**Figure 14.15**). These are special LTO system configurations that offer the ability to hold many LTO tapes at once and can switch from tape to tape unattended. The advantages of multiple tape drive units are convenience and speed. If you're working with several productions on a regular basis and need to back up a lot of footage, then libraries and autoloaders can easily justify their higher investment. One unit can sit rack-mounted on a network, configured to automatically manage data across many terabytes of tapes as needed while remaining physically unattended. On the other hand, if you're working with just one camera or production at a time, a single drive unit should be more than up to the task. It takes a while to copy onto a 400 GB or 800 GB tape, so you have plenty of time to manually swap tapes out as the backup progresses. Also, it's a good idea to leave a margin of free space on an LTO drive instead of completely filling it up. Each manufacturer recommends a specific amount to reserve in the owner's manual.

ARCHIVING SOFTWARE

Tape drive systems don't work like a regular hard drive or server; they are typically not visible on your computer's desktop as a regular hard drive would be. Tape drives with built-in Web servers allow access via FTP software, but otherwise you need special software to store and retrieve tape footage. In this section, I look at some of the more popular backup applications currently on the market. The nice feature is that tape-based technologies are essentially OS-unaware, so most of these archiving applications are available in both Mac and Windows versions (with some even in Linux).

EMC CORPORATION RETROSPECT

Retrospect (www.retrospect.com) is one of the older backup applications on the market and benefits from many years of development. It's available in several versions, depending on the type of access you need. Prices range from $129 for a three-user license up to $1,669 for a multiple-server license with unlimited clients and annual tech support. On the Windows side, Retrospect Professional is designed for a single-user direct connection to the drive setup. Also, server variations enable several users to access the drive as centralized storage. The Retrospect lineup on the Mac side is similar with single-user, workgroup, and server versions. You can easily configure Retrospect to manually back up or restore archives and schedule automatic backups daily, weekly, or as desired (**Figure 14.16**).

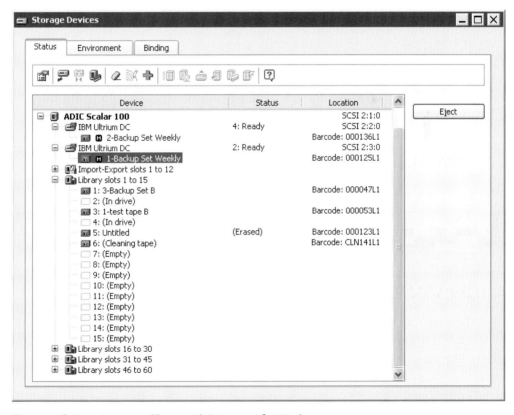

Figure 14.16 Browsing a tape library with Retrospect for Windows.

TOLIS GROUP BRU

Backup & Recovery Utility (BRU) is a relative newcomer to the archival software field. Interestingly, the $499 program was developed with lots of input from RED owners, so it's particularly well suited to creating RED archives. BRU Producer's Edition is specifically aimed at archiving creative assets. It supports archives by session, so you can easily organize all your RED digital magazines on a per-project basis. Producer's Edition also handles native project files from editing software such as Final Cut Pro and Soundtrack Pro and can automatically create and span multiple copies of each archive. BRU includes broad hardware support for single-tape and library drive units (**Figure 14.17**). Tolis also offers a budget-priced, single-user LE edition for $129 that offers many of the same features. Demo versions are also available at www.tolisgroup.com.

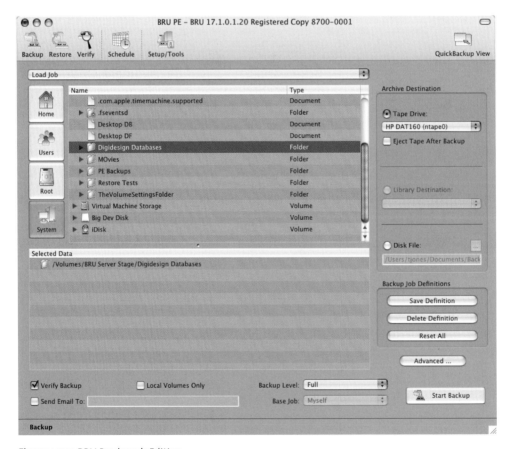

Figure 14.17 BRU Producer's Edition.

ARCHIWARE PRESSTORE ARCHIVE

PresSTORE Archive (www.archiware.com) is designed to be as scalable and intuitive as possible. The software costs about $1,200, depending on the options. Mindful of data integrity needs, PresSTORE automatically logs any errors or issues encountered during backup operation. It also offers a customizable search database capable of generating preview thumbnails and clips of video and audio data (**Figure 14.18**). As with the other solutions, PresSTORE writes archives to tapes without OS-specific data, enabling any operating system to restore from them. Finally, it can be set up to monitor folders and archive only those files that have changed according to user-definable parameters.

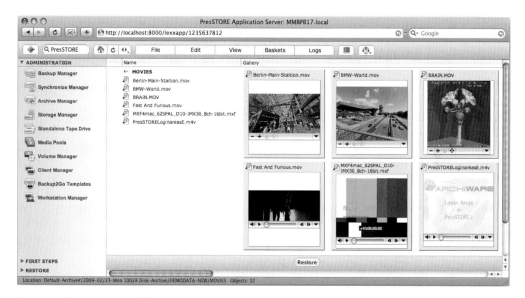

Figure 14.18 PresSTORE Archive.

ATEMPO DIGITAL ARCHIVE

Atempo's Digital Archive (contact www.atempo.com for current pricing) is a powerful solution that operates as server and client software. At this time, the Mac OS version is client only. This means that to set up an archive, you need at least one server system running Windows, Unix, or Linux. Centralizing storage offers a number of benefits, including consistent, single-administrator control over metadata and indexing (**Figure 14.19**). Additionally, data flow is constantly monitored to provide optimum performance across the network. Digital

Archive can also be integrated directly with Apple's Final Cut Server for a robust, automated workflow when working with many different projects at once.

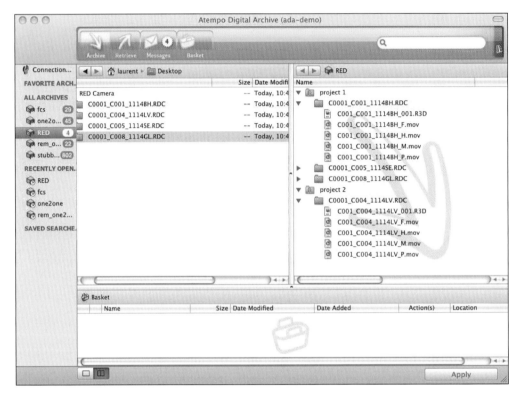

Figure 14.19 Atempo Digital Archive.

That concludes our survey of some of the archiving applications available for your RED footage. The good news is that a wide variety of hardware and software is available to handle this task, which you should consider critical. Before you purchase any tape drive solution, confirm that it has been tested and certified with the backup software you intend to use. Software developers usually maintain updated compatibility matrices of the hardware they support. Used properly, archiving software can mean the difference between spending some extra time restoring and completely losing all of your hard work.

Vaulting Services

Now that you've successfully implemented a long-term data archiving solution, what are you going to actually *do* with those tapes for the next few years (or decades)? What you'll do is store them in a cool, dry place out of the light and safe from vibration. You might consider an off-site *vaulting* service (**Figure 14.20**). For example, Underground Vaults & Storage (www.undergroundvaults.com), located in rural Kansas, operates a climate-controlled bank vault facility 650 feet below the earth's surface. The place is encased in a 400-foot-thick rock salt mine with only two vertical access points.

Figure 14.20 Underground Vaults & Storage stores traditional movies on film as well as LTO tapes.

The concept of putting data tapes into a salt mine might seem like overkill, but if you're working on a big-budget studio feature, it may be a requirement from the completion bond company. You ship your tapes to the storage facility, and they take care of the rest. Vaults with less elaborate facilities than Underground Vaults & Storage are available in movie-production cities such as Los Angeles and New York as well.

Vaulting services have been around for decades for film, tapes, audio recordings, and other important archives and have adapted themselves to the requirements of tape formats like LTO. Of course, there's no way to guarantee data tapes against *force majeure*. That said, storing your footage with a vaulting service is about as close as you can get, and archiving is all about considering the worst-case scenario.

> NOTE   *Force majeure* (French for superior force) is a common contract clause freeing both parties from liability during circumstances beyond their control, such as a war, strike, riot, crime, or "act of God" (flooding, earthquake, volcano, and so on). If any of these events actually happen to your data, losing your RED footage may be the least of your concerns.

As with other aspects of the RED workflow discussed in this book, preparation is everything. Have a detailed plan for archiving footage ready to go before you shoot. Decide on production-wide directory naming conventions and file-handling procedures, and then be consistent with them. Take great care to assure that not only is that footage transferred but also that verified copies are completed. You can manually check or run software with automatic copy verification to confirm copies. Guide your decision making by comparing the costs of archiving equipment and software with the costs of losing data.

You can think of archiving as a value-added service to offer your customers. If there's one issue that concerns newcomers to the tapeless workflow, it's how their footage will be preserved in lieu of tapes or film negative and what sort of master archive format they'll walk away with. You'll look that much more prepared to your clients if you already have your backup equipment and procedures in place when they inquire about archiving.

Photographer Greg Williams works with the RED ONE.

Greg Williams
PHOTOGRAPHER

U.K.-based photographer Greg Williams launched his photojournalism career in crisis zones such as Burma, Chechnya, and Sierra Leone in the 1990s. His photo-essays covered hard-hitting topics such as mad cow disease and brain-damage rehabilitation for children. In 1997, Williams started an assignment for the London *Sunday Times Magazine* covering the British film industry. He subsequently photographed behind-the-scenes and promotional material for more than 150 movies including *King Kong*, *The Talented Mr. Ripley*, *The Bourne Ultimatum*, *Casino Royale*, and *Quantum of Solace*.

Williams also shoots advertising, celebrity portraits, and fashion photography. His subjects have appeared on the pages of magazines such as *Vogue Italia*, *Vanity Fair*, and *Esquire*. Always keen to pioneer new techniques, Williams chose to create photos for recent magazine spreads by shooting footage with the RED ONE and extracting stills suitable for printing. His first published RED photo, featuring *Quantum of Solace* actress Olga Kurylenko, ran in the August 2008 issue of *Vogue Italia*.

Greg Williams' RED ONE still of actress Olga Kurylenko for *Vogue Italia* magazine.

Williams has followed the RED since its public introduction. "I saw a 4K still from Peter Jackson's short, *Crossing the Line,* on RED.com," he recalls. "It was a machine gun being fired in the trenches of World War I. I immediately thought the quality could be printed in a magazine with no worries. I put in a reservation, but there was a long wait before I received my camera, so I was renting at first."

Williams creates images with the RED ONE for print, short movies, commercials, and what he calls *motos* (moving photos), a hybrid of motion and still photography. "Motos look like regular stills," he explains. "Everyone thinks it's a photo because it has such high resolution, but then it comes to life like the newspapers in *Harry Potter*. I did that with Megan Fox for the online version of the *Esquire* cover. She's completely still, and then suddenly she rubs her leg and reveals her stocking."

"We also did moving posters for *Quantum of Solace* with Daniel Craig with the RED," Williams continues. "We ran those on LCD screens at the escalators of the London Underground. It looks like a regular movie poster with a portrait of Craig on it, and then he just turns his head a little. Those were up for the whole release of the movie."

Williams supplements his RED ONE with a Canon EOS 1Ds Mark III digital still camera. "I use the RED more than 50 percent of the time because I want to be at the forefront of what it can do," he says. "There's a massive convergence of photo and film happening right now, and RED is a catalyst for that. A RED still is not as high resolution as one from my Canon, but I don't need it to be because I already add grain and texture in post. It's only when I need very sharp, high-resolution glossy images for specific advertisers that I stick with only the Canon. I'm hoping RED's upcoming EPIC camera will tip the balance with its higher image quality."

Asked about the production tools he uses in addition to his RED and Canon, Williams details his lens kit. "I recently tried out the RED PRO PRIME lenses and thought they were very good but quite heavy for handheld use," he says. "I've been using ARRI T1.3 Super Speed primes: the 18mm, 25mm, 35mm, 50mm, and 85mm. I've never put a zoom on the RED or the Canon. As a photographer, I think zooms make you lazy because you zoom the lens instead of moving to reframe your subject, but I am sure I will use them for movies. I usually compose with the RED PRO 7" LCD screen instead of the electronic viewfinder."

Williams continues, "I'm also waiting on a Birger Engineering Canon adapter mount and excited to try my lenses with it. I have F1.2 and F1.4 primes, and I don't think I'm going to mind the breathing people describe when using them with the RED. It would also enable me to share lenses between the RED and the Canon in my travel kit."

Although many still photographers work with flash strobes, Williams learned lighting by observing movie cinematographers. "Working on movie sets has given me a real advantage," he notes. "I learned how to shoot with constant lighting and to light the environment rather than the subject. I like to light a room and let a person exist in there. It's not always important to have a key light hitting an actor in the face to get the best shot. If you look at a lot of movie cinematography, you'll notice the same thing."

 Running a RED camera constantly as opposed to shooting a frame at a time induces different reactions in Williams' subjects. "Models thrive on the click of a still camera shutter—they know to give you something new when they hear it," he observes. "Actors are different, especially the ones I have been lucky enough to shoot on the RED with like Robert De Niro, Jude Law, Daniel Craig, and Clive Owen. The shutter can grate their performance because they're best at acting, not posing, so I find the RED incredibly useful."

Actor Jude Law in a still from a Williams print ad shot with the RED ONE.

For postproduction, Williams works with a team to grade his images. "I supply my final work to clients as CMYK proofs ready for print," he explains. "I edit in RED Alert! with a maxed-out Mac Pro and export selected frames as 4K TIFFs for Photoshop. Then I add sharpening, work with color, and add grain, but I do very little cosmetic retouching. I like my images to look attractive but also realistic."

Peering into the future, Williams foresees a merger of still and motion imaging, culminating in a major change to the way photos are experienced. "The next step is screen-based magazines that are completely foldable and feel like paper but are Web-connected color screens," he predicts. "As soon as you've got that, there's no reason for photos to only be still anymore. They might be movies of a few seconds or a few minutes, like a portrait telling you about their life. I think nearly every photographer is going to have to become a filmmaker.

"RED started this collision of still and motion," Williams adds. "It was inevitable, but Jim Jannard is a daredevil who did it at least three years before anyone else was going to. Who knows how camera makers like Canon or Panavision are going to respond, but it's going to be interesting. I'm very excited to see what happens next."

Greg Williams's Web site is www.gregfoto.com. ∎

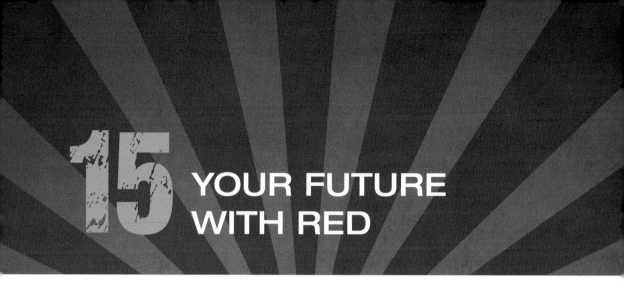

15 YOUR FUTURE WITH RED

If you've made it through most of this book without skipping ahead to this final chapter, congratulations, and thanks for sharing your time! As you can now see, the RED camera has a complex workflow both in production and in post. But if you take the time to learn and practice, it's really not that tricky.

To wrap up, I'll give you a few more tips regarding the potential for building a business around your RED camera. At the end of this chapter, you'll find some recommended Web sites to visit for more information, a map of the RED ONE's onboard menus, a gallery of stills, and a glossary.

Building a Business with the RED

If you read through Chapters 4 and 5 on putting together a RED equipment package, you probably noticed that all this stuff can get quite expensive before you even start shooting. So, how can you make your RED camera pay off? Let's look at some potential business scenarios and how to handle them.

DIGITAL IMAGING TECHNICIAN/ DATA WRANGLER

This is a relatively new field, and it brings plenty of opportunity. You're likely to find available positions as a data wrangler and/or digital imaging technician (DIT) in any major movie-production town (and not just for the RED but for other data-centric HD and better digital cameras). This is a job for which owning a RED camera is not a necessity, as long as you know the camera and its menus well. Chapters 4, 9, and 14 contain helpful information for potential DITs.

The single most important quality for this position is an utmost respect for data. Treat every CF card or RED-DRIVE as if it were a camera original negative, because that's essentially what it is. Be mindful of footage, and make sure you always know what's been backed up and which media can be recycled back onto the camera. Never lose a shot. Review the POV interviews with Evin Grant, Brook Willard, and Dean Georgopoulos for additional tips.

CAMERA RENTAL

If you own a RED ONE, chances are you're not going to be shooting with it every day. So, you might consider renting out your camera to other productions. If you explore this route, you should keep a few things in mind. First, take into account the production market where you're located. What's the competition like for RED rentals?

If you're in a big production town such as Los Angeles, New York, or London, watch out. You'll be up against major camera rental houses with multiple RED cameras and high-quality accessories and optics. More importantly, they will have an established infrastructure and staff ready to deal with all rental requests. That can make it difficult to compete as a lone-gun rental operation.

You also need to have your package insured against loss and damage. You would be surprised how roughly rental equipment gets treated sometimes. Before you lend out your gear, make sure the people renting it have properly insured your package with production equipment and liability insurance. For this and the reasons already mentioned, if you're in a major rental market area, I think it's wiser to align yourself with an existing rental facility and put your package into their consignment pool. You won't keep as much income from each rental, but you'll be protected against damages and loss, and you won't have to worry about having the absolute best of every piece of equipment to remain competitive in your market.

DIRECTOR OF PHOTOGRAPHY

Successful directors of photography (**Figure 15.1**) care more about composition and lighting than they do about specific cameras and technologies. A good DP adapts his or her techniques to whatever given medium a project is shooting on and makes the most of it. That said, owning a RED ONE package can make your services as a cinematographer that much more attractive, because it's one-stop shopping for a would-be producer. They get a camera package and someone who knows how to use it to its best potential from one source.

Figure 15.1 Director of Photography M. David Mullen, ASC, works on the set of *Manure*.

If you go this route, make sure you know the camera backward and forward and that you also are skilled at cinematography and lighting. I recommend practicing with a still camera to master the basics of composition and exposure. With a motion-picture camera this complex, it's not always practical to be a one-person band. You need to have an excellent gaffer and camera assistants you can rely on to make the most of your reputation. Review Chapter 6 and the POV interviews with cinematographers such as Arthur Albert; Nancy Schreiber, ASC; and Rodney Charters, ASC, for more hints on being a DP.

In addition to moving pictures, you can also use the RED for still photography since its 4K resolution offers sufficient quality for most print applications. This opens up a whole new opportunity as the worlds of photography and motion picture cinematography converge. It's possible to shoot movies on the RED and extract single frames for use as still photography. Short films, features, commercials, and print campaigns all can be conceivably captured within a single session. Check out the POV interview with photographer Greg Williams for details on this evolving trend.

EDITOR/POSTPRODUCTION SUPERVISOR

Half of this book is devoted to postproduction, so it's obviously very important to the RED workflow. It used to be the case that you would shoot a project and then turn it over to a film lab and postproduction facility to do all the heavy lifting. But nowadays you can do nearly all of the work yourself with a modest computer and editing and finishing software. Whether you're a camera owner/operator or a freelance editor for hire, a thorough understanding of the post process is essential to completing a RED project.

As evidenced by this book's chapters on Avid Media Composer, Adobe Premiere Pro, and Apple Final Cut Pro, there are many different approaches to completing a RED project. My advice is to pick one application to specialize in rather than trying to be a jack-of-all-trades. At the end of the day, audiences don't care which program you edited with, if they enjoy your story. If you can master the technical side of the workflow, all that's left is the art of the edit and the creativity of color correction. (For more specifics on artful editing, I recommend *The Lean Forward Moment* by Norman Hollyn [New Riders].)

Your Next Camera

If there's one question that comes up a lot, it's this one: "Is this the last camera I'll ever need to buy?" I wish I could say the answer is yes, but in fact it's an almost definite no. The movie-making industry is constantly evolving and developing new technology. Ten years ago, the possibility of using a high-definition camera was completely out of reach for most productions. Ten years before that, a video camera was something you shot birthdays with. In 2006, when RED first announced a 4K camera, the concept sounded like science fiction. Yet, just recently Regal Cinemas announced it would be outfitting 5,000 of its theater screens with Sony 4K digital projectors.

This year, several major motion pictures are being released digitally and in 3D. The trend for higher resolution and image quality is going to continue for the foreseeable future. You can see the roots of this happening already at RED with its upcoming 5K resolution (and beyond) cameras such as the RED EPIC. Will we ever reach a plateau with digital cameras, when we have sufficient resolution and standards set in stone? Personally, I think that might happen eventually. But not anytime soon.

Story First

So if you have to keep getting new cameras and learning new workflows every couple of years, what can you do to stay ahead of the curve? For my taste, the things you can always keep consistent are your own talents and skills as a storyteller. If you make a derivative movie with stock characters speaking clichéd dialogue, it's not going to play any better in 4K, 3D, or whatever the newest camera technology has become. Create a unique idea with interesting characters who change in major ways over the course of the story, and you'll have a potentially great project. Then, if it just happens to be shot on a RED ONE, so much the better.

ADDITIONAL RESOURCES

Here are some Web sites where you can share RED footage and techniques with other users.

www.peachpit.com/red	Support site for this book with latest updates
www.red.com	Homepage of RED with store and technical help
www.reduser.net	RED's official discussion forum
www.scarletuser.com	REDuser's sister forum
www.fxguide.com/redcentre	RED-centric podcast at fxguide
www.redrelay.com	Place to share RED RAW footage
www.provideocoalition.com	Group of bloggers focused on HD/digital production
www.broadcastnewsroom.com	Production-related news stories
forums.creativecow.net/redcamera	Creative Cow's RED Forum
www.2-popforums.com	Discussion forum with postproduction emphasis
www.dvinfo.net	Forum with production emphasis

A COMPLETE SYSTEM MENU MAP

Like all modern digital cameras, the operation of the RED ONE is controlled by a hierarchal system of menus. With the help of Scott Jones from XL Films (www.xlfilms.tv) we present a complete diagram of those menus in this appendix. The current build number has probably changed by the time you're reading this but in general the camera's overall command structure changes very little from build to build, so most of this information will still apply.

You'll notice some round icons at the top of each page. These correspond to the buttons on the back of your RED camera. Pressing one of these buttons initiates the related menu. The options for each button are listed beneath this circular icon. Each successive menu selection takes you further down the menu as noted in the diagram.

It may look like a lot of information to take in at first but take some time to practice with your RED ONE and before long you'll know these menus by heart—or at least enough to shoot your favorite settings.

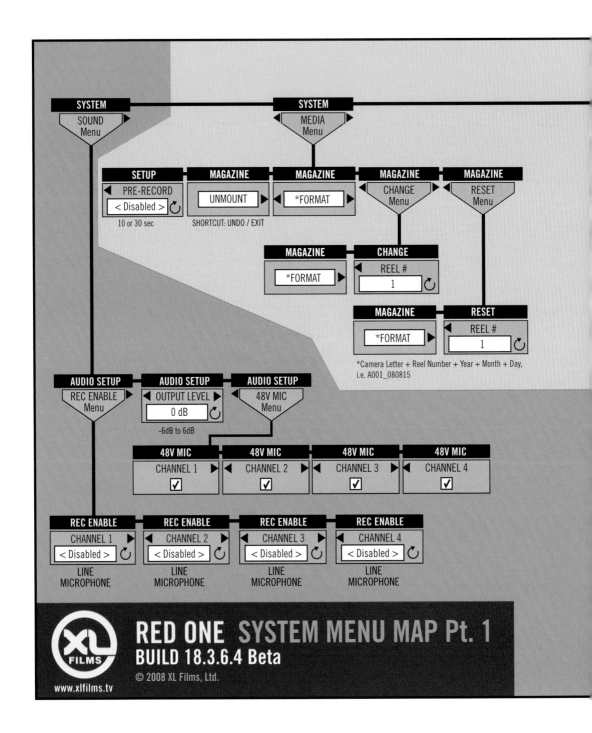

SYSTEM
SOUND
Menu

SYSTEM
MEDIA
Menu

SETUP
PRE-RECORD
< Disabled >
10 or 30 sec

MAGAZINE
UNMOUNT
SHORTCUT: UNDO / EXIT

MAGAZINE
*FORMAT

MAGAZINE
CHANGE
Menu

MAGAZINE
RESET
Menu

MAGAZINE
*FORMAT

CHANGE
REEL #
1

MAGAZINE
*FORMAT

RESET
REEL #
1

*Camera Letter + Reel Number + Year + Month + Day,
i.e. A001_080815

AUDIO SETUP
REC ENABLE
Menu

AUDIO SETUP
OUTPUT LEVEL
0 dB
-6dB to 6dB

AUDIO SETUP
48V MIC
Menu

48V MIC
CHANNEL 1
☑

48V MIC
CHANNEL 2
☑

48V MIC
CHANNEL 3
☑

48V MIC
CHANNEL 4
☑

REC ENABLE
CHANNEL 1
< Disabled >
LINE
MICROPHONE

REC ENABLE
CHANNEL 2
< Disabled >
LINE
MICROPHONE

REC ENABLE
CHANNEL 3
< Disabled >
LINE
MICROPHONE

REC ENABLE
CHANNEL 4
< Disabled >
LINE
MICROPHONE

RED ONE SYSTEM MENU MAP Pt. 1
BUILD 18.3.6.4 Beta
© 2008 XL Films, Ltd.

XL FILMS
www.xlfilms.tv

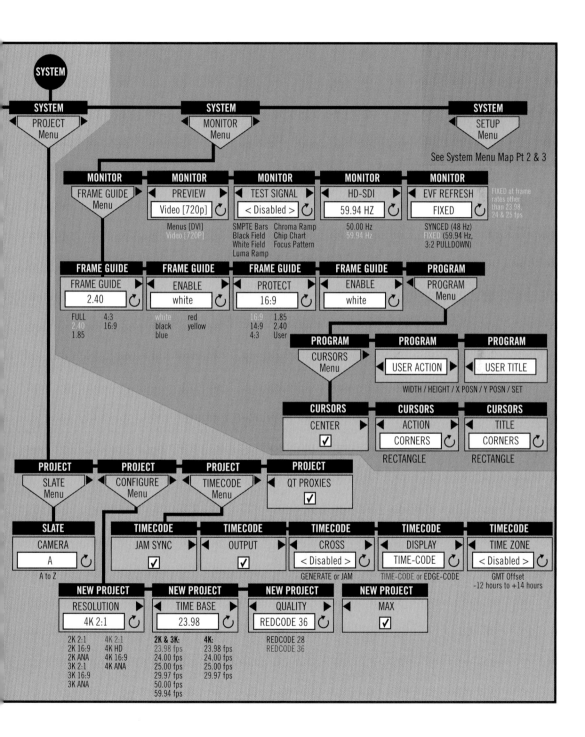

SYSTEM

SYSTEM	SYSTEM	SYSTEM
◄ PROJECT Menu ►	◄ MONITOR Menu ►	◄ SETUP Menu ►

See System Menu Map Pt 2 & 3

MONITOR	MONITOR	MONITOR	MONITOR	MONITOR
◄ FRAME GUIDE Menu ►	◄ PREVIEW ►	◄ TEST SIGNAL ►	◄ HD-SDI ►	◄ EVF REFRESH ►
	Video [720p] ↻	< Disabled > ↻	59.94 HZ ↻	FIXED ↻

FIXED at frame rates other than 23.98, 24 & 25 fps

Menus [DVI]
Video [720P]

SMPTE Bars   Chroma Ramp
Black Field   Chip Chart
White Field   Focus Pattern
Luma Ramp

50.00 Hz
59.94 Hz

SYNCED (48 Hz)
FIXED (59.94 Hz,
3:2 PULLDOWN)

FRAME GUIDE	FRAME GUIDE	FRAME GUIDE	FRAME GUIDE	PROGRAM
◄ FRAME GUIDE ►	◄ ENABLE ►	◄ PROTECT ►	◄ ENABLE ►	◄ PROGRAM Menu ►
2.40 ↻	white ↻	16:9 ↻	white ↻	

FULL   4:3
2.40   16:9
1.85

white   red
black   yellow
blue

16:9   1.85
14:9   2.40
4:3   User

PROGRAM	PROGRAM	PROGRAM
◄ CURSORS Menu ►	◄ USER ACTION ►	◄ USER TITLE ►

WIDTH / HEIGHT / X POSN / Y POSN / SET

CURSORS	CURSORS	CURSORS
◄ CENTER ►	◄ ACTION ►	◄ TITLE ►
☑	CORNERS ↻	CORNERS ↻

RECTANGLE   RECTANGLE

PROJECT	PROJECT	PROJECT	PROJECT
◄ SLATE Menu ►	◄ CONFIGURE Menu ►	◄ TIMECODE Menu ►	◄ QT PROXIES ►
			☑

SLATE	TIMECODE	TIMECODE	TIMECODE	TIMECODE	TIMECODE
◄ CAMERA ►	◄ JAM SYNC ►	◄ OUTPUT ►	◄ CROSS ►	◄ DISPLAY ►	◄ TIME ZONE ►
A ↻	☑	☑	< Disabled > ↻	TIME-CODE ↻	< Disabled > ↻

A to Z

GENERATE or JAM

TIME-CODE or EDGE-CODE

GMT Offset
-12 hours to +14 hours

NEW PROJECT	NEW PROJECT	NEW PROJECT	NEW PROJECT
◄ RESOLUTION ►	◄ TIME BASE ►	◄ QUALITY ►	◄ MAX ►
4K 2:1 ↻	23.98 ↻	REDCODE 36 ↻	☑

2K 2:1	4K 2:1	**2K & 3K:**	**4K:**
2K 16:9	4K HD	23.98 fps	23.98 fps
2K ANA	4K 16:9	24.00 fps	24.00 fps
3K 2:1	4K ANA	25.00 fps	25.00 fps
3K 16:9		29.97 fps	29.97 fps
3K ANA		50.00 fps	
		59.94 fps	

REDCODE 28
REDCODE 36

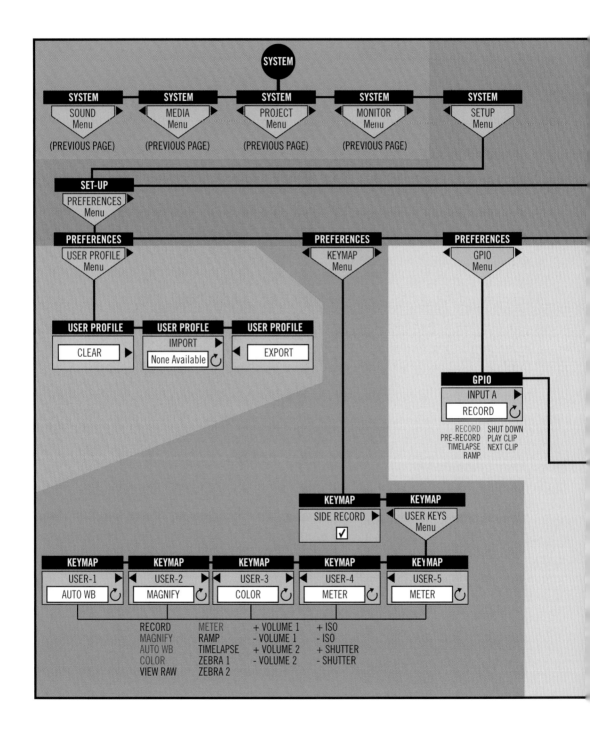

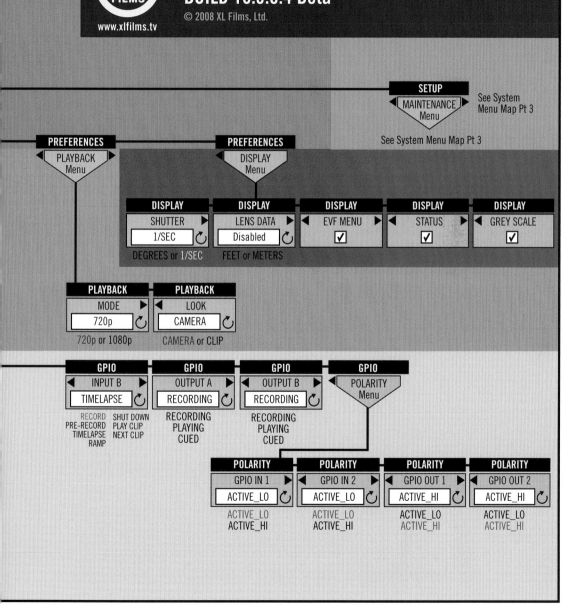

RED ONE SYSTEM MENU MAP Pt. 2
BUILD 18.3.6.4 Beta
© 2008 XL Films, Ltd.
www.xlfilms.tv

SETUP
MAINTENANCE
Menu
See System Menu Map Pt 3

See System Menu Map Pt 3

PREFERENCES
PLAYBACK
Menu

PREFERENCES
DISPLAY
Menu

DISPLAY
SHUTTER
1/SEC
DEGREES or 1/SEC

DISPLAY
LENS DATA
Disabled
FEET or METERS

DISPLAY
EVF MENU
✓

DISPLAY
STATUS
✓

DISPLAY
GREY SCALE
✓

PLAYBACK
MODE
720p
720p or 1080p

PLAYBACK
LOOK
CAMERA
CAMERA or CLIP

GPIO
INPUT B
TIMELAPSE
RECORD   SHUT DOWN
PRE-RECORD PLAY CLIP
TIMELAPSE   NEXT CLIP
RAMP

GPIO
OUTPUT A
RECORDING
RECORDING
PLAYING
CUED

GPIO
OUTPUT B
RECORDING
RECORDING
PLAYING
CUED

GPIO
POLARITY
Menu

POLARITY
GPIO IN 1
ACTIVE_LO
ACTIVE_LO
ACTIVE_HI

POLARITY
GPIO IN 2
ACTIVE_LO
ACTIVE_LO
ACTIVE_HI

POLARITY
GPIO OUT 1
ACTIVE_HI
ACTIVE_LO
ACTIVE_HI

POLARITY
GPIO OUT 2
ACTIVE_HI
ACTIVE_LO
ACTIVE_HI

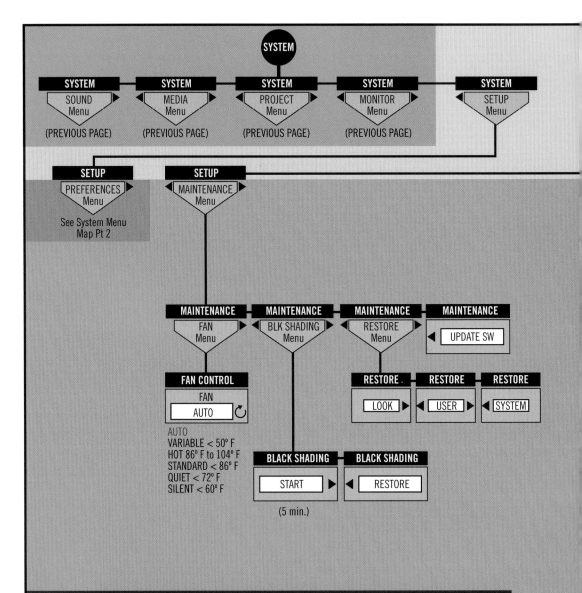

SYSTEM

SYSTEM	SYSTEM	SYSTEM	SYSTEM	SYSTEM
SOUND Menu	MEDIA Menu	PROJECT Menu	MONITOR Menu	SETUP Menu
(PREVIOUS PAGE)	(PREVIOUS PAGE)	(PREVIOUS PAGE)	(PREVIOUS PAGE)	

SETUP
PREFERENCES Menu

See System Menu Map Pt 2

SETUP
MAINTENANCE Menu

MAINTENANCE	MAINTENANCE	MAINTENANCE	MAINTENANCE
FAN Menu	BLK SHADING Menu	RESTORE Menu	UPDATE SW

FAN CONTROL
FAN
AUTO ↻

AUTO
VARIABLE < 50° F
HOT 86° F to 104° F
STANDARD < 86° F
QUIET < 72° F
SILENT < 60° F

RESTORE .	RESTORE	RESTORE
LOOK	USER	SYSTEM

BLACK SHADING	BLACK SHADING
START	RESTORE

(5 min.)

RED ONE SYSTEM MENU MAP Pt. 3
BUILD 18.3.6.4 Beta
© 2008 XL Films, Ltd.
www.xlfilms.tv

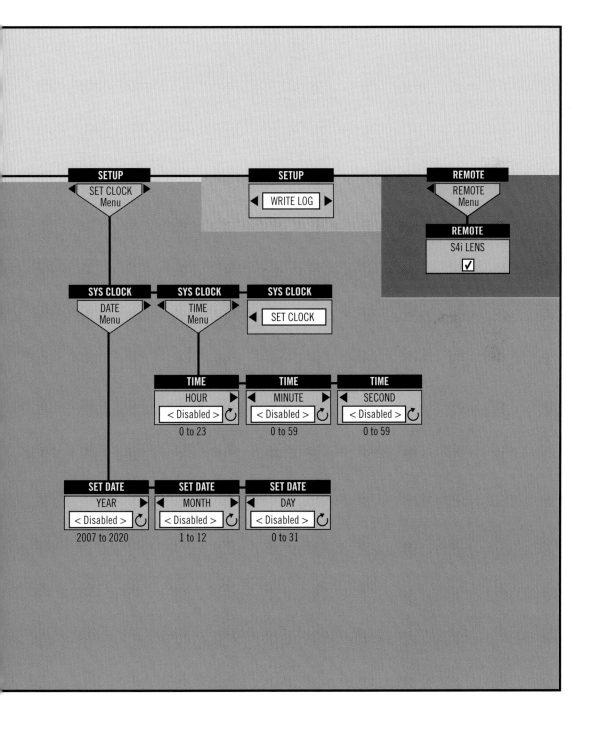

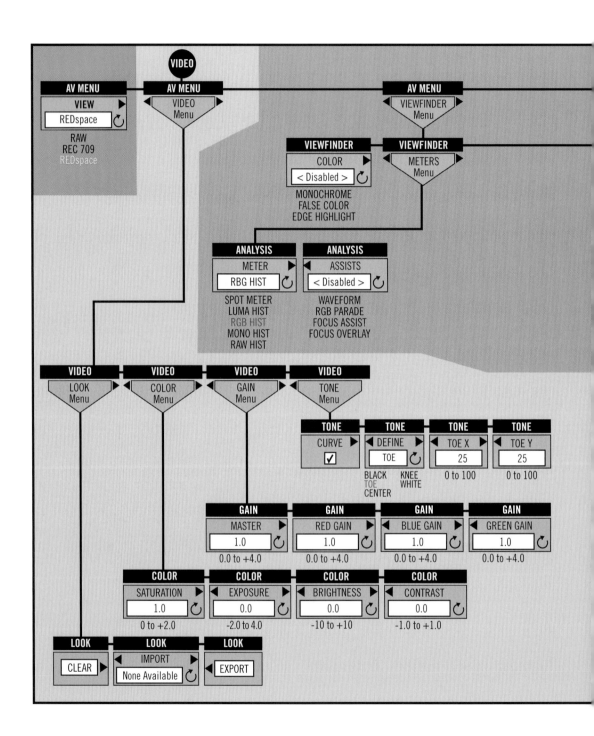

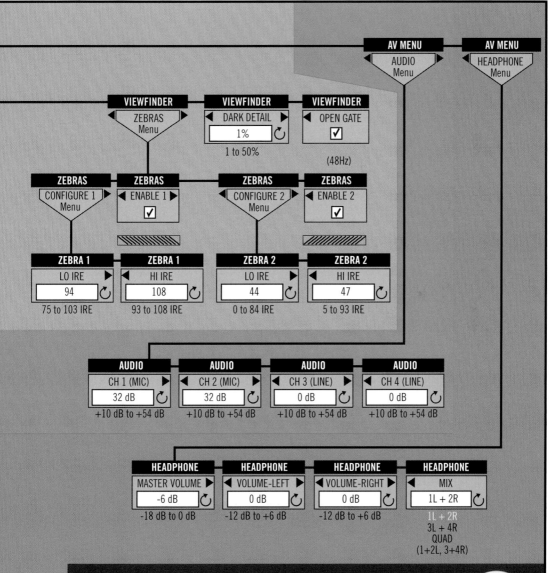

© 2008 XL Films, Ltd.

www.xlfilms.tv

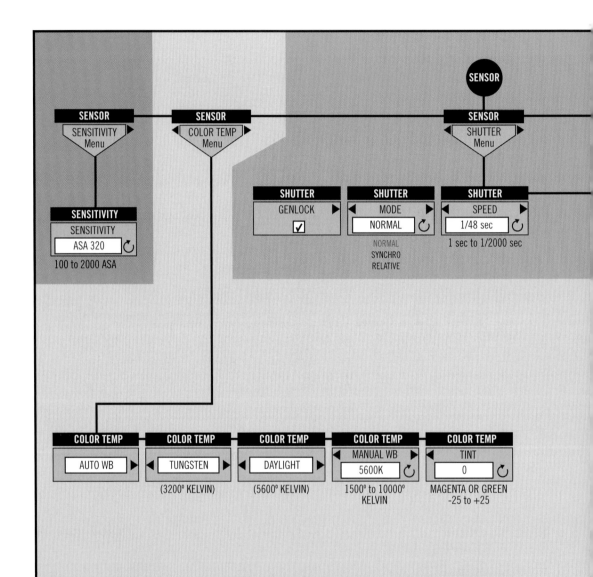

SENSOR

SENSOR	SENSOR	SENSOR
▶ SENSITIVITY Menu	◀ COLOR TEMP ▶ Menu	◀ SHUTTER ▶ Menu

SHUTTER	SHUTTER	SHUTTER
GENLOCK ▶	◀ MODE ▶	◀ SPEED ▶
☑	NORMAL ↻	1/48 sec ↻
	NORMAL SYNCHRO RELATIVE	1 sec to 1/2000 sec

SENSITIVITY

SENSITIVITY
ASA 320 ↻

100 to 2000 ASA

COLOR TEMP	COLOR TEMP	COLOR TEMP	COLOR TEMP	COLOR TEMP
AUTO WB	◀ TUNGSTEN ▶	◀ DAYLIGHT ▶	MANUAL WB	TINT
			5600K ↻	0 ↻
	(3200° KELVIN)	(5600° KELVIN)	1500° to 10000° KELVIN	MAGENTA OR GREEN -25 to +25

RED ONE SENSOR MENU MAP
BUILD 18.3.6.4 Beta
© 2008 XL Films, Ltd.

www.xlfilms.tv

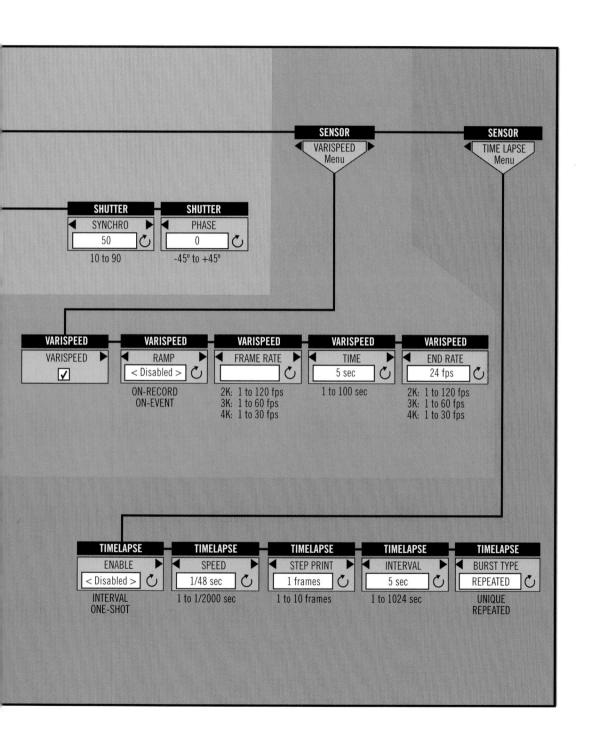

B RED GALLERY

For additional inspiration and to illustrate the possibilities you can achieve with the RED camera, the following pages show frames from various RED productions.

Glossary

Within this book, I've attempted to define the key technical terms and abbreviations when they are used for the first time. If you happen to be skipping around the chapters and you're unclear on a particular term that comes up, check out this glossary for the definition.

1080i High-definition, interlaced footage recorded at 1928 x 1080 pixels.

1080p High-definition, progressive footage recorded at 1920 x 1080 pixels.

16:9 Aspect ratio of high-definition footage; a wide, rectangular-shaped image.

2:1 The RED ONE's "universal" aspect ratio, suitable for use in film-destined projects.

24p Footage recorded at 24 frames per second progressive; also called 23.98 (see also *progressive*).

25p Footage at 25 frames per second in progressive (see also *PAL*).

29.97 Footage at 29.97 frames per second (see also *60i* and *NTSC*).

2K 2,000 lines of resolution; standard format for projects intended for film output (see also *DI*).

4:3 Square aspect ratio of standard-definition footage.

4K 4,000 lines of resolution; the RED ONE shoots 4096 x 2304 at 16:9.

60i Footage recorded as 60 interlaced fields per second (see also *NTSC* and *interlaced*).

A/D converter Analog to digital converter, for digitizing analog audio or sound into a digital format.

ADR Automated Dialogue Recording, rerecording dialogue in postproduction to replace production audio; also referred to as *looping*.

ASA American Standards Association measurement used to classify the speed of a negative film stock or the sensitivity of a digital image sensor (often used side by side with ISO).

ASC American Society of Cinematographers, a Hollywood-based Guild for distinguished Directors of Photography (DPs); also publishes *American Cinematographer* magazine.

aspect ratio The width of an image divided by its height.

B camera   An auxiliary camera shooting at the same time as the main unit camera; its footage is often referred to as *b-roll*.

bitrate   The amount of digital data being processed during a given time period.

block   To determine the geography and desired angles for a scene.

Blu-ray   A high-definition, recordable disc format developed by Sony.

breathing   Visible wobbling on the edges of the frame; happens as the lens focus is changed; typically more apparent with lower-quality lenses.

CF card   CompactFlash memory card used by the RED ONE to store footage (see also *RED-DRIVE* and *RED-RAM*).

chroma   The color portion of a video signal (see also *luma*).

Cineon   Image file format developed by Kodak for digital intermediates (see also *DI* and *DPX*).

clapper sticks   Wooden or plastic slate with production information and two sticks that come together at the start of a take to help assist with postproduction audio sync (see also *SMPTE*).

CMOS   Complementary Metal-Oxide-Semiconductor chip used in the RED ONE's Mysterium image sensor.

codec   Compression/decompression; a specific algorithm for compressing video or audio.

color space   A method of mathematically representing color for use with a specific display or medium.

color temperature   A method of describing the color characteristics of a light source.

cutlist   A list of shots used in an edit to be pulled from negative film rolls (see also *EDL* and *XML*).

D5   A professional digital videotape format developed by Panasonic; available in standard and high definition.

DAT   Digital Audio Tape, used for recording production sound.

DCP   Digital Cinema Package; a format used for digital files intended for theatrical exhibition.

debayer   The mathematical process of interpreting RAW image data from a sensor back into a full-color image.

DI   Digital Intermediate; the process of digitally color correcting footage for final output (see also *RGB* and *REC709*).

Digibeta   Digital Betacam tape, a standard-definition digital tape format developed by Sony.

DNxHD   Avid's high-definition postproduction codec.

DP   Director of Photography or cinematographer.

DPX   Digital Picture Exchange, an image file format for use in digital intermediates (see also *DI* and *Cineon*).

DSMC   Digital Still & Motion Camera, RED's concept of cameras that are capable of functioning as still cameras and motion-picture cameras (see also *EPIC* and *SCARLET*).

DV   Digital Video, a compression codec used to digitally capture and store standard-definition video.

EDL   Edit Decision List, a file format for exchanging completed edit sequences between NLEs and other postproduction software (see also *XML*).

ENG   A term used to indicate the individual or team involved in Electronic News Gathering; documentary and news productions are often referred to as *ENG crews*.

EPIC   RED's 5K camera successor to the RED ONE.

eSATA   External SATA hard drive (see also *SATA*).

EVF   Electronic ViewFinder used on the RED ONE.

firmware   RED ONE's user-upgradeable onboard software.

focus-puller   Crew member who manually adjusts lens focus during a shot.

follow-focus   A mechanical or electronic device for adjusting lens focus.

gain   Electronically amplify an audio signal or brighten an image.

gamma   Mathematical method for calibrating an image's brightness values for use with different displays.

grade   Color correct an image.

HD   High Definition footage has a resolution of 1280 x 720 pixels or 1920 x 1080 pixels; compared to the RED's maximum resolution of 4096 x 2304 (see also NTSC and PAL).

HDCAM   A high-definition tape format developed by Sony; originally intended as an HD version of Digital Betacam.

HDMI   High-Definition Multimedia Interface, widely adopted on consumer and prosumer video monitors and accessories.

HD-SDI   High-Definition Serial Digital Interface for monitoring.

Histogram   An analysis graph of image exposure; on the RED ONE, the higher the levels are to the right, the closer you are to overexposure.

interlaced   Footage stored as overlapping half-frames referred to as *fields* (see also *60i* and *progressive*).

ISO   See *ASA*.

jam sync   To electronically lock timecode between the RED ONE and an external audio recorder (see also *clapper sticks* and *timecode*).

latitude   The range of brightness and/or color values within an image; also a measurement of an image sensor's sensitivity.

LEMO   Cable connector used for various functions of the RED ONE including EVF, timecode, and auxiliary power output (named after LEMO company founder, Léon Mouttet).

linear   A method of expressing values of color and brightness equally across an entire range of latitude (see also *LOG*).

LOG   Logarithmic, a method of expressing brightness and color values on a curve (see also *linear*).

LTO   Linear Tape-Open, a digital tape format used to archive data.

luma   The brightness portion of a video signal, expressed from pure black to pure white (see also *chroma*).

LUT   LookUp Table, a set of instructions used to profile color and gamma to simulate their appearance on a given medium, such as an HD display or a specific film stock.

megapixel   One million pixels, a term used to describe the size of a digital image sensor; RED's Mysterium sensor measures 12 megapixels.

metadata   Footage attributes that can be altered in the REDCODE RAW format including exposure, color temperature, tint, color, and gamma space.

NAB   National Association of Broadcasters convention in Las Vegas, where RED and other camera manufacturers debut new technologies.

NLE   NonLinear Editor, such as Avid Media Composer, Adobe Premiere Pro, and Final Cut Pro.

NTSC   National Television System Committee, 29.97 frames per second, standard-definition analog television format used more in North America and Japan.

PAL   Phase Alternating Line, 25 frames per second, standard-definition analog television format used more in Europe.

pixel   The smallest component of a digital image.

PL mount   Positive-lock lens mount developed by ARRI.

postproduction   Activity that occurs on a project after principal photography.

POV   Point Of View, a shot taken directly from a character's perspective.

prime lens   A lens with a fixed focal length.

progressive   Footage stored as discrete frames (see also *interlaced*).

ProRes   Apple's high quality postproduction codec.

proxy   A file that translates the camera's RAW R3D files for viewing in the QuickTime Player on the Mac; available in various sizes for tailored performance.

QuickTime   Apple's video format and player; uses the .mov file extension.

R3D   RED's native recording format for footage.

RAID   Redundant Array of Independent Disks, a linked set of multiple hard drives for storing data with higher performance and reliability than a single hard drive.

RAW   Unprocessed image sensor data enabling extensive postproduction manipulation (see also *REDCODE* and *metadata*).

RDC   RED Digital Clip, file folder used to store individual R3D shots along with matching proxy files (see also *RDM*).

RDM   RED Digital Magazine, the top-level folder for storing RED footage on a CF card, RED-DRIVE, or RED-RAM.

REC 709   The display standards used for high-definition television signals.

REDCODE   RED's proprietary compression codec (see also *RAW*).

RED-DRIVE   An external SATA hard drive used to record RED footage directly from the camera.

RED-RAM   An external flash memory hard drive used to record RED footage directly from the camera.

REDSpace   A custom gamma and color profile used for viewing RED footage.

RGB   Color data separated into Red, Green, and Blue channels for viewing on a display.

S35   Image sensor comparable in size to a Super 35mm film frame.

SATA   Serial ATA hard drive, used for high-speed data transfer; eSATA is the external version.

SCARLET   RED's camera system, focused on the prosumer market.

SD   Standard-Definition footage has a resolution of 720 x 480 pixels or 720 x 576 pixels; compared to the RED's maximum resolution of 4096 x 2304 (see also *NTSC* and *PAL*).

SMPTE   Society of Motion Picture and Television Engineers, a group of standards to define common media production signals (see also *timecode*).

solid state   A memory card or hard drive with no moving parts (see also *CF card*).

sync   Synchronization, typically between separately recorded picture and sound.

timecode   Method of counting individual frames of recorded footage, used to determine shooting formats as well as ensure audio/video synchronization (see also *SMPTE*).

transcode   Convert video or audio data from one codec, resolution, and/or format to another.

T-stop   Measurement of a motion-picture camera lens' aperture; referred to as *F-stop* on still-camera lenses.

USB   Universal Serial Bus connector used on hard drives and many other computer peripherals.

video village   Location where a DP sets up production monitors for viewing by the director and crew.

XLR   A connector often used for audio peripherals (see also *LEMO*); three-pin for audio, four-pin for power.

XML   Extensible Markup Language, a customizable file format used to exchange data between postproduction applications (see also *EDL*).

zebra   A customizable striped pattern appearing in the EVF to indicate areas of an image falling within a defined exposure range (see also *EVF*).

zoom lens   Lens with a variable focal length.

Image Credits

While I managed to photograph or screen capture some of the imagery in this book, the rest was generously provided by fellow RED enthusiasts, companies, and individuals. We corresponded through e-mail, phone, fax, Skype, Facebook, Flickr, Twitter—you name it. I've attempted to credit each source below according to figure number, along with any related Web sites so you can check out more of their work. Thanks again. You all helped made this book look great.

COVER

The front cover features a Zacuto custom RED rig provided by Steve Weiss (www.zacuto.com) and was codesigned as a favor by my good friend Aaron Lea at Pixascope (www.pixascope.com).

INTRODUCTION

Page x *Remioromen* music video, Paul Leeming, (www.visceralpsyche.com)
Page xx *As The Dust Settles*, Mike Hedge, (www.asthedustsettles.com)

1. THE HISTORY OF THE FUTURE

Figure 1.1 RED NAB 2006 Booth, Graeme Nattress, (www.nattress.com)
Figures 1.3, 1.7 Crossing the Line, Milk Girls footage, Jarred Land, (www.red.com)
Figures 1.4, 1.6, 1.8 Prototypes, RED NAB 2007 booth, Robert Rex Jackson, (www.flickr.com/photos/r_jackson)

2. OVERVIEW OF THE RED WORKFLOW

Figure 2.3 SI-2K camera, Ari Presler, (www.siliconimaging.com)
Figure 2.4 RED Camera report, Fotokem, (www.fotokem.com/nextlab)
Figure 2.5 HD Monitor Pro, Ben Aein, (www.hdmonitorpro.com)
POV Interview, page 29 Rodney Charters, ASC, photo by Michael Klick, (www.rodneycharters.com)
POV Interview, page 31 Pyongyang, North Korea, Rodney Charters, ASC, (www.rodneycharters.com)
Page 32 *As The Dust Settles*, Mike Hedge, (www.asthedustsettles.com)

3. DEFINING YOUR PROJECT

Figure 3.2 Documentary footage, Jay A. Kelley, (www.mammothhd.com)
Figure 3.4 Music video, Dean Georgopoulos, (www.redone4rent.com)
Figure 3.5 Food footage, Leo Ticheli, (www.ltpro.com)
Figure 3.6 Short film, Paul Leeming, (www.visceralpsyche.com)
Figure 3.7 Saturation footage, Ric Forster, (www.lolseries.com)
Figure 3.8 Resolution diagram, Ben Cain, (www.hd-cinema.blogspot.com)

Figure 3.9   Sensor chart, Jon Farhat, (www.jfi.net)
Figure 3.10   ARRI lenses, Mike Hedge, (www.mikehedge.com)
Figure 3.11   Frame guide footage, Leo Ticheli, (www.ltpro.com)
POV Interview   Albert Hughes, Courtesy Greg Longstreet, (www.polarispr.com)

4. BUILDING A RED PACKAGE

Figure 4.5   Lens flare footage, Leo Ticheli, (www.ltpro.com)
Figure 4.6   Lens vignette footage, Scott Matthews, USAF
Figure 4.7   16mm lens, Arturo Jacoby, (www.loscoltrahues.com)
Figure 4.9   Birger Engineering mount (www.birger.com)
Figure 4.10   Long Valley Nikon mount, Douglas Underdahl, (www.longvalleyequip.com)
Figure 4.13   Sunset IR shot, Paul Kalbach, (www.PaulKalbach.com)
Figure 4.14, 4.20, 4.22   Schneider filter, Petrol case, and O'Connor tripod, Susan Lewis, Lewis Communications
Figure 4.16   Polarized footage, Mónica Reina, (www.simplemente.net)
Figure 4.18   Keson tape measure, Jude Nosek, (www.keson.com)
Figure 4.19   Preston FI+Z, Howard Preston, (www.prestoncinema.com)
Figure 4.24   Element Technica hardware, Chris Burkett, (www.elementtechnica.com)
Figure 4.25   RED monitor on set, Shawn Booth, (vimeo.com/channels/shawnbooth)
POV Interview   Mark Pederson, (www.offhollywoodny.com)
Page 88   Kyosuke Himuro concert, Paul Leeming, (www.visceralpsyche.com)

5. WORKING WITH SOUND

Figures 5.1, 5.2   Nagra gear, John Owens, (www.nagra.com)
Figures 5.3, 5.4   Shure gear, Davida Rochman, (www.shure.com)
Figure 5.5   Sennheiser, Stephanie Schmidt, (www.sennheiser.com)
Figure 5.6   Sony MDR headphones, Jim Barraud, (www.jimbarraud.com)
Figure 5.7   Field recordist, Victoria Lahti, (www.victorialahti.com)
Figure 5.8   Rycote, Simon Davies, (www.rycote.com)
Figure 5.9   Aaton Cantar, Martine Bianco, (www.aaton.com)
Figures 5.13, 5.14   Denecke slate, Kim Parra, (www.denecke.com)
Figure 5.16   Production Sound Report, Angelica Dewlow, (www.locationsound.com)
POV Interview   Dean Georgopoulos, photo by Noah Kadner, (www.callboxlive.com)

6. EXPOSING THE IMAGE

Figure 6.4   Greenscreen rain footage, Obin Olson, (www.dv3productions.com)
Figures 6.6, 6.7   Color temperature footage, Keith Brown, (www.flickr.com/people/keithdbrown)
Figure 6.9   Waveform monitor, Alex Vizbird, (www.compuvideo.com)
Figure 6.16   Football footage, Simplemente, (www.simplemente.net)
Figure 6.10   ChromaDuMonde color chart, Michael Wiegand, (www.dsclabs.com)

Figure 6.21   Restaurant footage, Leo Ticheli, (www.ltpro.com)

POV Interview   Arthur Albert, ER © Warner Bros. Entertainment Inc. All Rights Reserved.

7. EXPLORING SHOOTING FORMATS

Figures 7.3, 7.5, 7.14   4K–2K resolution, 2:1/16:9 comparison and timelapse clouds, Mark Andersen, (www.rubberball.com)

Figures 7.6, 7.10   Frame guides and slow-motion fire footage, Bob Glusic and Art Levy, (www.mammothhd.com)

Figure 7.7   24p motion, *Hybrid*, DP John Leonetti, RED Specialist Colin Hubick, (www.mindseyepictures.com)

Figure 7.15   Time lapse footage, Artbeats, Inc., (www.artbeats.com)

POV Interview   Nancy Schreiber, ASC, photo by Yousef Linjawi, (www.youseflinjawi.com)

8. BUILDING A POSTPRODUCTION SYSTEM

Figure 8.1, 8.7   Apple hardware, Courtesy of Apple, (www.apple.com)

Figure 8.2   Final Cut Pro footage, Leo Ticheli, (www.ltpro.com)

Figure 8.3   Adobe footage, Obin Olson, (www.dv3productions.com)

Figure 8.4   Avid footage, Scott Matthews, USAF

Figure 8.6   CalDigit RAID, Lauren O'Grady, (www.caldigit.com)

Figure 8.8   Decklink HD, Blackmagic Design, (www.blackmagic-design.com)

POV Interview   Michael Cioni, photo by Michael Cioni, (www.lightirondigital.com)

Page 172   Helicopter rig in Afghanistan, Scott Matthews, USAF

9. USING HELPER APPLICATIONS

Figures 9.1–9.3, 9.5, 9.6, 9.9, 9.25–9.27, 9.30   Racing and worker footage, Simplemente, (www.simplemente.net)

POV Interview   Brook Willard, (www.brookwillard.com)

Page 200   Car rig from *Hybrid*, Colin Hubick, (www.mindseyepictures.com)

10. APPLE FINAL CUT PRO WORKFLOW

Figures 10.2, 10.3   Log and Transfer and project window footage, *Naked Dawn*, Shawn Booth, (www.funnyordie.com)

Figure 10.7   Cinema Tools Database footage, Ric Forster, (www.lolseries.com)

POV Interview   Evin Grant, photo by Kiana Grant, (www.evingrant.com)

11. ADOBE PREMIERE PRO WORKFLOW

Figures 11.4–11.7, 11.9   Racing footage, Simplemente, (www.simplemente.net)

12. AVID WORKFLOW

Figure 12.2   Transcode settings, Dean Georgopoulos, (www.redone4rent.com)

Figure 12.3   Tula music video, *Snow*, (www.snowdrum.com)

Figure 12.5   Timecode burn-in, *Keep Strivin'* by Al Kapone, Director JD McDonnell, DP Adam Habib, (www.truesouthstudios.com)

Figures 12.10, 12.16   Football footage, Simplemente, (www.simplemente.net)

Figure 12.12   AFE file in DS, Shawn Nelson, (www.nelsonentertainment.com)

POV Interview   Michael Phillips, photo by Howard A. Phillips, (www.avid.com)

13. FINISHING YOUR PROJECT

Figure 13.4–13.6   SCRATCH screens, Nacho Mazzini, (www.assimilateinc.com)

Figure 13.7–13.9   IRIDAS screens, Patrick Palmer, (www.iridas.com)

Figure 13.11   Encore screen, Dave Helmly, (www.adobe.com)

Figure 13.16   DVD Studio Pro footage, Bob Glusic, (www.MammothHD.com)

POV Interview   Simon Duggan, ACS, photo by Vince Valitutti, (www.vincethephotographer.com)

Page 270   Sunset on the set of *Manure*, M. David Mullen, ASC, (www.davidmullenasc.com)

14. ARCHIVING YOUR MEDIA

Figures 14.1, 14.12   Quantum hardware, Alistair Washbourn, (www.quantum.com)

Figure 14.2   G-Tech hardware, Erin Hartin, (www.fabrik.com)

Figures 14.5, 14.6   Shotput Pro, Dan Montgomery, (www.imagineproducts.com)

Figure 14.7   R3D Data Manager, Conrad Hunziker III, (www.r3ddata.com)

Figure 14.9   Active Storage drive, Louie Santos, (www.getactivestorage.com)

Figure 14.14   HP hardware, Nora Upalawanna, (www.hp.com)

Figure 14.16   Retrospect, Kristin Goedert, (www.retrospect.com)

Figure 14.17   BRU, Paige Jones, (www.tolisgroup.com)

Figure 14.18   PresSTORE Archive, Isabella Holz, (www.archiware.com)

Figure 14.19   Atempo Digital Archive, Janet Lafleur, (www.atempo.com)

Figure 14.20   Underground Vault, Nancy Young, (www.undergroundvaults.com)

POV Interview, page 291 and 293   Greg Williams, © Greg Williams / Art + Commerce

15. YOUR FUTURE WITH RED

Figure 15.1   M. David Mullen, ASC, Anna Marie Fox, (www.davidmullenasc.com)

APPENDIX B: RED GALLERY

Page 312   Mumbai, India, Mike Hedge, (www.mikehedge.com)

Page 313   Artbeats, Inc. (www.artbeats.com)

Page 314, top   Rodney Charters ASC, (www.rodneycharters.com)

Page 314, bottom   James McAleer, STEADI-RED Ltd, (www.steadi-red.com)

Page 315, top   Thor Wixom, Mammoth HD Footage Library, (www.mammothhd.com)

Page 315, bottom   Watering Life, Mammoth HD Footage Library, (www.mammothhd.com)

Page 316, top   Dean Georgopoulos, (www.red31.com)

Page 316, bottom   Scene from *Hybrid*, DP John Leonetti, RED Specialist Colin Hubick, (www.mindseyepictures.com)

Index

F

_F QuickTime proxy, explained, 24

False Color tool, features of, 118–119

fast-motion effects, achieving, 138–139

feature films, considering length of, 34–35

file formats
  native, 155
  proxy, 156
  transcoding, 156

File Segments RAW metadata, displaying from single shot, 27

FileName RAW metadata, displaying from single shot, 27

files, storing in folders, 24–26

film
  compatibility of RED with, 17
  versus digital, 125

Film Composer, introduction of, 246–247

film finish, delivering for, 50–52

film workflow, overview of, 250–251

filters
  color-correction, 73
  diffusion, 73
  infrared, 70
  IR (infrared), 72
  ND (neutral-density), 71
  polarizing, 72
  Schneider TRU-Cut IR, 70
  softening, 73

Final Cut Pro
  Media Manager, 280
  saving XML file from, 217
  sending BWF to, 104
  using, 157–158, 170

Final Cut Pro 7, export options in, 211

Final Cut Pro workflow
  color correcting, 205–210
  editing, 204–205
  ingesting footage, 202–204

native-wrapped method, 212–214

proxy method, 214–218

sharing with other formats, 211

system requirements, 202

Final Cut Pro XML files, importing, 184–187

Final Cut Studio, using Cinema Tools in, 207–210

Finder, offloading via, 277

firmware, upgrading, 27–28

Firmware RAW metadata, displaying from single shot, 27

fishpole, using with microphones, 94

focus
  automatic versus manual, 73
  pulling with tape measure, 74

focus whip, using, 74

folders, storing files in, 24–26

follow-focus kit, components of, 74

food, shooting in commercials, 40

footage. *See also* RED footage
  ingesting in Adobe Premiere Pro, 223
  ingesting in Avid Media Composer, 232–236
  ingesting in Final Cut Pro, 202–204
  keeping track of, 20
  transferring, 273

footage transfers
  directory naming conventions, 278
  offloading utilities, 275–277
  offloading via Finder, 277

formats
  multiple, 45–46
  specification for RED ONE, 3

Formatt filters Web site, 70

Forrest Gump, 56

Fotokem camera report (figure), 19

FPS RAW metadata, displaying from single shot, 27

frame guides, activation of, 134

frame rates

of 4K resolution, 131

choosing for multiple formats, 46

choosing for PAL system, 46

considering for film finish, 50

effects, 139

for recording media, 128

selecting from TIME BASE menu, 138

specification for RED ONE, 3

frame sizes
  considering for formats, 45
  resolutions for, 48

FrameHeight and FrameWidth RAW metadata, displaying from single shot, 27

"Frankie" prototype, 5

Fraser, Brendan, 267

From Hell, 56

G

Gain RAW metadata, displaying from single shot, 27

gamma
  defined, 193
  differences in, 53
  space settings, 194–195

GammaSpace RAW metadata, displaying from single shot, 27

Georgopoulos, Dean interview, 107–109

Get Smart, 16

Gladiator, 140

Goldblatt, Stephen, 29

GPI connector, using trigger with, 141

Graham, Heather, 56

Grant, Evin interview, 219–220

G-Technology
  G-SAFE external hard drive (figure), 274
  Web site, 162

H

_H QuickTime proxy, explained, 24

Hansen, Rune, 9

Happy Gilmore, 125

Get free online access to this book for 45 days!

And get access to thousands more by signing up for a free trial to Safari Books Online!

With the purchase of this book you have instant online, searchable access to it for 45 days on Safari Books Online! And while you're there, be sure to check out Safari Books Online's on-demand digital library and their free trial offer (a separate sign-up process). Safari Books Online subscribers have access to thousands of technical, creative and business books, instructional videos, and articles from the world's leading publishers.

Simply visit www.peachpit.com/safarienabled and enter code EVQSPVH to try it today.